Terrace Heroes

CW00555922

The 1930s saw the birth of the football idol, the 'terrace hero' prototypes for today's powerful media sport stars.

The players of the 1930s were the first generation of what we now regard as 'professionals', yet until recently the lives and careers of footballers of this era have been little studied.

During the 1930s British football became increasingly commercialised, and the rise and development of both local and national media, in particular broadcast media, enabled players to become widely recognised outside of their immediate local context for the first time.

Tracing the origins, playing careers and 'afterlives' of several First Division players of the era, Graham Kelly's revealing history explores the reality of living in Britain in the 1930s and draws comparisons with lives of our contemporary 'terrace heroes', the football stars of today.

Graham Kelly is Head of Postgraduate Programmes and Research at the Lancashire Business School, University of Central Lancashire, UK. He is also a founder member of the university's International Football Institute.

Sport in the global society
General Editors: J.A. Mangan and Boria Majumdar

The interest in sports studies around the world is growing and will continue to do so. This unique series combines aspects of the expanding study of *sport in the global society*, providing comprehensiveness and comparison under one editorial umbrella. It is particularly timely, with studies in the cultural, economic, ethnographic, geographical, political, social, anthropological, sociological and aesthetic elements of sport proliferating in institutions of higher education.

Eric Hobsbawm once called sport one of the most significant practices of the late nineteenth century. Its significance was even more marked in the late twentieth century and will continue to grow in importance into the new millennium as the world develops into a 'global village' sharing the English language, technology and sport.

Other Titles in the Series

Terrace Heroes

The life and times of the 1930s
professional footballer

Graham Kelly

Routledge
Taylor & Francis Group

LONDON AND NEW YORK

First published 2005 by Routledge, an imprint of Taylor & Francis
2 Park Square, Milton Park, Abingdon, Oxfordshire OX14 4RN

Simultaneously published in the USA and Canada
by Taylor & Francis Inc
270 Madison Ave, New York, NY 10016

Routledge is an imprint of the Taylor & Francis Group

© 2005 Graham Kelly

Typeset in 10/12pt Goudy
by Graphicraft Limited, Hong Kong
Printed and bound in Great Britain by TJ International Ltd,
Padstow, Cornwall

British Library Cataloguing in Publication Data
A catalogue record for this book is available from the British Library

Library of Congress Cataloging in Publication Data
A catalog for this book record has been requested

ISBN 0-714-65359-4 (hbk)
ISBN 0-714-68294-2 (pbk)

To the memory of my parents, Joan and Laurie Kelly
and
with thanks to my wife, Jenny, and our son, Ben

Contents

Illustrations

Acknowledgements

My thanks go to each of the following football club historians and statisticians, whose valuable contributions have assisted me in the research for this book: R. Briggs of Grimsby Town FC; I. Cook of Arsenal FC; D.K. Clareborough of Sheffield United; R.J. Owen of Portsmouth FC; and B. Dalby of Denaby United FC.

Series editor's foreword

> After the ball was centred,
>   after the whistle blew,
> Dixie got excited and
>   down the wing he flew,
> He passed the ball to Lawton
>   and Lawton tried to score
> But the goalie took a dirty dive
>   and knocked him on the floor!

This passionate partisan piece of doggerel in support of past Everton heroes chanted *en masse* in my boyhood primary school playground, has continued to reverberate in my head down the years. Heroes sometimes achieve immortality in odd ways!

Dixie Dean and Tommy Lawton were 'Terrace Heroes' of my north-western childhood. Graham Kelly has added to this small but sacred pantheon with his study of the lives and times of his *Topical Times* Ten. He places them in their cultural context, explains their social purpose and explores their common significance. This makes good sense. His Heroes, in part or in whole, personified period values. Such Heroes came in more than one form: 'local' heroes – embedded in their communities, loyal to their team and parochial symbols of success for the proletarians packed on the home terraces with precious few life chances; 'moral' heroes who for some epitomised middle class missionary 'fair-play' in a rougher working-class world; 'anti-heroic' heroes who were admired for tilting at such conventions and offered vicarious escape from ethical rigidity.

These 'heroes on a muddy field' were actors on an outdoor stage, who offered their audience momentary release from drudgery, restriction and boredom. Roland Barthes put this point well when he commented that modern sports are analogous to the theatre of antiquity – contemporary dramatic contests with epic heroes from whose exploits the sporting public derives concentrated substitutional excitement which compensates for drawn-out everyday monotony.[1] Such culture heroes allow the non-heroic 'access to catharsis in culturally consecrated ceremonies.'[2] Norbert Elias pushed his analytical probe deeper, and arguably put the point even better:

If one asks how feelings are aroused . . . by leisure pursuits, one discovers that it is usually done by the creation of tensions . . . mimetic fear and pleasure, sadness and joy are produced and perhaps resolved by the setting of pastimes. Different moods are evoked and perhaps contrasted, such as sorrow and elation, agitation and peace of mind. Thus the feelings aroused in the imaginary situation of a human leisure activity are the siblings of those aroused in real-life situation – that is what the expression 'mimetic' indicates – but the latter are linked to the never-ending risks and perils of fragile human life, while the former momentarily lift the burden of risks and threats, great or small, surrounding human existence.[3]

Women, we are told, passionately venerated icons in early Christianity. Since their existence required divine sanction to make it more sustainable, these women clung to these icons tenaciously. Through them they had an outlet for their pent-up emotions.[4] What is sauce for the goose is often sauce for the gander. In the England of the 1930s a rather different kind of intervention resulted in Saturday icons which made the working man's weekdays more bearable. The urge to find heroes is thus enduring. It serves basic needs. However, in the modern world the mythical emphasis has shifted: '. . . myths are how heavily associated with sport and are social in function and secular in content – and since sport is now a substantial part of cultural existence, its myths, mythical heroes and mythical messages are central to modern cultures.'[5]

'I am specifically interested in sports popularly dismissed as 'mere sport' [and] . . . clearly separated in the American mind from serious activity or work' wrote Michael Oriard in *Dreaming of Heroes*. In an English setting so is Kelly.[6] In truth, of course, as Oriard also remarks, few activities embrace reality and fantasy in such a paradoxical way as does sport: the realities of hard work, discipline and failure jostle with the fantasies of freedom, perpetual youth and heroism.[7]

There is, however, more, much more, to be added to this partial parade of paradoxes: sport can purify and it can corrupt; it can motivate and demotivate; it can stimulate team work and stifle individual expression; it can humanize and dehumanize – and still the parade stretches back out of sight. Football is no exception to this rule. In the Anglo-Saxon world of 1930s football, the game and its players defined both patterns and polarities[8] in English cultural experience and held up a mirror to social values that were both time-trapped and timeless. *Terrace Heroes* melds performers, performance and period into a holistic piece. Here is its attractive originality.

J.A. Mangan,
Series Editor,
Swanage, August 04.

1 Professional footballers as 'terrace heroes'

'We simply must have heroes. They give us blessed relief from our daily lives, which are frequently one petty thing after another'.[1] Societies have always created heroes for themselves, not only to provide this 'blessed relief' but also to provide a vehicle to communicate, both internally and externally, the essential values, aspirations and ambitions that (if anything does) bind their populations together. Heroes also provide a means by which societies can celebrate their collective achievements and those of key individuals. Myths and legends inevitably develop, and become the subjects of story-telling across the generations. Historians clearly play their part in this process of intergenerational communication, seeking to set heroes, as R. Holt and J.A. Mangan have put it, 'in their cultural context, to explain their social purpose and to explore their communal significance'.[2]

Arguably, sport increasingly provides an arena in which individuals and, indeed, teams can display 'heroic' levels of performance and achieve success far beyond the wildest dreams of those who only stand and stare. Sporting heroes, whether Olympians, world champions or, indeed, FA Cup winners, all achieve their status by providing other people with sufficient vicarious excitement to establish a distinctiveness in those people's minds. There are clearly many winners in sport; in fact, this is the key characteristic of sporting contests. Very few spectators find drawn matches, dead heats or no-score draws quite as exciting as when there is a clear winner. Winners, however, do not all become heroes. Heroes, similarly, may not themselves be winners either. What, then, makes one person achieve the status of 'hero' and another, often equally successful, fail to achieve it?

The 'terrace heroes' who form the subject of this book have been given this epithet in an attempt to reflect one of the essential dimensions of heroes, and in particular professional footballers as heroes: that there needs to be a 'terrace' before there can be a 'hero'. The power lies with the mass, the crowd on the terrace, to confer a specific social status on an individual and then celebrate it. Such a status can bring benefits with it, but it can also impose significant responsibilities. Heroes, once 'ordained', can easily fall from grace. Many sporting heroes have found, to their cost, that it is far easier to achieve such a status than to maintain it, for the 'terraces' can be very fickle with their affections. A true 'terrace hero' may best be seen as one who is able to maintain power as a hero over a sustained period of time, in contrast to a footballer who rises in the collective rankings and then falls quickly away.

This book is focused on one sport, professional association football, in one country, England, and in one decade, the 1930s. It is argued and demonstrated that these years saw the emergence of what can now be recognised as modern professional football, with tactically minded team managers, increasing levels of organisation and planning, and players who, primarily through the medium of newspapers, radio and, ultimately, television, have become national as well as local 'terrace heroes'. While players were not given much celebrity or status by their employers, the League clubs, or by the public during the 1930s, the essentially working-class supporters who followed the game were already being exploited by the national press and the emerging BBC radio service. Relatively few football supporters were able to watch their favourite teams other than at the fortnightly home matches, but increasing newspaper and radio coverage of professional football enabled a growing band of 'stars' to emerge. Match attendance figures were influenced by the appearance of certain 'star' visiting teams and individual players. For example, Arsenal, the dominant team of the decade, drew larger than normal gates wherever it played, as did players such as Stanley Matthews or Bill 'Dixie' Dean.

Despite this growing media attention, many 'terrace heroes' remained embedded in their immediate local communities. While players did clearly make progress in their careers by moving around the country, sometimes by being transferred but more often than not following release by their previous club, there is an identifiable category of 'terrace heroes' who achieved their status by demonstrating a sustained commitment to one club, often a club near their birthplace or the community where they grew up; such a player was commonly referred to as a 'one-club man'. Their type of 'heroism' had a lot to do with being seen to place the needs of the club and, in particular, the supporters over and above personal ambitions. Cynics may claim that such players were often not good enough to attract the attention of other 'buying' clubs, while being good enough to warrant the employing club's retaining them rather than subjecting them to the normal end-of-season 'release and retain' system that was prevalent in the 1930s. It is clear, however, that most supporters of football clubs gave credit to those players who demonstrated the same loyalty that they themselves exhibited. They did so even though, while the social and economic mobility of most working-class male football supporters in the 1930s was about as low as one could imagine, many professional footballers were men from similar backgrounds who had, by good fortune, genetic endowment and/or sheer hard work, managed to claw their way out into the relative affluence and social prestige of professional football.

Other types of 'terrace hero' emerged both at the club and the national level. Some players demonstrated personal traits and patterns of behaviour that had traditionally been expected more of amateurs and 'gentlemen' than of working-class professionals. Jack Crayston, a long-serving player and later manager at

Arsenal, provides perhaps the classic example of this type of hero. He was widely known as 'Gentleman Jack', reflecting both his fair-play approach to the game on the pitch and his modest, teetotal, non-smoking lifestyle off the pitch. In the 1930s the management at Arsenal was well known for thoroughly investigating the lifestyles and habits of players whom it was thinking of buying and placed bids only for those who would fit into its carefully cultivated middle-class club culture.

Other players became 'heroes' for almost exactly the opposite reason: their lifestyles and their playing styles were those of anti-heroes – they were rebels, scallywags or individualists rather than team players. Some who were individualists on the field of play still managed to demonstrate the fair play and modesty expected of 'gentlemen', the legendary Stanley Matthews being probably the best example. Others sometimes developed 'hero' status primarily because of their attitudes to life off the pitch, as well as to authority figures both in their clubs and in the national game.

Heroes are created in the minds of the footballing public as figures who are to be respected and admired. They may also be figures who can be relied on to provide excitement and thrills. Occasionally there have been heroes who have had the ability, personality and style to be both. Other players achieve heroic status by proving themselves capable of overcoming setbacks. For a footballer recovering from a badly broken leg to score a hat-trick in his first game is a classic 'heroic' achievement. Matt Busby, a star in the 1930s, achieved some of his heroic status much later in life by surviving the Munich air crash that killed many Manchester United players and then going on to build the successful Manchester United team of the 1960s. Joe Mercer, another star of the 1930s, also achieved an element of his status in the game by managing to cope with injuries that would have ended the careers of lesser players. Mercer, like Crayston of Arsenal, was also known as a 'gentleman', reflecting his sense of fair play and his genial personality, both on and off the pitch.

Clearly, football, being a game that emphasises winning rather than merely avoiding losing, has a tendency to offer players in certain positions greater opportunities to achieve the status of hero. It is not surprising to find that forwards and, in particular, goal-scoring forwards have achieved the greatest degrees of support from fans and of publicity in the media. Clubs have always tended to pay higher transfer fees for these players, with the expectation that their fans will reward the transactions by turning out in even greater numbers on Saturday afternoons. This was just as true in the 1930s as it is today. Arsenal, probably the leading 'buying club' in England at the time, aimed to construct a winning team and to create instant heroes. While the team included some long-serving 'club men', such as Crayston, the club also paid record-breaking fees to bring in forwards, such as Bryn Jones. High fees did not in themselves guarantee success, or satisfaction on the terraces, in the 1930s, any more than they do today. Then as now, very few football supporters were satisfied for long with teams or players who seemed to play well but did not win many matches or, more importantly, any trophies. It seems that in order to sustain their status as 'terrace heroes' most players needed to score goals and, to a lesser extent, make goals for others to score. High levels of individual skill, especially in dribbling and in beating opposing players, were also sources of excitement for spectators. A player who consistently demonstrated that he had some special powers not found among either normal players or the watching public was well on his way to becoming a hero.

Individual status as a hero could also be conferred on members of a team, especially an outstandingly successful team. Winners of the FA Cup, for example, were all able to bask in the glory of that day at Wembley. Players who, in themselves, were distinctive neither as footballers nor as personalities could sometimes gain this status, albeit often only for a short time, if supporters saw them as contributing to the success of the team. Winning promotion, the Division One Championship or the FA Cup were all milestones in the professional career of any player. Being a member of a winning team could confer a special status on players of quite modest individual achievements and ambitions. However, while instant glory has always been available, it is often only in the longer term that these players have been held up as heroes. As increasing numbers of club histories and biographies are written and published, players who have come close to being forgotten have started to re-emerge as key figures. It is hoped that this book will bring individual players to the notice of contemporary club supporters with little or no previous knowledge of the players who contributed to their clubs' history and to the development of the English game itself during the 1930s.

Heroes, whether on battlefields or, more recently, on football pitches, in films, in schools or hospitals, or anywhere else, all have one essential feature in common: their behaviour is initially judged by others, and then this judgement is recorded and communicated to a wider public. The professional behaviour of footballers on a Saturday afternoon is very much a live performance before a crowd of thousands, whose judgements, even in the 1930s, could be transmitted to millions. Indeed, crowds at even quite modest clubs were much larger than they are today. Nevertheless, there was relatively little opportunity for others outside the immediate vicinity to observe and judge their performance for themselves. Reporting of major matches by the national daily and Sunday newspapers was on the increase, but their coverage tended to be primarily factual. Radio was starting to improve the population's ability to follow the game, but listeners' judgements were dependent on the judgements of the commentators to whom they listened. Television was in its infancy and during the 1930s it made little impact on ordinary football supporters.

Football heroes therefore tended to be local and closely associated with their clubs, primarily because the only major source of information for supporters was what they saw from the terraces during a match. Clearly, the discussions and debates that went on in pubs, factories and offices in subsequent days helped to firm up individual supporters' judgements. Without the benefit of video replays or Saturday night television highlights, which are taken for granted by supporters today, football fans in the 1930s depended on memory, third-party information and local newspaper coverage. Another feature of the more community-based environment of football in the 1930s was that players often lived within the community itself. Players' biographies frequently refer to walking or taking the bus to the ground on match days, alongside the fans. Being able to touch one's heroes and judge what they were like as ordinary people, rather than as icons on a muddy field, provided many with the opportunity to ground their views of particular players in face-to-face encounters. A player's attitude to ordinary fans thus became a key determinant of his status within his local community. Matthews, for example, was regarded by his loyal Stoke City fans as a 'god' on the pitch, but he was also seen as a 'decent bloke' who was not given to putting on airs and graces. The remarkable outburst in Stoke when it looked as if he was to leave the club demonstrates his status as a local hero. In his case this was reinforced, not superseded, by his growing status at the national and international levels of the game.

Finally, there have been some suggestions that before the Second World War football was characterised by the treatment of players as heroes to a greater extent in the North of England than in the South. As R. Holt has suggested, 'the composite northern hero was a tough competitor with a strong work ethic, not always a great stylist but highly effective'.[3] Northern teams, then as now, tended to cultivate, or have imposed upon them by the media, an image of being tough and hard-working. Players from the North, whether they were still playing in the region or had been transferred to the 'soft' South, were seen in this light (and perhaps still are). For example, Wilf Copping, a northerner who played for Arsenal in the 1930s, was typically described as 'the tough, blue-chinned Wilf Copping'.[4] Another northerner, who played alongside Copping at Arsenal and was a great friend of his, was Jack Crayston, who was described by Arsenal's coach, Tom Whittaker, as 'that elegant gentleman of the football field'.[5] Clearly, there are northerners and there are northerners, although perhaps Crayston played in the South, and with the dominant Arsenal team, for so long that he became contaminated with the 'southern' values of gentlemanly conduct and fair play.

R. Holt and J.A. Mangan have argued that 'The history of sport has been keen to establish its historical credentials by considering the social, cultural and political context of performance, rather than the performers themselves The individual has been rather overlooked.'[6] This book attempts to redress the balance by analysing the lives and times of professional footballers in the 1930s, with a particular focus on ten players who were celebrated by being included in a set of full-colour picture cards issued by what was then a leading weekly publication on football, the *Topical Times*. Before examining in detail their own particular claims to fame, if not fortune, the book focuses on the career pattern of the typical player of the 1930s: how his role as an employee of a leading professional football club was fulfilled; how his career was related to the increasingly professional process of football management at the club level; how he constructed his life and his lifestyle; and, finally, how the media increasingly played a role in creating and promulgating his status as a 'terrace hero'.

2 The career path of professional footballers

Professional footballers, like members of other occupational groups, may be seen as pursuing a 'career path' that involves a series of complex interactions between themselves and their employers, the football clubs, centring on the negotiation and the subsequent fulfilment of contracts of employment. In addition, players and clubs can also be said to formulate 'psychological contracts', implicit agreements based on mutual expectations relating to the exchange process involved. For example, a player may expect that he will work hard, always do his best and live up to the requirements of his manager and the club as a whole, and that in exchange the manager and the club will work to provide him with opportunities to make progress, to be rewarded appropriately for his efforts and to be given satisfactory working conditions. Where these expectations are not met by either party serious consequences may follow. For example, the player may become less committed to the club and less focused on working for the team, and the club may decide to relegate the player to the reserves or, at the end of the season, choose not to retain his services.

A football club, like other employing organisations, has to engage in a number of activities aimed at matching its players' needs, requirements and expectations with its own. Such matching activities include the initial recruitment and selection of the playing staff; the training and development of the players; the provision of specific playing opportunities, such as playing in the first team or in important cup matches; promotion to the status of first-team regular or captain; the general management and supervision of the players; and the provision of an appropriate reward system, including bonuses and other non-monetary rewards. How a football club manages these activities clearly influences the long-term outcomes achieved both by the club and by its players. Clubs aim to see long-term success both on the field, through league promotions and trophies, and on the balance sheet. Players, too, seek the personal rewards associated with success on the field but they also seek other outcomes, such as security, personal development and overall job satisfaction.

Professional footballers, like members of any other occupational group, ultimately engage in paid employment in order to survive within society. Footballers, in the 1930s as today, have a particular career cycle that is intimately linked with the biosocial ageing cycle, in that they can anticipate a predictable deterioration of work performance as they get older. The physical demands of the professional game and the accompanying mental demands make it clear to professional players, from the outset, that their chosen career will be time-limited. Some players take opportunities to extend their involvement in the game through second careers in management, coaching or scouting, or by moving into football-related areas such as sports goods or journalism. The extension of their career cycle through such activities is something that, even in the 1930s, players could be seen to be preparing for as they moved into the twilight years of their playing careers.

In the 1930s professional players, in the main, went through the same career cycle as their counterparts do today. However, it is clear that even the leading players then had significantly less personal control over their passage through this cycle. In the employment relationship between the clubs and the players the power was very much in the hands of the clubs in the 1930s. The view that a professional player was a 'servant' of the club, its manager and, most importantly, the directors was the norm, as will be examined in the remainder of this chapter and in the next.

Entry to the career

Not surprisingly, footballers growing up after the First World War spent much of their childhood and early teenage years engaged in schoolboy football. For many this included organised football with school teams and representative games at town, city, county and, for a few, international level. Jock Dodds, for example, experienced school and county football both in his native Scotland and then, later, in his adopted home of Durham. Joe Mercer and Stan Cullis, both brought up in the Cheshire town of Ellesmere Port, represented their home town in the same team. For others, such as Eddie Hapgood (later of Arsenal) or Peter Doherty (later of Manchester City), there was no such opportunity, since physical education did not rank high on the school curriculum. With a school-leaving age of 14, budding footballers soon moved on to play for local junior teams or works teams, where, typically, the really talented were spotted by scouts and managers from the professional clubs.

Stan Cullis's entry into professional football was unusual, in that he was spotted by a local Football League referee while playing for Ellesmere Port Schools and was recommended to Major Frank Buckley of Wolverhampton Wanderers, one of the most energetic advocates of bringing youth through into the professional game. Cullis was invited to meet Buckley at his home in Wolverhampton and was immediately, and without a trial, offered a position on the ground staff, playing for the club's 'A' team. Cullis also demonstrates the importance of significant others, in his case his father, in facilitating entry into professional football. The Cullis family had, like many hundreds of others, moved from Wolverhampton to Ellesmere Port with the Wolverhampton Corrugated Iron Company several years earlier. This background and club allegiance ensured that young Stan was only ever going to join the Wolves, at least if his father had anything to do with it. Stan Cullis went on to become one of the most famous and revered Wolves in the club's history. Similarly, Cullis's friend Joe Mercer, also playing for Ellesmere Port, was spotted by his local club, Everton, and was signed as a junior.

Jack Atkinson's entry into Bolton Wanderers is an example of the importance of works football as a source of new recruits to the professional game. Having left school, Atkinson joined a County Durham side, Washington Colliery, and was spotted by the First Division club Bolton Wanderers, which 'signed' him without paying a fee. Recognising that he needed regular match practice in order to develop, Bolton asked that he stay with the Colliery side until he was 18. Although a fee was not paid, Bolton did make a regular financial contribution to the colliery club's funds, thereby ensuring that their future star was not lost to another club. In due course Atkinson signed professional terms, and started playing in Bolton Wanderers' Lancashire Combination and Central League sides.

Professional clubs tended to scout regularly for talented recruits. Even in the 1930s the larger clubs used teams of scouts spread across Britain. Smaller clubs more typically covered only their own regions, with managers sometimes doing much of the scouting themselves. Scotland and the Northeast of England tended to attract many of the English clubs, perhaps reflecting the view that raw 'northern' players were more likely to be able to cope with the increasing physical demands of the professional game. Bob Baxter is an example. Born near Edinburgh and playing for a local club, Bruntonian Juniors, Baxter was spotted by Middlesbrough's manager, Peter McWilliam. McWilliam had come to Scotland to watch another player, but this player's match had been postponed; McWilliam dropped in to watch Baxter's match purely by chance. Baxter, then aged 20, was combining football with two jobs, since he was a coalminer and also the part-time manager of a dance band.

Entry to professional football was, then, largely dependent on being spotted by a roving manager or scout. Clubs could not sign players as professionals until they were aged at least 17, but this did not stop them employing them in various office and ground-maintenance roles. A key feature of this career entry process was the arrangements that professional clubs made for their young recruits during the summer months, when typically they either released their players and therefore avoided having to pay them, or offered them lower weekly wages. Eddie Hapgood, later of Arsenal, has told the story of how Bristol Rovers failed to sign him because they offered him only a summer job driving a coal cart for one of the club's directors.[1] Hapgood was already driving a milk cart for his brother-in-law's dairy and saw a 'social distinction' between the two. Kettering Town then came in with an offer of £4 winter wages and £3 in the summer, and the chance to keep his dairy job. Hapgood signed. Just twelve weeks later Hapgood and Kettering were visited by two gentlemen who turned out to be Herbert Chapman and George Allison of Arsenal. Hapgood recalls Chapman's 'selection interview' going something like this: 'Well, young man, do you smoke or drink?' Hapgood said, 'No.' Chapman replied, 'Good. Would you like to sign for Arsenal?' Chapman paid Kettering a fee of £1,000, including the receipts from a friendly match later in the season.

The experiences of Tommy Lawton, later of Everton and England, also reflect the non-footballing aspects of entry into professional football. Having been brought up playing schoolboy football in his native Bolton, Lawton, with the aid of his grandfather and his headmaster, was able to negotiate with his local League club, Wanderers, over the type of job that he would be offered if he signed terms as an amateur. Offered a choice between becoming an office clerk on 10s. a week, or working as a butcher's delivery boy on 7s. 6d. a week, Lawton very quickly turned them both down, much to Bolton's regret, and increasingly so as the years went by. Liverpool and Sheffield Wednesday were also interested in signing the young Lawton, but neither was able to provide him with a suitable non-footballing job. Eventually Burnley came into the picture and, with Lawton's headmaster acting on his behalf, the club offered him a job in its own offices. In addition, Lawton's grandfather was found a job on the club's ground staff and the club found a house in Burnley for Lawton, his mother and his grandfather to live in. Lawton was just 15½ when he 'signed' for Burnley. Two years later, having just taken the next step on his career path by signing professional terms, Lawton was on his way to a First Division club, Everton, for a then record fee, for an under-21-year-old, of £6,500. He was recruited as an understudy for Bill 'Dixie' Dean.

Lawton's entry to the professional game clearly illustrates the role that relatives and schoolteachers played in protecting the interests of these talented youths. Lawton and Hapgood both show that football could not be relied upon as the sole source of income by young men aspiring to become professional footballers. Then as now, entry into the professional game was very much a lottery and relatively few winners achieved the pinnacle of establishing themselves as full-time professional footballers.

Progression along the career path

Once he was established as a contracted professional, a footballer's career in the 1930s was primarily determined by a combination of his own developing prowess and the attitude taken to him by his employers, the latter being influenced by the club's own success (if any) in winning championships and cups. An examination of the career patterns of the footballers of the time reveals that a select few, such as Joe Mercer or Bert Sproston, were able to start at the top and remain there throughout their playing years. Others, such as Cliff Parker or Jack Crayston, entered the professional game at a relatively low level, had their abilities recognised, and then moved onwards and upwards into the higher divisions. Others travelled the other way: having entered the game by joining, for example, a First Division club as an apprentice or junior professional, they moved downwards through the ranks, often because they did not fulfil their early promise, or fell prey to injury or other adverse circumstances. Finally, there were the vast majority of professional footballers, who spent their careers in the lower reaches of the game, never achieving wider recognition or attracting the interest of the larger clubs, but still playing the game and, it is to be supposed, making a living sufficient to survive on.

The players who attracted national attention through media coverage were those who played for all or some of their careers at the top level. These were the 'terrace heroes' who were written about in the national newspapers and football magazines. However, there were many other players who were the objects of 'hero worship' even if only from a few thousand supporters of a small club playing in the Third Division. The exploits and achievements of these heroes were celebrated every week in the local public houses, factories and schools. The celebrity status of many players was very much a local affair, but it provided them with sufficient satisfaction and recognition to keep them in the professional game, often despite the insecurities associated with the clubs' ruthless application of the policy of 'release and retain' at the end of each season.

As will be discussed later, at the end of every season a club's directors decided whom they would retain on the payroll across the summer and whom they would release. Financial pressures encouraged clubs to release many of their journeymen professionals, only to take them on again at the start of the next season. While summer wages were always lower than wages during the season itself, even at the top level, clubs were keen to offload all but their essential players. With no income from gate receipts clubs were reluctant to pay their players for doing nothing. This policy meant that players often had playing careers that involved many different clubs, with all the resulting social and financial disruption that could be expected.

Despite this, some players managed to maintain allegiance to a club over many seasons. These 'club men' became famous for this alone and achieved a degree of 'hero' status as a result. Charlton Athletic's famous goalkeeper Sam Bartram played for the club for more than twenty years, including those years in the 1930s that saw the team rise to a high position in the First Division. Jack Atkinson of Bolton Wanderers similarly played for his club through most of the 1930s, during the Second World War and on into the late 1940s. Bob Baxter, another inspirational centre-half, had a similar career with Middlesbrough, as did Harry Betmead at Grimsby Town. Jack Crayston, having joined Arsenal in the mid-1930s, not only played there up to and through the war years, but also extended his one-club career by joining the backroom staff, eventually becoming manager in the mid-1950s.

Gaining representative honours and/or international recognition counts as a milestone in any footballer's career. During the 1930s the Football League organised regular interleague matches with its counterparts in Scotland, Wales and Ireland. These matches, which were usually played at First Division club grounds, provided opportunities for players on the fringe of gaining full international honours to be tested. Most of the full England team of the 1930s gained such honours before receiving their full caps. Stanley Matthews, probably the game's ultimate terrace hero, first appeared for the Football League in a 6–1 win over the Irish in 1934, as part of a forward line comprising Raich Carter of

Sunderland, Ray Westwood of Bolton Wanderers, and the Manchester City pair of Tilson and Brook. The legendary goalkeeper Frank Swift first appeared for the Football League in 1935, in another match against the Irish, along with two other debutants, Jack Crayston of Arsenal and Sam Barkas of Manchester City.

Since England did not play in the fledgling World Cup championships, international recognition tended to come in the form of matches against the other home countries and other European rivals on end-of-season tours. Such matches inevitably attracted maximum media coverage and lifted many players from being club heroes to becoming, even if only briefly, national heroes. Such recognition further enhanced their status within their own clubs and local communities. Partly because of the committee-based selection policy for internationals, the era saw a high turnover of players being picked for England duty. Without the appointment of an international manager, which did not come about until after the Second World War, players fell in and out of favour, and some of the top stars of the First Division ended their careers with relatively few international caps. Dixie Dean is a case in point. Although he scored 18 times in 16 matches for England between 1927 and 1932, and continued to be a major goal-scoring force with Everton in the First Division until 1937, he was never selected again. Eddie Hapgood of Arsenal, England's captain for much of the mid- and late 1930s, was an exception, appearing a total of 43 times. Describing his feelings about gaining an England cap, Hapgood recalled:

> To me, at any rate, there was the natural excitement of being considered good enough to play for my country, the pride of achievement of a workman, the tools in this case being my feet, head and football brain, that his work was considered top-notch, and a great thankfulness that the step I had taken those years ago – to pit my youth and confidence against the masters of the game, which, while still a game, was one of the testing grounds so many fail upon – had proved myself right . . . I knew then that, all things being equal, I could become a great footballer, and I had, to the extent of national recognition.[2]

Here Hapgood expresses the sentiments of many footballers who have reached this career milestone.

Finally, the 1930s proved to be a unique decade for any assessment of the career patterns of professional footballers as it ended, of course, with the outbreak of the Second World War, just a few days into the 1939/40 season. All club contracts with players were suspended and professional footballers suddenly found themselves out of work, although the clubs held on to their registrations. Although football was restarted, in a variety of forms, just a few weeks later, the call to national service seriously truncated many players' careers as full-time professionals. Regional competitions commenced in October 1939, with teams being allowed to have guest players to compensate for the loss of many of their full-time regulars to the armed forces. Guesting not only helped players to increase their incomes but also brought some national stars to the most unlikely of venues, especially those close to army and Royal Air Force locations. Players were paid just 30s. a match and little training took place. For the leading players, however, there were still some opportunities to play in international and representative games.

The war brought the playing days of those players who were already reaching the latter stages of their professional careers to a premature end. Other players, however, emerged as a new generation of footballing stars. Young players who had been just entering the professional game in 1939, such as Nat Lofthouse, Tom Finney, Billy Wright and Jackie Milburn, all established their professional careers at this time, and went on to become terrace heroes of the 1940s and 1950s. Jock Dodds, one of the terrace heroes discussed later in this book, became nationally famous during the war years with his record goal-scoring exploits. Having been Sheffield United's prime striker between 1934 and 1939, with 113 goals in just 178 League games, Dodds moved to Blackpool in the months just before the outbreak of war. Blackpool, based in a town that contained a large RAF base, emerged as 'the' team of the war years. Led by Dodds, and aided by 'guests' including Matthews of Stoke City, Dix of Tottenham Hotspurs and Burbanks of Sunderland, Blackpool went on to win the Northern Championship and the War Cup, and in 1943 the team beat Arsenal to become 'champions of England'. Dodds scored 223 goals in just 161 games: in the 1941/2 season he scored a record 66 goals. Dodds himself also guested for other sides, notably Manchester United, Fulham and West Ham.

Exit from the career

Professional footballers' careers have always been relatively short-lived in relation to their overall working lives. In the 1930s footballers knew that their days were numbered almost from the very start. While serious injury on the field of play has always been a danger to any player, of any generation, in the 1930s players' careers were also subject to the whims of club directors applying the retain and release policy. Many young players were released every summer, and this meant the termination, or at least the suspension, of their careers as professional footballers. Since very few of these players had developed other work skills they found themselves being either absorbed into the ranks of the unemployed or forced to retreat into manual occupations in factories, down mines or on farms. Those players who managed to survive the annual cull could have their careers extended into their thirties, when physical decline set in and they were forced to retire.

Career exit could be a gradual process for professional footballers. Within each club players who could no longer make the grade found themselves relegated to the reserves, and playing only occasionally in the first team. Others were placed on the transfer list and then sold to clubs in lower divisions. For some this demotion extended to having to end their playing days in non-League football.

Clubs typically did little to prepare their employees for life after playing, whether to guide them towards second careers or to encourage them to save for the future. Arsenal, being Arsenal, was an exception. There was a savings scheme within the club, so that players were able to build up nest-eggs against the time when they retired or left the game. Some players had the foresight to develop other strings to their bows and set up businesses while still playing. Joe Mercer famously ran a grocery business on the Wirral. Tom Finney, the 'Preston Plumber', also demonstrated this kind of foresight. Other players developed skills that helped them to launch second careers, Charles Buchan and Frank Swift being famous examples of players who developed as journalists.

However, the ambition of many footballers nearing the end of their playing days was to stay in the game in one role or another. Going into management could seem the ideal second career, and it became a reality for many of the leading players of the 1930s. The decade saw the gradual emergence of the 'manager', rather than the 'secretary–manager', at club level, and this trend provided many opportunities for experienced and well-connected players to move on after hanging up their boots. In addition, most clubs had coaches, trainers and scouts, and many players also took on these roles, some doing so as the first step on the career ladder to eventual club management.

A few examples of star players of the 1930s who went on to football-related second careers, often achieving more success than they had as players, will illustrate this pattern. Joe Mercer, the terrace hero first of Everton and later of Arsenal, probably had one of the most successful of all second careers. Having managed to overcome serious injury into the 1950s, Mercer made a smooth transition into club management, first with Sheffield United, then with Aston Villa and then, famously, with Manchester City, working with Malcolm Allison to take the club to heights that it had not reached since its Championship-winning heyday in 1936/7. Mercer then moved into general management and directorship with Coventry before capping his career by becoming temporary manager of England. He had had quite a journey since his schoolboy footballing days in Ellesmere Port alongside another famous player who later turned manager, Stan Cullis.

Another terrace hero, Bert Sproston, also achieved a lengthy second career in the game, taking on the various roles of trainer, physiotherapist and scout with Bolton Wanderers after playing top-level football, first with Leeds, briefly with Tottenham Hotspurs and then with Manchester City, and of course, with England. Sproston ended his playing days by leaving the professional ranks and joining the non-League club Ashton United for one final season.

'Gentleman Jack' Crayston of Arsenal also extended his career into football management, staying with his own club well into the mid-1950s, having joined it as a young professional in 1934. Crayston had also gained some training in accountancy during his playing days and this assisted him in taking on the role of assistant manager under Tom Whittaker's managership, a role that included book-keeping duties as well as maintaining the club's extensive files on players whom it might wish to buy at some future date. Crayston also played a role on the coaching side. Arsenal had a long-standing commitment to continuity among its staff, so it was no surprise when Crayston eventually took over from Whittaker as manager, although he remained in this post for only two years before he resigned after a dispute with the board. He then had a spell as manager and secretary–manager at Doncaster Rovers before buying himself a newsagent's and general store in the Midlands, where he stayed until he retired.

An interesting example of a player who stayed in the game but did not enter management is Jimmy Guthrie. Having become famous as the captain of the giant-killing Portsmouth team that beat the favourites, Wolverhampton Wanderers, to win the FA Cup in 1939, Guthrie developed a second career as a professional trade unionist, becoming full-time chairman of the Players Union (formally known as the Association Football Players and Trainers Union, later to become the Professional Footballers Association). Having been the union's rep while he was at Portsmouth, he played on during the war years, combining his growing interest in the union with playing. He was transfer-listed with a fee at the end of the war, but he felt that this was unfair treatment and, after spending the summer months coaching in Norway, he returned to England to take up a similar role with Crystal Palace. In 1946 he was appointed as the union's first full-time chairman and left Palace in order to concentrate on his new duties. He went on to play a key role in the growing debate over players' representation during the 1950s.

Not all players ended their playing days at the top level by moving smoothly into management positions within the game. Jock Dodds, for example, who had plundered goals galore with Sheffield United and Blackpool during the 1930s, and then again during the war years, spent a brief and inglorious period in the late 1940s with Shamrock Rovers in Ireland, then went to Everton, before ending his playing days with Lincoln City and retiring from the game in 1950. Despite being offered football management jobs, he decided instead to enter the world of commerce. Over the years he ran several businesses, including a hotel, a sweet-manufacturing company, betting shops and night clubs, and later got involved in distributing health foods.

Dixie Dean also had a varied career, which included what seemed to some a sad exit from the game. Having become the country's most famous player with Everton, Dean first found himself relegated to the reserve side playing in the Central League, being replaced by the young upstart Tommy Lawton. To every-one's surprise, including Dean's, he was then transferred to a Third Division (South) club, Notts County. Plagued by injury, he then moved to an Irish side, Sligo Rovers, before the outbreak of the war induced him to return to Mersey-side, where he took a job in an abattoir before joining the army. After the war he took on the 'typical' job of many former professional footballers: he ran a public house. Over the next fifteen years Dean's pub in Chester became the haunt of many journalists and former players. Dean eventually ended his working life as a security officer at Littlewoods, ironically linked once again with Everton, the club that had let him go in the late 1930s without so much as a leaving ceremony. Dean, one of the game's genuinely legendary figures, perhaps exemplifies the way in which professional footballers of this era were, like most working men of their generation, at the beck and call of the labour market. For many professional football players, even the very best, being a terrace hero turned out to mean very little when it came to the day they finally hung up their boots.

3 Footballers as employees

The dole queue has cast a long shadow over the nation's collective memory and many people still associate the period most strongly with the spectre of unemployment.[1]

The first half of the 1930s saw unemployment consistently above 2 million and it peaked in the winter of 1932–3 at 3 million, or about one quarter of the insured working population of Britain. As the decade went on, however, world trade started to recover and Britain's economy started showing signs of modest growth. The heavy industries, including steelmaking, shipbuilding and coalmining, all started to revive, although in the late 1930s their output remained below the levels achieved before 1914. Manufacturing also moved forward in the latter years of the decade, especially in newer industries such as electricity supply. By 1939 two thirds of all homes had mains electricity, compared with one third in 1930. Cars and other motor vehicles also became more commonplace during this decade, and increasing numbers of families could realistically aspire to owning them as prices fell significantly. The wider engineering industry also expanded as increasing numbers of consumer durables came onto the market. The second half of the decade, in strong contrast to the first half, was a period of growing economic prosperity, with an increasing proportion of the population being able to consume more as well as to produce more. Retailing expanded, partly aided by improved transport and, arguably, the increasing branding and promotion of goods by manufacturers. The media, especially the press and cinema, provided opportunities for the advertising of all types of new consumer goods, fuelled by the rapid expansion of hire purchase schemes for the more expensive products. Unemployment began to decline, as indicated above, from 1933 onwards. The living standards of those in work rose sharply. However, life for those in the depressed regions of the country remained relatively unchanged, and their plight was brought into even sharper focus by the very obvious affluence in the Southeast and the Midlands, which were rapidly becoming the new industrial hub of the country.

The lot of professional footballers

Set against this social and economic backcloth, professional football in fact remained 'relatively unaffected by these general industrial trends'.[2] Clubs tended to seek to cut their costs where they could and, while wages were, as always, kept under very close control, most of the larger clubs managed to retain sufficient players to turn out three teams each.

Professional footballers, even in the lower reaches of the League, still managed to keep one step ahead of their working-class comrades. The differences between those on the terraces and those on the field were clearly in evidence. Players received pay that was significantly higher than what those putting in hours at the local factory received. With a maximum wage of £8 a week during the playing season and £6 in the close season, footballers compared very well with, for example, skilled engineering workers, who in 1938 were on wages of £3 10s., or factory labourers, who were on £2 10s., while secretaries at Preston North End, for instance, earned just £1 10s. a week.[3] George Summerbee, a reserve team player at Preston (and later the father of the England and Manchester City star Mike Summerbee) received an annual wage of £250, as compared with coalminers on £100 a year or provincial bank managers on £350.[4]

George Hardwick, who played for Middlesbrough in the late 1930s, recalls in a recently published autobiography that 'in those days, with so many people out of work, it was a real privilege to play football for a living . . . football was a profession which was well-respected'.[5] Hardwick's somewhat rosy recollections of life as a professional in the 1930s are not shared by all his contemporaries. One England star, Len Shackleton, admittedly writing in 1955, described their contract as 'an evil document'.[6] Jimmy Guthrie, captain of Portsmouth when they won the FA Cup in 1939 and later chairman of the Players Union, has suggested that 'advantage was taken of the love a player had for the game'.[7]

Even so, the lot of professional footballers in general must be regarded as significantly better than that of the ordinary working men who spent their shillings on ninety minutes of vicarious excitement on Saturday afternoons. However, then as now, there were professional footballers and there were professional footballers. While the star players were able to live life to the full, at least during their playing days, there were far more professional footballers for whom the game was a much less well-rewarded occupation and, probably more significantly, a more insecure and exploited one. Playing in the lower reaches of the Third Division, or in the 'Stiffs' or reserve team of a higher-level club, did not offer much job satisfaction or security.

The employment contract

> Footballers, with a weak union and with few alternative means of employment, were effectively controlled by a system of work discipline which would have proved intolerable to any other group of workers.[8]

Footballers didn't complain, they muttered. The power in football rested firmly with the Football Association and the Football League at the highest level, and the provincial businessmen who ran the clubs, the 'little shopkeepers who govern our destiny' as Billy Meredith contemptuously termed them.[9]

Professional footballers in the main were employed by their football clubs on a one-year contract that expired at the close of the playing season in May. One of three things could then happen to them: they could be placed on the transfer list, in an attempt to find another club that would purchase their services in return for a fee; they could be 'released', or, as we would now say, be made redundant; or they could be offered a new contract.

A new contract might not, of course, be on the same terms as the one that had just expired. For up and coming young stars the terms might well be enhanced; for the stalwarts already on maximum terms the contract might well represent more of the same; and for those who had failed to fulfil their potential, or had lost form and/or fitness during the past season, the terms might well be less attractive. Some clubs had sliding scales of pay for their players, a system that many directors saw as essential, given the overall size of their playing staffs, which could be between forty and fifty players in the larger clubs. George Summerbee, for example, signed for Preston North End in 1935 on a contract promising £5 a week during the season and £4 in the summer, then the standard terms. He did not make it into the first team, but, having done enough to justify retention, he was re-signed in 1936, as a Class 2 player. One of his colleagues, Bill Shankly, was also re-signed, but as a Class 1 player on weekly wages of £8 in the season and £7 in the summer. Summerbee continued to slide down Preston's hierarchy, in 1937 becoming a Class 3 player. It should also be noted that Preston still held out the carrot of playing in the first team, with the promise of a weekly wage of £6 if he ever reached such heights. 'The extra pound for a first-team appearance and the chance to pick up a win or draw bonus was as important in those times as the prestige that accompanied a regular first-team place.'[10] Summerbee did eventually receive that extra pound, but only three times throughout his career with the club, his debut coming in 1938 when he was called in to cover for Shankly, who was playing for Scotland against England at Wembley.[11]

Underpinning this retain and release system were the maximum-wage regulations, which decreed that the highest weekly wage that could be paid to any player, whether at Arsenal in the First Division or Clapton Orient in the Third Division (South), was £8 during the playing season and £6 during the summer months. These rates had been fixed in 1922 and remained unchanged throughout the 1930s. Estimates suggest that 'probably only 20–25 per cent of players were on the maximum at any one time and, as ever, many professionals found themselves in a trade from which they could be removed by injury, loss of form or their club's response to financial vicissitude'.[12] Sheffield United, for example, guaranteed the maximum wage to only four of their twenty-one professionals during the 1934/5 season.[13] Clubs were known on occasion to release a player in May and then re-hire him in late August, thereby escaping payment of summer wages to a player who might well be enjoying a few weeks of cricket or taking on some other form of paid employment. In addition, a player might well be taken on again at a lower weekly rate.

Other players were retained across the summer and into the next season, but on reduced terms. As Jimmy Guthrie of Portsmouth has commented: 'The married man had little choice, he either accepted the cut to ensure that his family could eat during the summer months or tried to find another job, knowing his chances of getting something to do for the close season were small. The form for the single man was the same but many were independent and refused to sign.'[14] The clubs won either way:

> If the man signed they saved money on his wage packet, if he did not sign until the start of the following season they saved the summer wages. If the player refused, after being offered his old terms near the start of the new season, he could not kick a ball for pay until another club came in and bought him, and the player, for his 'rebellion', would lose the accrued share of the transfer fee.[15]

The general uncertainty of employment and of wage levels led players to concern themselves more with their own personal positions than with the collective position of their fellow professionals. Football was a competitive business for players, both on and off the pitch. Established players were always wary of new recruits or of up and coming youngsters who might threaten their regular first-team places and thus their incomes.

At the top end of the football labour market, where the maximum wage was virtually guaranteed for the likes of Tommy Lawton, Joe Mercer or Eddie Hapgood, there was still concern over the matter of pay: 'Money dominated their thoughts and even a cursory examination of the respectful and usually bland autobiographies written by players whose careers were subject to the tyranny of the maximum wage reveals a preoccupation with the fact that they all considered themselves grossly underpaid.'[16] Lawton, for example, put into his memoirs, published in 1946, a breakdown of his income between May 1938 and May 1939, which, while it totalled more than £500, included his weekly season wage of £8; his summer wage of £6 per week, augmented by additional payments for international appearances at £8 per match; a £1 bonus for each League point accrued during the season; and a further bonus of £25 for being a member of the winning team in the League Championship.[17] Such was the lot of a typical star player. Lawton, Bill 'Dixie' Dean and other crowd-pullers increasingly saw themselves as 'sporting entertainers', comparable to professional boxers and golfers in Britain, or even to baseball and ice-hockey players in the United States, whose salaries were already way beyond anything to be found in the Football League.

A further dimension of the professional footballers' lot was the benefit system, which was designed to reward individual players for their loyalty to their clubs.

Under the Football League's rules a professional player became eligible for a benefit payment of £650 after playing for a club for five years. Such payments were not an entitlement, although most leading players were fairly certain to be awarded one and at the maximum level. This, however, was not always the case. Sheffield United, for example, awarded no benefit payments between 1931 and 1936.[18] Probably the most notorious case relating to the benefit system in the 1930s focused on Stanley Matthews and Stoke City. Offered a benefit payment of only £500, Matthews decided to seek a transfer. Stoke's directors had clearly made a serious error of judgement and were faced with one of the country's first public protests regarding a footballer. Local industrialists, mainly from the potteries, organised a public meeting that was attended by 3,000 fans, while 1,000 more were locked out of the hall. The directors backed down: Matthews was offered the maximum benefit payment and was persuaded to withdraw his transfer request. Matthews later wrote: 'As far as I was concerned, I'd shown great loyalty and it had not been reciprocated. What's more, the belligerent attitude and hard line taken by the club put a dent in the implicit trust I had in those running the club.'[19]

Other rewards

While the leading players' financial circumstances were constrained by the Football League's rules regarding contracts, wages and benefits, there is clear evidence that a few of their number were able to augment their incomes by engaging in non-playing activities. Even as early as 1929 Arsenal had to find Alex James further sources of income in order to lure him away from Preston North End. In James's case this meant becoming a sports equipment demonstrator in the department store Selfridges. He had a weekly newspaper column ghostwritten for him, again for a fee. Dixie Dean was also able to attract up to £50 a session for advertising or endorsing products. Even less well-known players were able to generate 'commercial' income, usually by being involved in events that would attract a high level of public interest. The FA Cup Final was clearly the major event of the football year. Newspapers typically featured stories about the two finalists in the week or so before the match and then again in the few days afterwards. Players, teams and even managers and trainers were featured in advertisements during this period. For example, Cherry Blossom boot polish was endorsed by Harry Hooper, the captain of Sheffield United, finalists in 1936; Wolves' captain Stan Cullis declared that Ward's Hats had made 'the best hat I've ever had'; and even the Wolves' trainer, J.H. Davies, extolled the virtues of an inhalant, Vapex, explaining 'how the Wolves keep colds from the door'. This last example seems somewhat ironic, as the Final in 1939 became famous, not just for Portsmouth's giant-killing performance, but also for the alleged use of 'monkey glands' by the Wolves' manager, Major Frank Buckley, to keep his players fit (see Chapter 15). While players and others were featured in such advertisements this was not an era of agents or players' representatives, so the rewards accrued were minimal and may have been little more than free supplies of the products endorsed.

Another less innocent aspect of players' efforts to gain extra income from their involvement in the game centred on the payment of, or at least the search for, 'under the counter' money during transfer negotiations. Jimmy Seed, Charlton Athletic's long-serving manager during that team's remarkable rise from the Third Division to the upper reaches of the First Division in the 1930s, wrote in the late 1950s about how he had missed out on signing some big stars because of his refusal to give such payments: 'I nearly signed a Scottish international. He was quite willing to join Charlton, but then he informed me that if I gave him £1,000 in his left hand, he would sign with his right.'[20] Another player, this time an ageing English international, also asked Seed for a 'bit over the top' in order to persuade him to sign for what was then a Third Division club. By his own account, Seed again refused. As Seed commented:

> If you sign on the so-called 'Golden Boy' who does a financial deal for himself, he will either corrupt the loyalty of other members of the team by boasting of his deeds and telling them to get wise to themselves, or he will soon be looking round for another 'easy touch' and this means trouble in the team. He will ask for a transfer and if his request isn't granted he becomes a non-trier.[21]

While Seed was a critic of the use of such tactics by players, at least in retrospect, he may well have been a little out of touch with some of his fellow managers. Players who sought such perks probably did so only because others around them were already getting similar payments. Perks were also available in forms other than cash payment. Stories of clubs buying their players' cars for far more than their market worth, or offering 'free' houses as inducements to move, were commonplace. Non-wage rewards, both legitimate and otherwise, were thus starting to appear within the professional game even as early as the 1930s.

The Players Union

'A Red Cross rather than a Red Army'.[22] This is an accurate statement of the role and effectiveness of the Players Union, or, as it was formally known, the Association Football Players and Trainers Union, which focused during the 1930s on handling compensation claims for players who were forced to retire from the game through injury. Achieving significant power within the professional game was always an aim for the union in the years between the wars, as its membership rose from 398 in 1924 to almost 2,000 at the outbreak of the Second World War. Club directors generally treated players as 'employees in a capitalist labour market',[23] using the Football League's rules to impose what the union's leaders regarded as a feudal system upon a workforce that, apart from a few select stars, was a transient group of working men who, at the end of each season, could be retained or discarded at will. Those journeymen professionals who were released every year were sometimes reappointed at the beginning of the next season, and sometimes left to drift out of the game entirely, to take on, if they could find them, 'normal' working-class jobs in the burgeoning factories of the late 1930s. For many the professional game became no more than a memory of an unfulfilled youth, and football eventually became no more than a pastime to be fitted in somehow alongside necessary paid employment.

The appointment of Jimmy Fay as secretary in 1929 marked the start of a key period for the union as it increased its membership and started to put pressure on the clubs and the football authorities. Not surprisingly, the maximum wage and the contract system formed the main focus for players' sense of grievance, although the leading players tended to be more concerned about their personal positions than about the lot of their colleagues in the lower divisions. Even the less well-established players were likely to accede to locally negotiated deals offered by their clubs if the only realistic alternative was to be placed on the 'release' list. Seeking union representation of their individual wishes and grievances was not something that many players had in their minds as they struggled to maintain their places in the full-time professional game; and the clubs' directors did not, of course, encourage them to contact the union in any case.

Players who did join the union were expected to pay a weekly subscription, which in the 1936/7 season was 1s. In its attempt to build up its membership the union worked hard to establish a network of delegates at all the League clubs. Each delegate was expected to recruit members from among his teammates and then collect the subs. Jimmy Guthrie, for example, moved from Dundee to Portsmouth and became not only the club's captain but also its union delegate. He held weekly meetings to hear the complaints and suggestions of the other players, which tended to revolve around conditions of service and wages. Guthrie recalls that at one such meeting the players came up with the idea that the club should form a first-team 'squad' and that all players in the squad should receive first-team wages whether they were picked for that week's match or not. The manager, Jack Tinn, and the directors agreed to the suggestion, and Portsmouth thus became the first club in the League to start a squad system, with sixteen players being involved.[24]

Clubs developed consistent attitudes to union membership over the years. Manchester City, Manchester United, Newcastle United and Sunderland tended to have relatively large memberships, while Everton, for example, remained non-unionised until 1937, when Joe Mercer got involved. Arsenal, the most successful team of the decade, also tended to be non-unionised, possibly reflecting the culture of the club and its paternal attitude towards its players, especially under the manager Herbert Chapman. Things at Highbury did, however, start to change after Chapman died, coinciding with Wilf Copping's arrival from Leeds United, where he had been a successful union delegate. By 1937 only eleven clubs in all four divisions did not recognise the union and membership was at its highest since 1920.

The union's attempts to gain compensation payments for players gradually bore fruit during the 1930s. In 1938 such payments totalled more than £9,000, compared with just over £1,200 in 1928. Jimmy Fay travelled the country talking with players and stressing the value of union membership as providing some form of protection against the day when injury struck. However, under his secretaryship the union was hardly a militant force fighting for improved wages, especially in the first half of the decade. Fay seems to have had a hard time getting his message across, as players tended to place their day-to-day needs over and above preparing for what might lie ahead. Stanley Matthews recalled a visit by Fay to Stoke City in 1932: 'You could buy a few pints of beer for a couple of bob, and some of the boys thought more of their pint than of Mr Fay's arguments.'[25] Fay needed to get the stars of the First Division clubs on his side if he was to encourage the less well-established majority to join the union, yet without strong union influence in the boardrooms there was little reason for the star players to become members. On the whole they appear to have taken the view that their future was likely to be better if they used their own playing prowess and crowd appeal to press their directors into making good deals with them. Nevertheless, by 1939 the union had managed to recruit more players from the First Division than from any other.

As the decade went on the players, with the union's help, started to 'assert themselves, take themselves and their professional position more seriously, and, through their union, claim some of the privileges of "ordinary" citizens'.[26] One example of this new assertiveness was the increasing tendency of players to raise objections to newspaper coverage of the game, especially when it was critical of individuals and, in their view, unfair or even libellous. The union's solicitor achieved several payments of compensation to players who felt aggrieved by newspaper reports and even more often he made newspapers print retractions and apologies. The union also succeeded in heading off a move within the Football League to reduce the players' rights relating to injury. C.E. Sutcliffe, the League official who proposed to change the rules on this matter, went into print increasingly often, in publications such as the *Topical Times*, to complain about 'lazy' players who, he claimed, were feigning injuries and causing clubs to pay increasingly high medical bills. Fay and the union raised objections, and Sutcliffe's resolution on injured players was withdrawn before being put to a vote. There was also a move to restrict what players could write, or have ghostwritten for them, in newspapers. As newspaper articles provided a useful source of additional income for some of its members, the union quickly objected and again the authorities backed down, although the League still insisted that players could not make personal criticisms of other players in their columns.

The Football League remained essentially dismissive of the union and its activities, seeing it as, at best, an irritant. However, in 1938 the union, with its membership rising and its bank balance improving, started to formulate a set of demands that, in 1939, forced the League to hold its first meeting with union officials in many years. Fay cleverly put together a set of proposals that met the needs of both types of players. The leading players wanted the maximum wage to be raised, for the first time in sixteen years; the other players wanted the contract system to be changed, especially in relation to summer wages, loyalty benefits and bonuses. The union's claim was for:

- an immediate increase in the maximum wage to £9 a week;
- a minimum wage of £4 a week;
- payment for the pre-season training period at the winter rate rather than the summer rate;
- contracts to run from the start of August to the end of July, preventing clubs from keeping players out of contract to save on wages;
- a larger share of any transfer fee to go to the player concerned;
- increases in bonus payments; and
- compensation and injury payments to be fixed and made compulsory.

The threat of a players' strike and increasingly supportive newspaper coverage of the issues the union was raising eventually brought the League to the point of arranging a meeting with Fay and his team. Predictably, the League rejected the union's proposals, leaving the union to start preparing for 'drastic action' at the start of the 1939/40 season.

Unfortunately for the union, just two days after September arrived so too did the war. The suspension of all professional football, at least initially, was sufficient for the whole issue of players' rights and conditions to be placed on hold until after the cessation of hostilities. The union was suddenly faced with the prospect of its members being out of work and having to support families with little or no income. Luckily, its accumulated reserves, built up during the late 1930s, enabled it to provide hardship support for many of its members.

As Jimmy Guthrie has recalled: 'When the game, for purposes of morale, was re-started players were paid a miniscule appearance fee and, although the player had no claim on his club, he, the player, was not allowed to kick a ball anywhere or for anybody, without permission from the club, with which he had no contract.'[27] The outbreak of war had changed nothing in relation to the position of professional footballers as employees. As J.P.W. Mallalieu, MP, commented in his introduction to Guthrie's autobiography: 'The football industry was one of the last relics of feudalism.'[28]

4 Directors, managers, trainers and coaches

During the 1930s the national game continued to be administered by two essentially conservative national bodies, the Football Association (FA) and the Football League. At the international level the FA's apparent priority was to keep the national team sheltered from the rapidly developing and improving game as played in other countries. Having left FIFA twice during the 1920s, the FA and its counterparts in the other home countries ensured that none of them played any role in the World Cup championships, which started in the 1930s. England, for example, played the other home countries every year and occasionally played other European national teams, such as Germany or Italy, notably during end-of-season continental tours. This relatively isolationist policy protected the image of British football in general, and English football in particular, as being the best in the world (something that was to change significantly after the Second World War).

Domestically the Football League remained even more of a force for stability and the status quo. Dedicated to preserving its own versions of the sporting values that had seen the game develop over the previous fifty years, the League worked assiduously to resist the creeping commercialisation of the game. Its opposition to the growth of football pools and associated forms of betting was characteristic. Other examples of 'dangerous' developments, as far as the League was concerned, included women's football, playing matches on Sundays, playing under floodlights and clubs using their grounds for non-football pursuits, such as greyhound racing or speedway. Given that the League was dominated by the directors of many of the larger clubs, it is hardly surprising that this essential conservatism was to be found at the club level too.

Directors

As limited-liability companies League clubs had to place administrative and financial control in the hands of boards of directors. Directors tended to be representatives of local business and professional communities, broadly the same constituencies as the clubs' shareholders. Directors were expected to offer their various occupational skills, unpaid, to their clubs, although, as will become clear, they were also liable to extend their brief to include team selection and even the offering of advice on team tactics. Many clubs were run as fiefdoms by powerful businessmen who took great pleasure in running 'their' clubs as extensions of their business empires. Preston North End, for example, was run by the autocratic James Taylor, who not only turned up at the Deepdale ground every day, but also made every key decision on the team's affairs, paying especially close attention to the buying and selling of players, team selection and tactics.

Many directors saw the success of 'their' team on the field as a stimulus to the local economy and, indirectly, their own businesses. Sheffield United's victory in the FA Cup Final in 1935, for example, was reported to have helped to attract industry to the city, reducing its large pool of unemployed men. Directors, then as now, also sought to gain personal kudos in their own professional and social circles by being associated with successful clubs. The opportunity to invite their business clients and friends to watch famous teams, and meet the star players whom they normally only read about in their morning newspapers, was an important side-benefit for most directors. Thus the motives of directors were essentially self-serving, although not in any way directly related to financial gain.

As the 1930s proceeded most directors increasingly recognised that to maintain a successful team on the field they would have to adopt more 'modern' business management techniques and approaches. The growing power of the mass media, coupled in some cities and regions with the increasing spending power of football fans, meant that the directors had to turn their attention to marketing and publicity, and to ensuring that their club balanced its books. Sustained footballing success, especially at the highest level, led many clubs to invest more in their primary assets: their grounds. The more enlightened directors also saw the wisdom of adopting a 'buying' policy in respect of their playing staff. Traditionally clubs had attempted to attract and keep youngsters, combining them with a number of more experienced and older players. With the maximum-wage regulations in operation there was little motivation for players on the maximum wage to voluntarily seek to change clubs. Towards the end of the 1920s and increasingly in the 1930s the leading clubs started to change their approach. Arsenal, under its manager Herbert Chapman, took the lead in putting together a team that was bought rather than 'home-grown'. Transfer fees gradually increased during the decade: in 1938 Bryn Jones's transfer to Arsenal from Wolverhampton Wanderers for £14,000 broke the previous record by £3,000. Arsenal was not known as the 'Bank of England' club for nothing; George Allison, its manager at the time of Jones's transfer, was nicknamed 'Moneybags'. Arsenal was an exception to the rule, however. Clubs in the lower reaches of the Football League were, then as now, forced to be 'selling' rather than 'buying' clubs, surviving by identifying talented schoolboy and youth players, and grooming them for eventual sale to the relatively cash-rich First Division. As a result directors at the lower levels of the game were forced to concentrate on the search for raw talent. Many clubs established scouting systems, both locally and further afield. Charlton Athletic managed to rise from the depths of the Third Division (South) to the upper reaches of the First Division during the 1930s partly because of the efforts of their scouts, especially in the Northeast, where the club's manager, Jimmy Seed, had been born. The goalkeeper Sam Bartram was one of their finds.

While it was rare for any club director to have been a professional football player, lack of experience on the pitch does not appear to have inhibited directors' involvement in the game. Their activities in many clubs made a direct impact on the men occupying the next level down in each club's hierarchy: the managers or, at most clubs, the secretary–managers.

The rise of professional managers

Since directors persisted, in the early 1930s, in holding onto the reins of all but the most mundane aspects of the footballing side of their clubs, the clubs were characterised by an essentially administrative culture. Most clubs, even as early as 1900, had established the post of club secretary as the operational officer of the board of directors. Playing essentially a clerical and office-based role, the secretary was charged with ensuring the smooth running of the club as a business organisation. Matches were organised and publicised, tickets were sold, players and other employees were paid, and the paperwork to be found in any organisation was efficiently and effectively processed. The nearest that most clubs got to having a 'football manager' in the sense understood today was the trainer, who was charged with keeping the players fit and treating the wide range of injuries suffered throughout the season. Scouts were used by many of the larger clubs, even before the 1930s, and they tended to be paid on a 'match watched' basis.

The secretary's role started to evolve, however, as the pressure on clubs to succeed, both on and off the field, increased, and secretaries were increasingly required to engage directly with the players. Many clubs reflected this develop-ment by adopting a new title for the post: the 'secretary–manager'. During the 1920s and increasingly in the 1930s secretary–managers became the primary representatives of most clubs in relation to both fans and the media.

An analysis of club records for the 22 clubs that were in the First Division in the 1932/3 season, and again in 1938/9, reveals some interesting insights into the posts being filled and the changes that took place over this relatively short period. In 1932/3 5 clubs had secretaries but no managers; 13 had secretary–managers; and the remaining 4 had both secretaries and managers. In 1938/9, in contrast, only one club still had just a secretary; 10 clubs had secretary–managers; and 11 had both secretaries and managers. Of the 5 clubs that had had only secretaries in 1932/3, Everton alone continued this arrangement in 1938/9, while West Bromwich Albion had a secretary–manager and the remain-ing 3 had separate secretaries and managers. Of the 13 clubs that had had secretary–managers in 1932/3, 9, including Arsenal and Wolverhampton, re-tained this arrangement in 1938/9. The other 4, including Liverpool and Leeds, had moved over to having separate secretaries and managers, alongside the 4 clubs that had already had this arrangement in 1932/3 – Derby, Huddersfield, Middlesbrough and Newcastle United – and still retained it.

It is clear, then, that the significance of distinct managerial responsibilities was well and truly recognised, at least among the leading clubs, towards the end of the 1930s. What were the reasons for this shift of focus and where did the stimulus for the change come from?

A widespread view is that the two individuals who did most to shape the role of the manager as the single most authoritative figure on football matters within a club were Herbert Chapman, first of Huddersfield and ultimately of Arsenal, and Major Frank Buckley of Wolverhampton Wanderers, who have been described as 'to some extent the prototypes of the "technocrat" professional manager'.[1] While they had quite different personalities, Chapman being a paternalist and Buckley a 'martinet',[2] they both managed to negotiate relationships with their directors that enabled them to exert control over all matters to do with football. Both had taken over the management of clubs going through poor patches, where the directors were only too pleased to rely on a single individual who claimed to be capable of leading them to the promised land of footballing success. Both managers or, more accurately, secretary–managers, went on to establish new norms within their respective clubs. Whether paternalistic or authoritarian, both Chapman and Buckley saw their future success as being linked to building a team on the basis of enhancing the welfare of the players, making careful tactical preparations, and imposing training regimes that emphasised the development of playing skills and not just stamina or physical fitness. By contemporary standards their approach seems unremarkable, but in the early 1930s they were both very much ahead of their time. Managerially inspired match tactics were unheard of and so too was the idea of running training sessions during the week with the aid of a football. The norm at most clubs in those days was to have players build fitness and, especially, stamina by running round and round the pitch or across country, leaving it to the individual abilities of the players to conjure up some magic on a Saturday afternoon in order to win three points. This was not Chapman's way, nor was it Buckley's. Writing in 1934, just before his untimely death, Chapman demonstrated just how his view of football management was some thirty years ahead of his time. In his view, 'A manager should pick his team alone and his professional expertise in doing so should be expected.'[3] He continued: 'We have been compelled to scheme, to produce the results which the public demand.'[4] His approach was to build the team up as a collective unit, not a disparate set of eleven often ill-fitting individual stars. His pursuit of the 'team ethic' extended to checking up not only on the playing capabilities of potential Arsenal players but also on their general character. As he put it, 'Today, there is only room for the decent fellow in the dressing room.'[5]

Chapman and Buckley also shared a common approach to dealing with matters off the field. Both were conscious of the need for publicity for their clubs and, indirectly, for themselves. The growing demand for newspaper coverage of football in the 1930s saw managers become the prime source of stories about current players, future players and all matters relating to the clubs' affairs. Players were barred from providing copy to newspaper reporters and were restricted as to what they could write, or have ghostwritten for them, in columns published under their names. Directors, meanwhile, were generally reluctant to cooperate with reporters at all. Thus the managers became all-important as the public faces of the football clubs. Through this increased exposure they soon became closely associated with the level of performance on the field of play; and having managers as scapegoats for poor results suited directors and fans alike. Success was usually attributed to the feats of the players – especially, as usual in football, the star goal-scorers, such as Dean, Lawton and Drake, or the mazy dribblers, such as Matthews. Those managers who, like Chapman and Buckley, had control over team selection and tactics generally found this situation acceptable, but the public were starting to hold the same view of all managers, whether or not they had the same level of authority.

Chapman, Buckley and a few other 'real' managers were thus, all unwittingly, placing increasing psychological burdens on other managers, most of whom still lived much the same essentially office-bound existence as secretary–managers did. Selling players, which has always been controversial among fans in any era, often proved to be problematic for such managers. With the directors still running things in most clubs, even where there was a manager or a secretary–manager in post, the sale of players, especially 'stars', always created unwanted press coverage and public criticism. Wherever directors refused to comment or hid behind the need for confidentiality, the managers would often have to take the flak. Even Buckley, one of the few 'star' managers of the era, was not immune: he had to be protected by the police when Bryn Jones was sold to Wolverhampton Wanderers' arch rivals Arsenal.

The growing public presence of football managers at the local level and of the managers of the leading clubs, such as Arsenal, at the national level fuelled a stereotypical image of this new occupational group: 'The football managers now began to acquire a mystique. They became canny wheeler-dealers hanging furtively around railway platforms and hotel lobbies waiting to conclude secret business.'[6] They were also seen as 'tricksters',[7] forever attempting to deceive the parents of talented schoolboys into signing them for their clubs, or trying to sell players with hidden injuries to their fellow managers. As far as managers were concerned, being 'professional' was increasingly linked with engaging in dubious or unethical behaviour, albeit it could be understood as doing what was necessary if a given club was to succeed. This instrumental 'win at all costs' approach was widely perceived as becoming pervasive in the game. Buckley, for example, is reported to have asked the local fire brigade to heavily water Wolverhampton Wanderers' pitch before an important game, in the belief that his team played better on heavier ground. This tactic backfired on him, however, as an unexpected drop in night-time temperature led to the pitch becoming frozen and the match being postponed. Buckley, a strong believer in the physical side of the game, is also said to have regularly rallied his team with the saying, 'It's easier to beat nine or ten than 11.'[8]

Not all managers who were involved with the playing side of things adopted the authoritarian management style favoured by Buckley and others such as Storer of Coventry. Far from it. Herbert Chapman, one of the greatest managers the game has ever known, was firm when he believed that there was a need to be, but was far more of a father figure around Highbury. His paternalistic approach extended to the lifestyles adopted by his players. He actively encouraged them to jettison what he saw as working-class habits centred on drink, gambling and women, and to replace them with abstinence, saving and home-building. As Wagg has commented: 'Some managers were doing more and more homework, and, in doing so, were becoming unwitting agents for an obviously middle-class morality.'[9] Chapman, for example, interviewed players before signing them, asking them whether they drank or smoked and taking the transfer talks further only if they denied doing either. He was concerned not only that their on-field performance might be impaired but also that they might bring the club into disrepute if the press reported any embarrassing incidents, especially as many of his signings were not used to living near the 'fleshpots' of London. The Arsenal 'family' involved not only the players but also the club's backroom staff, among whom Chapman and his successor George Allison both stressed the need for continuity. The club's 'boot room', comprising Whittaker (who later became manager), Shaw, Peters and Wall, proved that continuity was invaluable, as they were able under Allison's leadership to help to continue Arsenal's successes, drawing heavily on the methods and values laid down by Chapman in the late 1920s and early 1930s.

However, Allison's style was in marked contrast to Chapman's when it came to dealing with players and getting his ideas across. While Chapman was a forceful man, used to having his team accept his authority without question, Allison adopted a more cooperative and negotiated style, probably reflecting his general lack of experience of the game at the top level. Alex James, for one, reported that he found Allison's style more acceptable, although Arsenal's captain, Eddie Hapgood, also noted in his post-war autobiography that the players, in general, were initially not very keen on having Allison as Chapman's replacement, because of his lack of tactical ability.[10] Allison, however, made excellent use of the cumulative experience of his backroom staff, especially Shaw and Whittaker.

The rise of professional football managers within some of the leading clubs during the 1930s is relatively easy to trace. In contrast, the evidence from other clubs in the four divisions of the Football League is patchy, although some general observations can be safely made. To begin with, employing both a secretary and a manager, rather than just a secretary or a secretary–manager, would presumably have given the less wealthy clubs in the lower divisions even greater financial problems than they already had, operating as most of them did on a virtual shoestring. Nevertheless, the increasing publicity being given to the First Division clubs and the exploits of their high-profile managers can only have intensified the pressure on the directors of these lower-level clubs to pursue just one over-riding strategy: to seek promotion by any means. An analysis of the club records of clubs in the two Third Divisions, South and North, again comparing 1932/3 with 1938/9, suggests that Chapman at Arsenal and Buckley at Wolves were indeed setting an example that even clubs without much financial strength tried to emulate. Of the 22 clubs that were in the Third Division (South) in 1932/3 12 had secretary–managers, 2 had secretaries and 8 had both secretaries and managers. By 1938/9 13 of the 22 had both, while the other 9 all had secretary–managers. In the Third Division (North), 4 clubs had separate secretaries and managers in 1932/3, but 11 had such an arrangement in 1938/9. Two of these clubs, Darlington and Rochdale, employed player–managers, and one, Mansfield, employed a manager–trainer, indicating perhaps that there was still a need to economise while creating a post with specific responsibility for the footballing aspects of the club.

Even so, at many clubs the manager or secretary–manager still did not control all aspects of the team, and its training and development. Clubs large and small still remained the preserves of directors taking time away from their main businesses to seek personal kudos and contribute to their communities. Puppet managers were still commonplace even as late as 1939. In this regard, Everton's insistence on retaining the post of secretary, rather than appointing someone as a manager, may have been more honest than the practice of appointing a manager but giving him little or no decision-making power. Joe Mercer,[11] recalling his Everton days under the club's secretary Theo Kelly, and the attempt by the players to copy Arsenal's 'third back' system, pointed out that the real power within the club remained in the hands of the chairman, Will Cuff. After the team was beaten 6–0 by Middlesbrough, while using the 'new' approach, Cuff arrived in the dressing room before the next game, against Preston, to deliver his 'team talk': 'Thrills and excitement are what they want. This bloody third-back game will bankrupt us! Get out there and start to play as Everton are expected to play!' Mercer notes that that is what they promptly did: they were beaten 6–5 by Preston, having led five times. At Everton the secretary was clearly not a manager under a different job title. Instead Cuff obviously regarded his role as including the determination of football tactics, even on behalf of a team that included the likes of Mercer and Tommy Lawton.

Another example of management quite unlike anything that would be understood by that term today was recalled by Raich Carter of Sunderland.[12] Johnny Cochrane, Sunderland's secretary–manager from 1928 to 1939, was infamous for his pre-match team talks. As Carter recounts: 'Just before a game, this man wearing a bowler hat, smoking a cigar and drinking whisky would pop his head round the dressing-room door. He'd ask "Who are we playing today?" We would chorus "Arsenal, boss." Johnny would just say, "Oh, we'll piss that lot!" before shutting the door and leaving us to it.' Cochrane and Chapman were both secretary–managers in the First Division during the 1930s, yet they clearly had significantly different interpretations of their role. The fact that both men managed teams that won the First Division Championship suggests that, whatever job title was held by the man with formal management responsibilities, and whatever real power he may have had, there was more than just management involved when it came to winning at football.

Trainers and training

'Gentleman George' Hardwick, who played for Middlesbrough in the late 1930s, has described training in his time as consisting of 'jogging aimlessly around Ayresome Park' and claimed that 'to be given a ball was considered a treat'.[13] T.G. Jones of Everton recalls the beginning of the season as being 'very, very hard, a lot of leg work and running. Long-distance running, short distances, sprinting and gymnastic work, it really was hard.'[14] Stanley Matthews, recalling his early years with Stoke City, has similar memories: 'training at most clubs consisted of a few laps of the running track, some exercises, then off for a bath and a Woodbine. Often a ball wouldn't feature at all.'[15]

These recollections reflect the majority view on the training of players during the 1930s. Football has always been an essentially physical game and, in an era when, as we shall see later, most managers and players were opposed to coaching, it is not surprising to find that clubs placed their highest priority on building physical strength and stamina, especially at the start of the season. It must also be remembered that, with just a few exceptions, most clubs had few, if any, facilities that could be used for training. Only the larger clubs had their own gymnasiums; very few had sufficient land for special training pitches; and training equipment was expensive. Club trainers had to make do with whatever space and resources they could find. With many clubs either paying lip-service to the concept of management or ignoring it altogether, it was often down to trainers to take the lead in preparing the players for their weekly matches. Most trainers were also required to act as physiotherapists, finding ways of healing the normal day-to-day injuries suffered by players in this toughest of games. As Gordon Watson of Everton recalls, this generally meant 'iodine for cuts and whisky for sprains'.[16]

'Special' training was starting to characterise the game at this time, especially before important cup matches. Taking the players away from their normal surroundings, often to a coastal resort or a spa town, so that they could be prepared for the big match became the norm for most of the more affluent clubs and was regarded by the players as something of a perk. Newspapers loved to report on such happenings, as they were among the few off-the-field activities that could not only be written about but also be photographed. How special 'special' training was is hard to ascertain from such reports: more often than not players were shown playing golf, walking along a beach or taking a brine bath. Derby County's players, for example, were taken to Rhyl in North Wales for two weeks before an important Third Round cup tie in January 1937,[17] while Manchester United sent not only all eighteen players and the manager, but also the chairman and the board of directors, to a spa, also in North Wales. The *Daily Dispatch* reported that they had 'used different types of baths at the spa, their up-to-date gymnasium and private golf course, as well as visiting an Odeon picture theatre'.[18] Special training seems to have had as much to do with preparing mentally for the rigours of the forthcoming match as with honing the players' leg muscles.

While training was generally somewhat basic by today's standards, there were clubs that adopted different practices. Arsenal, not surprisingly, led the way in its approach both to training and to the treatment of injuries. With Chapman's full backing, the trainer, Tom Whittaker, developed the club's medical facilities to a level then unsurpassed in British sport. As Chapman himself commented, 'If trainers were transferred like players his fee would be beyond price.'[19] Under Whittaker's tutelage the Arsenal players willingly turned up for five days of training a week, which was not the norm elsewhere. As with other clubs, running was still a mainstay activity, although players were trusted to put in whatever amount of training they thought was needed. Arsenal also experimented with a variety of mechanical devices and initiated the practice of 'head tennis'. Everton also led the way in its approach to training, as befits a club known at the time as 'the School of Science'. Tommy Lawton, the centre-forward in the Everton team that won the Championship in 1939, has recalled: 'We just played it by ear. We did nothing else but play five-a-side football. No tackling and, if it got a bit too easy, one-touch and two-touch . . . it gives you mastery of the ball . . . and above all it gives you understanding of other people.'[20] Lawton also recalls that the players used to come back in the afternoons to work with their trainer, Harold Cooke, on any problems identified in their morning sessions. Everton's approach was essentially training through playing, rather than training through merely running, but few clubs were prepared to countenance this in an era of strong defences and tough tackling.

Coaching and tactics

While managers varied in their interpretations of their role and duties, and trainers varied in their approaches to the development of fitness, there was one aspect of the game in the 1930s that almost all managers, trainers and, indeed, players agreed about: that footballers could not be coached to play in particular ways in order to win particular matches. This widespread resistance to coaching was, according to Wagg, a reflection of the commonly held view that it was 'anathema' as 'it undermined the hero, transferring his rightful credit to dry off-the-field boffins'.[21] Wagg goes on to suggest that, with both managers and players coming, in the main, from the urban working classes, they brought with them an 'ingrained suspicion of book learners, chalkers on blackboards and purveyors of purely theoretical knowledge'.[22] Coaching was seen as something alien to the majority of players and their managers, representing an affront to those who regarded themselves as 'natural' players, born to play the 'people's game'. Stanley Matthews, for one, certainly held this view, stating that he would 'defy any coach to make a really good player out of a youngster who hasn't got what it takes'.[23]

Inevitably, perhaps, a few key individuals held the opposite view. In particular, Herbert Chapman, Frank Buckley and Stanley Rous were to play major roles in the development of the game, both in the 1930s and, indirectly, long after their own time. Chapman was a strong believer in the value of teamwork over individuality and organised his own coaching scheme in conjunction with the amateur club Corinthians. Buckley, who had himself represented England as a player, became probably one of the first managers to put on a tracksuit and train with his team, organising coaching for his young recruits at Wolverhampton, often refereeing practice matches and passing on instructions.

However, it was Rous who made the greatest impact on the introduction of formal coaching into the English game. Appointed secretary to the Football Association in 1934, he set about trying to ensure that football coaching became established, from schools to the international level, as a key ingredient in the making of a successful team. He took the view that, if England's national players were to hold their heads high in the increasingly competitive and skilful international game, youngsters at school would have to be taught the principles and skills of football alongside other subjects in the curriculum. In the 1920s schools had started to switch their allegiance to the rugby code of football, which was seen as more of a 'gentleman's game'. Association football had to hit back if the national team was to prosper. Rous saw the development of hundreds of FA-qualified football coaches, working not only in clubs and at the international level, but also, and more importantly, in schools and at youth level, as the key to the game's long-term success. The FA's first coaching course was organised in London in 1936 and was attended by, among others, Whittaker of Arsenal, Grimsdall of Tottenham and Jimmy Hogan of Fulham. Rous believed that players should attend the courses so that they could not only pick up some additional earnings through coaching in their spare time, but also have a second career open to them after they retired from playing. He also believed that their playing abilities might well benefit too. Sadly, many players saw the notion of gaining a certificate to prove their knowledge of a game that they dearly loved and had practised for many years as a threat rather than as an opportunity. The courses also meant that anyone could become qualified to coach football, not just players or former players, so any player who anticipated moving into management at the end of his playing days could be forgiven for seeing this new breed of coaches as likely to limit his employment prospects.

While Rous, with his FA-backed courses, and managers such as Chapman and Buckley were preaching the benefits of formal coaching to all who would listen, there had for many years been significant numbers of former players undertaking coaching across Europe and even as far away as South America. Jimmy Hogan, for example, had pursued a very successful career as a coach in European clubs and international football, including being coach for the Austrian national team. Back in England, however, Hogan found it hard to get his ideas accepted, either by players or by directors. When he was managing Aston Villa in 1936, just after the team had been relegated to the Second Division, Hogan came up against a less than supportive club chairman, who once declared: 'I've no time for all these theories about football. Get the ball in the bloody net, that's all I want.'[24]

While coaching was anathema to most, the use of tactical planning by forward-thinking managers was also denigrated by many, including those players who had built their careers and their status as heroes on their own individual skills and their fair but hard style. As 'Gentleman George' Hardwick recalls, 'tactical discussions were kept to a minimum. Games were won or lost by the individual ability of the 11 men on the pitch. We always concentrated on our own strengths and were never immersed in the quality of the opposition.'[25] Bill 'Dixie' Dean, the icon of Everton, also actively resisted Theo Kelly's attempts to introduce a tactical system in an attempt to match the ever-successful Arsenal. Stanley Matthews recalled that 'we picked up tricks by watching others and by playing as often as we could'.[26] Such 'star' players saw themselves as being above the need for teaching, forgetting that they were very much the exceptions to the rule. Coaching offered players and teams with more modest abilities a means of making the best use of their talents and harnessing the strength of the team over and above the special skills of a small number of individualists. Some players and managers still saw discussion of tactics as a form of deviousness and gamesmanship, running counter to what Wagg has called 'the dominant football ideology of the time'.[27] For most working-class men football was about playing the game fairly but hard, so that 'anyone who shrank from this placed an ominous question mark against his masculinity'.[28] As the Everton star T.G. Jones recalls: 'There were a lot of dirty tricks practised. Going over the top was the worst thing. You had to be very skilled, very well-practised to really be effective at this sort of thing.'[29] For Jones and his contemporaries football was a much harder and more physical game than it is today.

5 Footballers' lifestyles

Professional football and footballers were increasingly in the public eye during the 1930s (see also Chapter 6). As national newspapers increasingly competed for readers, and the new media of radio, cinema and, latterly, television offered additional coverage, every professional player 'plied his trade under a much brighter media spotlight'[1] than ever before. A select few, such as Bill 'Dixie' Dean and Stanley Matthews, came close to being national household names, but for the vast majority of players coverage remained mostly local, the town newspaper being the primary means by which their exploits, on and off the field, were revealed to their adoring public.

Competition among newspapers, especially but not exclusively at the national level, resulted in increasing amounts of space being given over to football coverage, but with matches being played only once a week, reporters were always short of copy to fill their midweek columns. News of injuries or of potential and actual transfers could be taken only so far without repetition. Players were generally barred or discouraged by their protective clubs from speaking to the press, although some star players, with their clubs' approval and, usually, cooperation, were able to speak through regular ghostwritten columns, in which they discussed their activities, their views on football and their feelings about particular games. Since (as mentioned in Chapter 3) the FA frowned on players making public criticisms of other players, these columns usually ended up being relatively bland, although they did enable some players to reach audiences far beyond the terraces of their own club. Meanwhile, given that most directors maintained a generally dismissive or uncooperative attitude, the managers became the primary internal sources of stories for the reporters. Indeed (as discussed in Chapter 4), the managers themselves often became the story: their wheeler-dealing, the special diets and medical treatments that they favoured, and their own job prospects all became 'news'.

In addition to newspapers, there was a widespread readership for specialist publications in the 1930s, including, for example, the *Topical Times*, with its detailed coverage of sport in general and football in particular. Such publications regularly included photographs of players, both on and off the field. They also ran circulation-boosting give-aways in the form of usually black-and-white but occasionally full-colour photo-cards, which could be mounted in albums also available from the publishers. These cards became the subject of many playground and terrace negotiations, and spread the images of players across the country.

The rise of the cinema and the showing of newsreels between feature films also led to increased coverage of football, in particular of the FA Cup Final and international matches. The British film industry itself also got onto the football bandwagon, notably when Arsenal's manager George Allison and some of his players, including Jack Crayston, appeared in Thorold Dickinson's film *The Arsenal Stadium Mystery*, a comedy thriller made in 1939 but still occasionally shown on television (most recently in June 2003).

Through newspapers, specialist magazines, newsreels and films the leading professional footballers of the 1930s were starting to become terrace heroes far beyond their own clubs. While this helped to promote the game in general, it also helped to boost attendances when a visiting team contained players who were regularly featured in the national media. The increased public attention also meant that the social standing of the players themselves was changing. Football was suddenly not just a job of work, put on public show on a Saturday afternoon, but a phenomenon that had an impact on their overall lifestyles. Suddenly they had to concern themselves with the effect on their public personas of what they did in their leisure time, how they dressed, what they said in public, and so on. Players had no social preparation for this new status. There were no agents or public relations officers in those days. Although some clubs and players benefited from having publicity-minded managers, such as Herbert Chapman and then George Allison at Arsenal, most clubs took the opposite approach and actively restricted the flow of information into the public arena. The media were not yet called by that name, but they could already be seen as potential enemies. Clubs regularly imposed news blackouts on the private lives of their players and were fearful of any indiscretions leaking out.

'Respectable young men'

Analysis of newspaper coverage reveals either that in the 1930s professional footballers really were as 'respectable, amiable, fun-loving in a fairly innocent way and hard-working'[2] as they were portrayed at the time, or that their images were already being manipulated by clubs that were highly skilled at managing their relations with the press. Photographs of young men wearing suits in posed groups, or dressed in golfing attire while on 'special' training at a seaside resort or a spa, show that these well-paid working-class lads really had moved on from their roots in the terraced housing that has become so familiar an image of British towns and cities in the 1930s.

In Russell's view, 'this image probably genuinely reflected the lifestyles and attitudes of most professionals'.[3] Certainly, those players who later wrote their autobiographies, or had them ghostwritten, presented very similar images of life as young players in the 1930s. Eddie Hapgood of Arsenal, for example, recalled his team-mates as non-smokers and non-drinkers who loved nothing better than a game of cards on away trips and plenty of golf in the afternoons. Saving their earnings for later life was also actively encouraged by Arsenal, which had a club savings scheme that guaranteed a 6 per cent return. As Hapgood comments: 'many of the players saved for the first time in their lives when they came to Highbury'.[4] Peter Doherty of Blackpool and Manchester City has written in a similar vein, stressing that this era saw footballers starting to take their 'professional' status more seriously. Having left his native Ireland, Doherty found that the order of the day for a young player starting his career was no smoking, no drinking and no women. Occasional nights out at the pictures with a couple of team-mates before returning to their digs appear to have been the norm. Doherty also advocated the value of getting married as a way of ensuring that a player took his career seriously.

Players and their local communities

The careers of many professional footballers began, continued and ended within their local communities. The transfer system meant that many other players were required not only to relocate to a new club, often at short notice, but also to move from one local community into another. This social disruption was regarded as a 'given', but it created its own tensions for players. For example, Bert Sproston, capped by England at full-back in the 1930s, was involved in an unfortunate move from Leeds to Tottenham Hotspurs: having failed to settle in London, he was very quickly sold, this time to Manchester City.

Those players who retained their usefulness to their current clubs and were therefore regularly retained on contract over the summer months gradually became fixtures in their local communities, the best example probably being Stanley Matthews, with his grounding in the community of Stoke on Trent. In 1938 the prospect of his departure provoked public uproar and protest. Such local heroes, by their character on the field and their loyalty to the club and, by implication, their community, epitomised much of what average citizens wished to see, in both themselves and their neighbours. Many such players led their private lives in the same living spaces as their fans. Manchester City's legendary goalkeeper Frank Swift, for example, recalls travelling home after a particularly gruelling match with his wife on the top deck of a bus in the midst of City fans, having a debate with one particular fan, who did not recognise him in his 'civvies', about whether or not the goalie should have let in a goal.[5] T.G. Jones of Everton also recalls travelling to the ground for a match by ferry and tram alongside the Goodison faithful.[6]

Arsenal players, on the other hand, once established as regulars, were encouraged by the club to invest in property in the leafier suburbs of North London, well away from Highbury. In this respect as in others, the leading club of the 1930s was a harbinger of changes that were to come to other clubs in later decades.

Working patterns, in season and out of season

Footballers in the 1930s typically played matches only on Saturdays. With no floodlights, evening matches were still many years off, despite the far-sighted proposals of Herbert Chapman and others. The working week of the typical professional was still dominated by the game, nevertheless. Training was under-taken on most weekdays during the season and even Sunday was a working day in many clubs, since players turned up at the ground to receive treatment for injuries received during the Saturday match. Eddie Hapgood, for example, recalls that in the early years of Chapman's reign at Arsenal Monday was a day off, but the players came to enjoy training so much that they soon volunteered for Mondays too, so by the early 1930s Monday had become part of the normal working week.

Training tended to take place collectively in the mornings. Clubs with stricter codes of discipline expected their players to sign in by 10 o'clock and penalised them if they turned up late. Those players who had families living nearby usually ate lunch at home, while the others gathered in a local café after the morning's exertions. Afternoons tended to be used by the players for a variety of other sporting and leisure pursuits, but still as a group. Golf features frequently in accounts of players' lives at this time, perhaps surprisingly, in view of the fact that many golf clubs were bastions of the middle class at the time. Players also engaged in snooker and billiards, visited the local picture house or dance hall, or played cards. The social networks of professional footballers were largely restricted to their families and their team-mates. With most other adults either working long hours in factories or offices during the day, or, if they were unemployed, lacking the financial resources to fund leisure outside their homes, players were effectively cocooned from their fans.

As local celebrities, players were also sought after to take part in a variety of 'good works', through charity dinners and other social functions. The clubs regarded such activities as useful means to demonstrate that they were putting something back into their local communities, off the field as well as on it. Indeed, many club directors justified their own involvement in football as both representing and assisting their local communities, and expected their employees to take the same attitude. Local press coverage of such 'ambassad-orial' activities was also an asset.

As discussed in Chapter 4, many of the leading clubs sent their players away for 'special' training before important cup matches. These days or, sometimes, weeks away provided the players with a welcome break in routine and appear to have been regarded as paid holidays rather than periods of intensive work. Training periods gave players who were used to living in 'digs' or relatively modest housing opportunities to sample a lifestyle based on hotels, spas and other forms of luxury. Opportunities for foreign travel were also far beyond the expectations of almost all working-class men at this time. Clubs regularly organised end-of-season tours, usually on the continent, and these too were regarded as holidays with a little football thrown in, rather than as occasions for serious, meaningful competition.

The summer months, in close season, offered varied experiences for professional footballers, depending upon their contractual positions. For a club's regular first-team players the summer meant a possible club tour, followed by a paid holiday during which they could rest before the start of pre-season training or pursue other interests such as cricket, a sport followed by a fair number of footballers including the Arsenal stars Denis and Leslie Compton, Joe Hulme and Ted Drake. For less fortunate players the summer months were to be feared as a period with no wages coming in and little prospect of gaining short-term work. The ultimate fear was that they would not be offered a contract at the start of the following season, or that, if they were, it would be on worse terms. The insecurity of most professional footballers in the close season led to many in the lower divisions drifting out of the game, at least in a full-time capacity.

A week in the life: a case study

The following extracts are taken from an article published in the *Topical Times* in January 1939. Although the player is not identified he is referred to as a 'player who has been capped 14 times'. The article is presented in the form of a daily diary across the Christmas period. It is evident that while a footballer was on duty his life was highly organised and that many decisions were made by the administrators at the club on his behalf. Then as now, professional footballers led relatively sheltered and privileged lives, certainly as compared to the lives of their working-class fans. While they may have complained that they were poorly paid, they were also subsidised, at least while they were away from home: how many other working-class men in 1938 had ever been inside a taxi, let alone had taxi journeys paid for by their employers?

> Wednesday [21 December 1938]: The taxis take us along to the ground at Harrogate where we do our training. Our trainer has rigged up a punch ball for us. We finish our training for the morning, running back to our hotel . . . we pass the afternoon playing table tennis . . . in the evening we are taken along to a boxing match at a local hotel.

> Thursday [22 December]: We run to the ground after breakfast and do the rest of our training in the dressing rooms. Later on we run back to our hotel . . . I later take a walk round the shops, buying a few presents and Christmas cards. After dinner we go to the station to meet our secretary coming back after attending our directors' board meeting. He tells me I will be captain of our team on Saturday, and that there are two changes . . . We all retire to a café, where we have a sing-song over a cup of tea.
>
> Back to the hotel for tea.
>
> After dinner, we are taken to the pictures to see Harold Lloyd in *Professor Beware*.

Friday [23 December]: We are taken by taxis to our training ground, where we do some sprints in the slush. We also do some exercises and skipping, and then back to our hotel, where we have a quick bath.

Next comes a walk round town . . .

Back to our hotel for dinner, and in the afternoon we all go into a café, where we have another sing-song. We have tea early, pack our bags and entrain for Manchester.

The journey is passed playing cards and when we arrive in Manchester taxis take us along to the Midlands Hotel, where we have the good fortune to witness a cabaret show.

Saturday [Christmas Eve]: After breakfast, we have a walk before entraining for home, where we have a lunch of tea, fish and toast. Taxis come along and take us up to our ground.

Soon we are stripped, and I lead our team onto the field . . .

The player reports that his team wins the match 4–0 and that he scores his first ever goal. He goes on to describe his evening:

At night, a friend and I go into town, where we have a walk round the shops and also watch all the people making whoopee.

Sunday (Christmas Day): After breakfast, I go along to the ground, where our trainer is very busy preparing our football kit for our game on Monday against the league leaders.

Later in the afternoon a friend and I take a run in the electric train as far as Southport, where we have tea in a café and book seats for the pictures.

The film they go to see is one of the hits of 1938, *The Adventures of Robin Hood*, starring Errol Flynn, but the player finds it 'disappointing'.

Monday [26 December]: I lie in bed until noon, and then have a light lunch of poached egg, tea and toast. I pack my case once again and off I go to the ground.

The player reports that there are two changes in his team. A crowd of 55,000 turns up, which the player regards as 'very good considering the weather'. The match ends in a 2–2 draw, with this player scoring once again: he considers the draw 'a fair result'. He then continues his diary:

We set off by taxi to the station, where we have dinner in the grill room. There are three teams having their food at this place – our opponents and ourselves, and Manchester City, who have been playing Tranmere.

After food, our opponents and our own team set off by train on our first stage to play in the return match. In our party there are 18 players . . . It is rather a tiresome journey.

When we reach our destination our opponents stay at the same hotel as us. This is more like friendly matches – until, of course, we go on the field.
After a light supper, upstairs to bed.

Tuesday [27 December]: Down for breakfast, and I learn that there is one change in our team. Our centre forward is fit.
Taxis to the ground, where I do a friend of mine a good turn.

A friend of the player's, and a group he has arrived with, cannot get into the ground anywhere, but the player manages to get them some tickets. The match is watched by 35,000, with a 'few thousand' turned away. The match ends with a 2–1 defeat for the player's team, although he scores yet another goal. Then:

After the game we have food and entrain for Dorking. The journey is passed playing cards, and when we reach London a bus takes us the rest of the way. We are allotted our various rooms and so to bed.

The player concludes his diary on Wednesday 28 December, commenting that the last time he was in Dorking 'we had just won the English Cup. Maybe being here once again is an omen!'

6   Footballers and the media

The 1930s saw unprecedented changes in the British mass media. The national newspaper industry became more concentrated, with a reduction in the number of titles published, yet also more competitive, notably with the emergence of the popular press, which aimed to exploit the increasing social acceptance of newspaper-reading as a habit among all but the very poorest. The British Broadcasting Corporation (BBC), formed in the mid-1920s, significantly expanded its radio service as technology developed and manufacturers found ways of producing wireless sets at affordable prices. Towards the end of the decade television, which was eventually to become the primary mass medium, started to reach out to small numbers of households the length and breadth of Britain. Football both contributed to the growing popularisation of the media and was significantly influenced by it, becoming a truly national game for the first time. As football itself became institutionalised as a seemingly 'natural' element of British society and culture, so too did its main participants, the managers and, ultimately, the players.

By the 1930s national, regional and local newspapers constituted the main form of mass communication in Britain. By the outbreak of the Second World War daily papers were being read by 69 per cent of all adults and Sunday papers by 82 per cent. Newspapers' circulation figures had risen significantly during the 1920s and continued to rise throughout the 1930s. In 1920, for example, only the *Daily Mail* had had a circulation of more than 1 million, but by 1939, when the *Mail* was selling 1.5 million copies a day, the *Daily Express* was selling 2.5 million, the *Daily Herald* (forerunner of, though very different from, today's *Sun*) was selling 2 million and the *Daily Mirror* was selling 1.5 million. The Sunday papers experienced a similar expansion in their circulation during this period. Sales of the *News of the World*, for example, rose from 3 million in 1925 to 3.85 million in 1937, while those of the *People* (later renamed the *Sunday People*) rose from 2.5 million in 1930 to 3.4 million in 1937. While the Sunday papers remained more popular, the bulk of the growth in newspaper circulation benefited the weekday papers, especially those targeted at the increasingly literate working classes. Between 1920 and 1937 daily papers saw an 80 per cent increase in sales, while the Sundays experienced only a 20 per cent increase. The rise of the major titles was to some extent at the expense of lesser ones, and a number of daily and Sunday titles disappeared, usually through mergers. The rise of the 'popular' papers, with their more sensational approach to news reporting, reinforced the established distinction between them and the 'quality' press – especially, again, in circulation figures. In 1939 *The Times*, for example, had a circulation of just 213,000, while the *Daily Telegraph* sold 640,000 copies a day. Regional and local newspapers also underwent a process of concentration during this period. Between 1921 and 1937 the numbers of regional daily papers declined from 41 to 28, of regional evening papers from 89 to 79 and of regional weeklies from 1,485 to 1,162.

In contrast, weekly publications aimed at specific groups of readers expanded rapidly, both in circulation and in range of subjects. Women's magazines grew in number, as did children's comics. The 1930s saw the birth, for example, of both the *Dandy*, in 1937, and the *Beano*, in 1938.

While newspapers and magazines went on expanding their overall readership, probably the most significant development in the mass media between the wars was the introduction and acceptance of the wireless (or radio, as it later became known). In 1922, when regular broadcasts began, only 1 per cent of British households had a wireless licence, but this figure rose to 30 per cent by 1930 and 71 per cent by 1939. It has been estimated that there were nearly 9 million wireless sets in British homes in the latter year, giving about 34 million individuals the opportunity to receive broadcasts. This exponential growth was fuelled by the ability of British manufacturers to launch a series of cheap radio sets onto the market. At prices between £1 and £3, and with opportunities to buy them by hire-purchase agreement, wirelesses became familiar objects in the vast majority of British homes. For those without the means to purchase their own sets there were also opportunities to gather in local radio shops in order to listen to reports of the major events of the day, such as the Cup Final, the Grand National or speeches by the King or the Prime Minister. Instant access to the latest news and to all forms of light entertainment through the BBC radically altered British society. The radio can be regarded as having played a key role in enhancing national unity and cultural homogeneity.

The cinema also continued to provide many towns and cities with one of the few social amenities that could be used, without reservation, by families and by unaccompanied women. With tickets being relatively cheap, even the unemployed could be found attending day-time showings of films. The number of cinemas (or picture houses, as they were sometimes known) rose rapidly, from 3,000 in 1914 to 5,000 in 1939. Bolton, for example, boasted 14 cinemas, serving a population of 180,000, in 1937. In many industrial conurbations it was quite common for people, especially the young, to go to the cinema several times during any one week. The newsreels, shown between the two feature films that formed the standard programme in those days, became an important if slightly outdated visual representation of news stories that cinemagoers had previously only read or heard about, in the newspapers or on the radio. Sporting events, including football matches, made up a significant proportion of the content of these newsreels, allowing people to see what particular players looked like, as well as seeing them engaged in their various exploits.

Finally, television, courtesy of the BBC, joined the ranks of the mass media in Britain in 1936, only to be suspended as soon as war broke out in 1939. Although it was very much a minority pursuit, television was to bring sport, and in particular football, into the living rooms of the masses. September 1937, for example, saw the very first attempt at a public broadcast of a football match by the BBC: a practice match between Arsenal and Arsenal Reserves was seen in a few thousand homes in the vicinity of Alexandra Palace in North London. The following year saw the very first live television broadcast of football's showpiece event, the FA Cup Final at Wembley.

Interplay between the mass media and football

Football became increasingly popular, both as a sport and as a social phenomenon, during the 1930s. Attendance figures rose, and clubs invested increasing amounts of money in improving their grounds and in players' transfer fees. As large sections of the working population overcame the scruples of their parents' generation to take up the pools and other forms of football-related gambling, football became part of most households' everyday experience. This trend and the rising popularity of the mass media reinforced each other. The development of football as the 'national game' was partly an outcome of the media's increasing attention to it, and the media's increasing presence in the everyday lives of British people was also partly an outcome of the use of football to gain readers and listeners. Each fed off the other, to their mutual benefit.

In particular, the coverage of football by the national press helped to give the game a national stage. While the local press retained its essential parochialism, the national papers, especially the 'populars', gave individual clubs, managers and players a nationwide appeal. Clubs suddenly found themselves with supporters in areas and regions well outside their own local communities. Arsenal, in particular, found that its away matches swelled its opponents' gate receipts, as people swarmed in to see stars such as Ted Drake, Eddie Hapgood and Cliff Bastin, whom they had previously only read about or seen in newsreels. The FA Cup Final and international matches, especially the traditional fixture between England and Scotland, became truly national events, followed by millions who would never think of attending a match at a local football club.

Football journalism developed to reflect this increased popularity. Facing an increasing need to compete for readers, papers such as the *People* adopted an approach that marked them off from papers that maintained the tradition of factually based reporting. While match reports were still the main form of coverage, they were increasingly written in an American style, with shorter sentences and paragraphs, and a more aggressive tone, and they were accompanied by photographs of action from the game. More column inches were also given over to football gossip, especially relating to possible transfers, injuries and happenings off the field. The *People* was the first paper to take its sports news out of the main body of the paper and move it to its current location on the back pages. It also significantly increased the number of column inches given over to football, while reducing its traditional emphasis on horse racing. The *People* also adopted a more irreverent attitude to the football authorities, both nationally and at the club level. Humour started to play an increasingly important role, as did the search for evidence of corruption and wrongdoing, particularly on the business side of the game. Reporters were becoming adept at searching out the 'inside story' and also tended to adopt a more campaigning stance, especially when it was believed that players or supporters were being dealt with harshly or unfairly. Predictably, the Players Union and the maximum-wage issue came in for considerable comment from many of the columnists employed by the popular daily and Sunday papers. Even the *Daily Worker*, the newspaper of the Communist Party of Great Britain, got in on the act with criticisms of football clubs' directors and their alleged sharp practices.

Football at the local level had always attracted a certain degree of loyalty from local newspapers. Criticisms, if any, tended to be mild and advisory rather than hostile. This, perhaps, was not very surprising, given that local football reporters were almost entirely reliant on maintaining good relations with clubs and their officials in order to get their copy. The growth in the popularity of football led many local newspapers to launch special Saturday editions to provide scores and match reports. Normally printed on pink or green paper, these instant special editions tended to display a strong bias towards local teams and also gave inside information on the latest developments behind the scenes. The clubs themselves also attempted to use local papers to communicate with fans *en masse* and with the wider local communities. In 1939, for example, Sheffield United, aware that rumours were abounding that its star centre-forward Jock Dodds had left the club of its own accord, gave the Sheffield *Star* a special briefing so that its side of the story could be told.

Local newspapers fulfilled an additional role within their communities: that of providing opportunities for fans to have their own say on football-related matters through letters to the editor, which were usually critical. Such letters could provide a newspaper's reporters with the chance to have things stated in public that they themselves would find it difficult to write without damaging their access to the club in question, as well as the chance to establish their paper as the forum for local debate and discussion. Alan Hoby, later to become a famous national football writer, recalls being banned from Brentford's ground following the publication of a reader's letter that attacked the team's performance.

One of the most sensational footballing incidents of the late 1930s, involving the Stoke City legend Stanley Matthews, demonstrates the role that local newspapers could play.[1] Matthews was in dispute with the club over a benefit payment and sought a transfer. Faced with the possible loss of the city's most famous player, the local *Evening Sentinel* took it upon itself to campaign for a change of heart by both the club and Matthews himself. It ran an editorial declaring: 'Without Stanley Matthews, Stoke City would not be Stoke City.

He is a star of the first magnitude. He cannot be replaced . . . Stanley Matthews must not be allowed to go.' It went on to appeal directly to the player: 'To Stanley Matthews, it must be said that a vast public will be very grateful if he can see his way to withdraw his transfer request, with firm assurances that his position shall be as happy as any player could desire.' Prompted by the *Sentinel*'s front-page coverage, local employers organised a protest meeting, which was attended by thousands, again providing the paper with even more column inches. It also published thirty-five readers' letters in one week, all but one supportive of Matthews staying. Eventually the club and the player came to an agreement, and the crisis was over, at least for the time being. The *Sentinel* had demonstrated the centrality of football to the local community. Its own view was that there had been no news like this since the abdication of Edward VIII three years earlier: football, and in this case one remarkable player, had managed to drive all other stories off the front page, as the *Sentinel* reflected and reinforced the cultural values of its readers. (The *Sentinel* never lost sight of Matthews, the quintessential local terrace hero, even as he moved on in his footballing career to Blackpool. The 'son of the Potteries' was still afforded front-page coverage when he won his Cup Final medal in 1953 and a full commemorative supplement was published after his death.)

The local press also used football as part of what has been called 'telling ourselves stories about ourselves'.[2] In relation to the significance of the FA Cup Final to the two towns or cities directly involved, it has been suggested that the local press has been 'not simply a passive reflector of local life and thought, but an active source in the creation of local feeling'.[3] Coverage of the event itself, at an often distant Wembley, and then of the return of the conquering or defeated team, provided local citizens, both fans and others, with an opportunity to participate in the creation and strengthening of local identity and distinctiveness. Football, especially in the form of major events such as the Cup Final, provided the 'social glue' for many normally divided communities. Local newspapers, with their emphasis on communicating the activities of a community back to that community, had an important part to play in this process.

Football also made a contribution to the spread of the wireless, adding to the public appeal of the medium and benefiting enormously from the mass audience offered by it. This was, it must be said, despite the best efforts of the football authorities. Having initiated live radio broadcasts of football matches in 1927, with coverage of a match between Arsenal and Sheffield United, followed in 1928 by coverage of the FA Cup Final between Huddersfield and Blackburn Rovers, the BBC came up against the conservative FA and the even more conservative Football League. While the FA was generally supportive of the medium, its leaders soon realised that it was missing a commercial opportunity by allowing the BBC to broadcast the event free of charge. In 1929, after the BBC refused to meet the FA's demands for payment for broadcasting rights, the Final was not broadcast nationally, although a national newspaper funded local broadcasts of the match with the BBC's lead commentator, George Allison (later to become Arsenal's manager), providing fans in Bolton and Portsmouth with a match commentary via loudspeaker vans. By 1930 the dispute between the FA and BBC had been resolved, with the BBC paying a £100 fee. During the 1930s the BBC continued to broadcast the Final and England's international matches, with commentary by Allison among others. By 1937 its coverage had been extended to include the FA Charity Shield and mid-week FA Cup semi-finals. The Football League, on the other hand, was not so flexible as the FA. Taking the view that many of its member clubs were suffering financially because of the live broadcasting of important matches while their teams were playing their own games, the League resolved in 1931 to prohibit live radio broadcasts of League matches. A public debate ensued, with newspapers, politicians and others arguing that the ban was denying the 'blind, infirm and hospitalised' the benefits of listening to matches. The League refused to back down from its position and even insisted that the BBC delay broadcasting any sports news at all until after 6:15 p.m. It did, however, permit the broadcasting of matches to other parts of the British Empire. The difference in the attitudes of the FA and the League to the BBC has, in part, been explained by reference to the physical location of the two bodies: the FA was based just a few miles away from the BBC in London, while the League's headquarters were in Preston. In addition, Stanley Rous, secretary of the FA from the mid-1930s, was one of the more farsighted administrators of the time and a keen advocate of gaining more publicity for the game as part of his drive to improve England's standing as an international force in football.

George Allison, the BBC's original radio commentator, continued to play a key role in the development of football broadcasting throughout the 1930s, including during his time with Arsenal. Although he was a native of Durham, Allison's 'southern' tones gave his radio broadcasts and, by implication, football itself a respectability that helped to broaden its appeal beyond its traditional base of support in the working class. His enthusiastic and dramatic approach to describing matches led to his being nicknamed 'By Jove' Allison. His voice became so well known that a cigarette firm produced miniature records of it to be given away with its products. His growing fame was also reflected in his being included in a cigarette card series of radio stars, and photographs of him appeared regularly in radio magazines. As Fishwick has commented:

> Footballers and officials made polite broadcasts over the wireless, and reassuringly refined voices described matches or discussed the game. At the same time, broadcasting helped further to establish the game as the national game, no longer appealing just to the working class in the traditional areas. Millions who might not have grown up in a footballing family or neighbourhood now heard live commentaries or caught glimpses of the game through newsreels, and stars' names and skills were inevitably better-known.[4]

Football was becoming a game that was talked about throughout the country, in all walks of life, by women and girls as well as men and boys, and by people of all ages. This wider audience was one that the clubs and the football authorities eventually found themselves having to address in the second half of the twentieth century, as football became part of the leisure industry.

Finally, we must mention television, the revolutionary medium that was eventually to transform football and much else besides. Initiated as a means of conveying visual excitement to the nation, the televising of football commenced in the late 1930s, again with the cooperation of Arsenal, the most forward-looking of the clubs, and of the FA under Rous's stewardship. After experimental broadcasts from Highbury in September 1937, the Cup Final between Preston and Huddersfield in 1938 was the subject of the first major live football broadcast. While television ownership was limited to members of the moneyed classes, this broadcast once again helped to give the game some respectability and social kudos.

The impact of the mass media on the players

What effects did these developments have on the individual players? Were they just actors on the footballing stage, written about in the papers, commented on in radio broadcasts and, eventually, watched on flickering television screens, or did they play a more proactive role? Players were certainly influenced by the enhanced media coverage given to their game during the 1930s. Most players, even those in the lower divisions, were capable of gaining some degree of fame, even if it was just within their own local communities. Some also gained a degree of infamy, more often than not because of activities off the field. The leading players playing for the most successful teams predictably gained more than most, acquiring extra prestige within the game itself, among their adoring football public and even in society more generally. Their role, however, was to play the game that they were being paid to play, while leaving publicity to others. Individual performances and team achievements were the primary means to achieving personal glory. Players, like children, were, in general, expected to be seen but not heard. Given the social and educational backgrounds of most of the players at the time, this may not have been too misguided a policy.

There were, as always, exceptions, however, and, as usual in the 1930s, the chief exception was Arsenal. Starting the decade under the inspirational and publicity-seeking Herbert Chapman, and ending it under the urbane but equally publicity-seeking George Allison, Arsenal led the field when it came to media relations. Allison, who was (as described above) a journalist turned football manager, commented in his autobiography, published in 1948, that 'I have never left journalism'.[5] Having worked with the showman 'Buffalo Bill' and the US press baron William Randolph Hearst, as well as the BBC, before joining Arsenal, Allison probably contributed more to the positive image of football than any other individual during the late 1920s and 1930s. His attitude to the media clearly rubbed off on his players and his backroom staff: Tom Whittaker, Arsenal's trainer (and later manager himself), contributed to BBC radio programmes on football; Alex James, or rather a ghostwriter in his name, contributed a regular column to a London evening paper; and (as mentioned in

Chapter 5) Allison and several of his players took part in the feature film *The Arsenal Stadium Mystery*, released in 1939. Arsenal's captain, Eddie Hapgood, summed up his own views of the press in his autobiography, published in 1944, with the possibly somewhat naive comment: 'I found that if you play fair with them, they play fair with you.'[6] As the captain of the decade's most successful club side, Hapgood had been the regular target of newspaper reporters for most of his career. There is also evidence that Hapgood, captain of the England team that gave the Nazi salute at the start of an international against Germany in 1938, was quite prepared to express his views to the press, including views contrary to those being communicated by the football authorities.[7]

In conclusion

The 1930s saw the development and institutionalisation of new forms of mass communication within Britain. Football emerged from its traditional working-class enclave to capture the minds and the hearts of a much wider audience, albeit comprising people most of whom had never stood on the terraces on a cold Saturday afternoon in mid-January. For them the terrace heroes were characters on a stage recreated by the mass media through the means of print and broadcast technology. Yet they were still very much terrace heroes, as we shall see in the remaining chapters of this book.

JACK ATKINSON,
Bolton Wanderers F.C.

7   Jack Atkinson – Bolton Wanderers

A stalwart of Bolton Wanderers in the 1930s, Jack Atkinson was 'a giant of a centre half around whom the entire defence would mould itself'.[1] His 'no nonsense' style of play enabled many of the more skilful players around him to demonstrate their art, knowing that any undue foul play would be quickly dealt with by 'Big Jack'.

Off the field Atkinson was anything but aggressive and tended to be the 'archetypal strong, silent type'.[2] Stories about his wife, who was 'petite yet very demonstrative', used to cause amusement among his team-mates: she had made herself well known to them by 'storming into the changing room after a match or a training session to make sure [that] her errant husband was on his way home, and not taking a short cut via the nearest hostelry'.[3]

As Nat Lofthouse has recalled, 'Bolton people liked honest guys, they liked people who tried. If a player was putting it on then they didn't want to know.'[4] Jack Atkinson was certainly one of the 'honest guys' who served the club well throughout much of the 1930s, during the war and on into the boom years of the late 1940s.

Football within the Bolton community

'Huddled figures in cloth caps, mufflers and clogs walking towards a football ground in the North of England':[5] this was the scene on a typical Saturday afternoon in many industrial towns and cities in the 1930s, as captured by the artist L.S. Lowry in his painting *Going to the Match*, which depicts the streets around Bolton's ground at Burnden Park. For most football supporters in Bolton leisure meant spending time trying to recover from the long hours and arduous manual work undertaken in the mills, bleach works and factories that dominated the town. Only 20 per cent of the town's adult population had wireless licences and few had enough disposable income to take trips out of the town, so residents had to rely on local events and activities to relieve the drudgery of their day-to-day existences. By 1938 the Bolton area boasted more than 300 public houses, over 200 churches and chapels, numerous cinemas, theatres and music halls – and one football club. A study undertaken in Bolton by the pioneering social research group Mass Observation in 1937 and 1938 concluded:

'On the whole, people care about their homes and their few personal dreams (security, a holiday weekend at orientalised Blackpool, a fortune on the pools), and nothing else matters much except the progress made by the town's football club, whose stadium draws each Saturday more people than go into the pubs and churches.'[6] For Boltonians the club and its players, including Jack Atkinson, were the fulcrum of their non-working lives, providing regular opportunities to demonstrate their civic pride, and to gain the emotional release of gathering with their peers to escape into the realm of heroes and villains. The town's Wembley track record in the 1920s still fuelled the imaginations of many middle-aged and elderly Bolton supporters, and raised their expectations.

Atkinson's career up to 1939

Born John Edward Atkinson on 20 December 1913 in New Washington, County Durham, 'Big Jack' grew up to play for the same Durham schoolboy side as Raich Carter. From there he moved on to a local works team, Washington Colliery, where he was spotted by a scout for the First Division team Bolton Wanderers. Bolton signed him but came to an agreement that he would benefit more, by playing regularly, if he stayed with the Colliery side. Seeing that he lacked a little in speed, Bolton encouraged the Colliery side to play Atkinson in their forward line. Bolton did not pay a transfer fee but it did make a number of contributions to the Colliery club's funds.

Atkinson eventually became a full-time professional with Bolton at the beginning of the 1931/2 season. Being more than six feet tall, he quickly took on the role of centre-half, playing in Bolton's Lancashire Combination and Central League sides. At the time Bolton were going through a period of transition as they attempted to recapture the halcyon years of the 1920s: Atkinson was just one of the young players signed in an attempt to replace the ageing team that had ended the previous decade with yet another FA Cup victory.

It was not until the last few weeks of the 1932/3 season that Atkinson made his breakthrough into first-team football. Unfortunately, this was just days away from Bolton's relegation into Division Two, after they finished equal on points with their Lancashire neighbour Blackpool. In March 1932 Bolton had sold their regular centre-half, Tom Griffiths, to Middlesbrough; Atkinson, his successor, made his debut in a home draw with West Bromwich Albion. The *Bolton Evening News* anticipated 'a trying baptism . . . against such a business-like attack as Albion's', but its match report stated that 'young Atkinson made an encouraging start'.[7] Its columnist, 'The Tramp', commented: 'No youngster could be better equipped for the game in a physical sense, for at 21 he stands over six feet, and weighs nearly 12 stone of good bone and muscle.'[8]

Atkinson played in the next game too. Although Bolton lost 2–0 to Sheffield Wednesday, the match report described him as 'a real success at centre-half. All through the game he played real football.'[9] Bolton then faced their final League game knowing that their chances of avoiding relegation depended as much on

Wolverhampton Wanderers' performance against Everton as on their own showing against Leeds. Unfortunately for Bolton and Atkinson, their 5–0 victory was to count for nothing, since Wolves also won. Bolton were doomed to play Second Division football for the first time in twenty-two years. Atkinson, however, had done enough in three games to cement his position as the regular first choice for centre-half. Despite being relegated, Bolton managed to end the season with profits of £2,000 and went into the summer in search of new players who could bring an instant return to the First Division. Support for the club had waned as the season had worn on, falling from a record crowd of more than 69,000 at a fifth-round FA Cup tie against Manchester City, which Bolton lost, to just 3,000 for a League game against Portsmouth, only four days later, which again Bolton lost. Bolton's fans were nothing if not unforgiving. A diet of success in the 1920s had established the expectation that Bolton was a winning club.

Bolton finished the following season, 1933/4, in third place, just one point behind Preston North End, who had been promoted, while the long-time leaders Grimsby Town achieved the championship in early April. Bolton and Preston both went into the last day of the season with promotion a possibility, but Preston's 1–0 victory at Southampton sealed second place and promotion, as Bolton was able only to draw 2–2 at Lincoln. Bolton were described as a 'solid side' with a 'clever' forward line, but they had some bad lapses at home, losing five games at Burnden Park. In the FA Cup tournament Bolton reached the sixth round before going down to the eventual losing finalists, Portsmouth. Not surprisingly for a centre-half, Atkinson only scored one goal throughout the season, although it was the only goal in a home victory over Oldham in October. Building on their relative success in the previous season, Bolton managed to win promotion in 1934/5, finishing second behind the champion side, Brentford. Bolton was roundly praised as the team of the season, not only of the Second Division but of the whole Football League:

> Their career was splendid. So varied indeed were their achievements that they nearly fell between two stools and lost promotion, and it was only by goal average on the last day that they regained the status which they lost in 1933. Although West Ham (third placed) had sympathy, it is certain that the public in general were glad that Bolton did not miss the reward. But for a prolonged run in the Cup, in which they received no aid from luck as they were drawn away in each round, they would almost certainly have finished in the first place. Although they won no trophy to show for it, they had as successful a season as they have ever enjoyed, their three Cup successes notwithstanding.[10]

Bolton's relative success as a Second Division side in the FA Cup tournament took the team all the way to the semi-final, where, after a replay, they eventually lost to West Bromwich Albion, which then lost 4–2 in the Final in a thrilling match against Sheffield Wednesday.

Atkinson was a first-team regular throughout the season and was the side's youngest player. He scored just 2 goals out of the 96 scored that season in the League, in a team dominated by the fire-power of the forwards Jack Milsom and Ray Westwood. Atkinson also scored the equalising goal in Bolton's away fifth-round match against Tottenham Hotspurs, a fixture that took three matches to conclude.

Atkinson obtained his only major representative honour during this season, being picked for a Football League XI to play a Combined Wales–Ireland XI at Everton, in celebration of King George V's Silver Jubilee. The League's team consisted exclusively of Lancashire players and contained three of Atkinson's team-mates. They won 10–2, with Hampson of Blackpool scoring 5 of the goals. The match was controlled by two referees. Atkinson never managed to achieve full international recognition, playing as he did at centre-half, a position dominated by some of the game's stars such as Stan Cullis of Wolves.

Having returned to the First Division once more, Bolton expanded the capacity at its Burnden Park ground to 70,000, in anticipation of larger attendances. Bolton finished in respectable mid-table positions throughout the rest of the decade, apart from 1936/7, when they just escaped relegation, finishing once again in twentieth place, mainly because of comparatively poor form at home and a run of injuries to key players. Throughout this period Atkinson continued to be the 'defensive kingpin' of the side, which was augmented with four new signings, three from Scotland – Alf Anderson from Hibernian, Alec Carruthers from Falkirk and John Calder from Morton – and the fourth being the left-back Harry Hubbick from Burnley. While relegation was avoided, the club was left with losses of £12,000 at the end of the season. To help offset the losses George Eastham was sold to Brentford for £4,500.

Bolton had a better season in 1937/8, finishing in seventh place despite losing the services of their key goal-scorer, Milsom, who sought a transfer to Manchester City during the year. Luckily, Bolton was able to replace him quickly with George Hunt, formerly at Tottenham and Arsenal, who went on to form a productive relationship with Bolton's other goal-scorer, Westwood. Bolton turned down a £12,000 bid for Westwood from Chelsea, in a desperate attempt to hold on to one of their key players despite its poor financial position.

Ray Westwood had sufficient charisma to draw large crowds. His stylish, skilful and speedy game made him a hero to the Burnden Park faithful, and a magnet to many other clubs, who wished to avail themselves of his goal-scoring prowess. As Chelsea discovered, Bolton was not going to let him go at any price. Westwood, despite his northern location, was one of the few players who were sufficiently well known to attract business sponsorship and to socialise with visiting stars of show business, such as George Formby. His face and, more significantly, his hair appeared on hoardings advertising the merits of Brylcreem, an endorsement for which he received the princely sum of 5s.

In the 1938/9 season Bolton again produced reasonable results, finishing eighth, with Hunt dominating the goal-scoring through the season. Westwood was out of the side, because of injury, from November to February.

The war years and after

With war looming, in April 1939 the FA wrote to all professional clubs encouraging them to allow their players to set a good example by joining the Territorial Army (TA) or other national service organisations. Bolton's captain, Harry Goslin, addressed the crowd at a home match, exhorting the men to join the TA and the women to volunteer to become nurses or ambulance drivers. On 10 April all of Bolton's first-team players joined the TA and then spent their leisure time preparing for what was to come. Gas masks were arriving and the population was soon trained in how to use them. Sandbags were being stored in key locations throughout the town. Air-raid shelters were being constructed.

At the outbreak of the war, just a few days into the new season, the League suspended all football. Bolton had been one of just two League clubs, the other being West Ham, where the players had signed up, virtually to a man, earlier in the year. As a result 15 of Bolton's players were immediately called up. These players spent much of the war together in the Bolton Artillery, being involved in Dunkirk, Italy and the Middle East. They continued to play football against many other armed forces teams throughout these years. Eventually, 32 of the club's 35 professionals joined the armed forces, while the other 3 took jobs in local munitions factories or in the coalmines.

Atkinson lost many of his best playing years because of the war. Having initially volunteered to join the police force, he continued to play for Bolton as well as guesting for both Everton and Blackpool. He then joined the army and became a non-commissioned officer in the Lancashire Fusiliers. It was during this period that he gained his first experience of football management and led an army team playing in Austria. His team had the distinction of being the first side ever to beat the then-renowned 8th Army team. He also saw service in Africa, in Sicily and elsewhere in Italy.

Bolton joined the North-West Regional League once football was restarted, later in 1939, but attendances were extremely small and there were difficulties in recruiting a team, so the club decided not to continue after the end of the season. Locally based players had to find opportunities to guest for other clubs, and the ground was turned over to the local education authority and the Ministry of Supply. Friendly matches were played against other teams in the region whenever Bolton's manager, Charles Foweraker, could find sufficient youngsters and soldiers on leave. Then in January 1941 Bolton's directors, under pressure from Foweraker, changed their minds about competing in the regional league and rejoined it. Playing in front of crowds of less than 3,000 Bolton managed to get through 33 League and Cup matches, using a total of 66 players. One such player was Nat Lofthouse, then 15 years old, who made his scoring debut for the club in March 1941 against Bury, a landmark in the history of Bolton Wanderers. Most players received 30s. a game, with no bonuses for winning and no payment for training; Lofthouse, still an amateur because he was too young to sign as a professional, received just 2s. 6d. as 'expenses'.

The war years also saw Foweraker's retirement, due to ill health, after he had served the club, in a variety of capacities, for forty-nine years. He is still regarded as the most successful manager in Bolton's history, having steered the team to three FA Cup victories in the 1920s. During the war he served in a voluntary capacity, reflecting the club's shortage of funds. Bolton's trainer, Walter Rowley, was promoted to replace Foweraker and went on to complete thirty-eight years' service before he too retired on grounds of ill health in 1950.

With the return of peace and the recommencement of League football, Jack Atkinson, having been demobilised from the army, returned to play full time with Bolton. Along with other loyal team-mates he was awarded a benefit payment of £650 in recognition of his long service. The 1945/6 season saw Bolton achieve both a creditable third place in the First Division and a place in the semi-final of the FA Cup. However, the season is remembered less for these achievements than for the events of 9 March 1946, which became famous across Britain as the 'Burnden Park tragedy'. Playing in the second leg of the FA Cup sixth-round tie against Stoke City, Bolton experienced one of the game's worst disasters when 33 people lost their lives and more than 500 were injured following the collapse of barriers due to overcrowding. Although the official attendance figure for the match was 65,000, it was later estimated that more than 85,000 had been present to watch Stanley Matthews and Stoke City take on Bolton Wanderers for a place in the Cup semi-final. Although Jack Atkinson was still playing for Bolton at the time, he was not selected for the match, but he was present at the ground, providing support and encouragement to his team-mates.

In the minutes before the match supporters were to be seen climbing over turnstiles, scrambling up the railway embankment that overlooked the ground, forcing holes in fencing and using an exit that had been opened by those already inside the ground, who were attempting to escape from the crush. Although the crowd was spilling onto the perimeter track around the pitch, the match started, and play continued for 12 minutes before it was stopped as it became evident that there had been fatalities and many injuries. The referee took the players off the pitch and they spent the following minutes back in their dressing rooms, unaware of what was happening outside on the terraces. It appears that many of the supporters in other parts of the ground were also unaware of the tragedy that was unfolding before them. It was not until bodies started to be laid out on the pitch itself that the full consequences become apparent to everyone. Amazingly, at least in hindsight, the match was resumed at 3:25 p.m., on the advice of the town's Chief Constable, as a way of avoiding panic. Play continued without a half-time break until the match was completed. The score was 0–0, so Bolton went through to the semi-final with a 2–0 aggregate win.

News of the Burnden Park disaster generated shock not only in Bolton but throughout the country. The Home Secretary, James Chuter-Ede, ordered an inquiry, a relief fund was set up and collected £52,000, and alterations to the ground were put in hand. The report of the inquiry made strong recommendations about the control of crowds at all football grounds, having concluded that the disaster was, in a sense, the result of the crowd's own behaviour, rather than the direct fault of the club, the police or the local authorities, even though there appeared to be little evidence of effective planning to cope with the expected full house, let alone with numbers exceeding the official capacity of the ground. Burnden Park was open for business again just four days after the tragedy, for a League match against Bradford. Just over 5,000 people turned up, demonstrating the impact that the tragedy had had on the majority of Bolton's supporters. Whether their attitude to attending matches was affected over the longer term is difficult to say, although just two weeks after the tragedy more than 7,000 fans travelled to support Bolton in the FA Cup semi-final against Charlton Athletic. The local newspaper published a photograph of some of these fans under the heading, 'Wanderers Followers in Merry Mood'.[11]

During the 1946/7 season Atkinson maintained his position in the first team, making 25 appearances. The following season, however, saw him lose his place to Lol Hamlett and, after making only 6 appearances throughout 1947/8, he was given a free transfer in April 1948 to New Brighton, where he took on the dual role of player–manager. His new club had had to seek re-election to the Third Division (North), and Atkinson was brought in to build up a new team, the club having given 15 of its players free transfers. With Atkinson putting himself at the heart of the defence he managed to turn the club around and achieved two seasons' worth of League respectability. Unfortunately for Atkinson, 'stringent economy measures' led to his being let go. He had made 52 appearances for the club. (New Brighton finished bottom of the Division in the following season. Re-election did not come this time and they were replaced by Workington, a well-supported Cumbrian club. New Brighton continued to play in non-League football until the club closed in 1983.)

'Big Jack' Atkinson eventually retired from the game having played 263 League and Cup matches for Bolton Wanderers between 1933 and 1948. Like many of his contemporaries retiring from the game, Atkinson took over a licensed house, in his case a pub in his beloved Bolton. He also maintained his interest in golf, an activity that featured strongly in many clubs' pre-match training regimes, playing off a handicap of seven. Jack Atkinson, the 'no nonsense' centre-half, protector of the skilful and long-time servant of Bolton Wanderers, died in 1977, aged 64.

ROBERT BAXTER,
Middlesbrough F.C.

TOPICAL
TIMES.

8   Bob Baxter – Middlesbrough

The word 'inspirational'[1] has been used to describe one of Middlesbrough's greatest centre-halves and captains, Bob Baxter. With his square jaw, his sunken eyes and his black, slicked-down hair, Baxter was an imposing figure at the heart of Boro's defence throughout much of the 1930s. Good in the air and a great tackler, he was a leader both on and off the pitch. His wicked sense of humour was often seen in his own penalty area, as he insisted on dribbling the ball past opposition forwards instead of responding to the shouts and screams of his team-mates to 'just boot it clear'. Off the field Baxter was known for his ability to impersonate others, including his team-mates. As Boro's right-half Duncan McKenzie commented in an article published in 1939, 'Most of the fun at Ayresome is started by skipper Bob Baxter. He could make a living any day with his impersonations, and mimics the boys so well that, at times, it's like looking into a mirror.'[2] As another team-mate, George Hardwick, recalled, 'He was an inspirational sort of player and also a natural comedian.'[3] Baxter is still regarded by many as the club's best ever captain and was certainly seen as a terrace hero by supporters in the 1930s.

Baxter's career up to 1939

Baxter was born Robert Denholm Baxter in Gilmerton, near Edinburgh, on 23 January 1911. He started his career playing youth football for a local club, Bruntonian Juniors, and it was there that Boro's manager, Peter McWilliam, spotted his potential. Having travelled north to watch another player whose match was called off, McWilliam dropped in on Bruntonians on the off chance. Baxter at the time was combining playing with a full-time job in the local coalmine as well as the unusual part-time occupation of managing a dance band.

Playing as a forward, Baxter signed professionally for Boro in May 1931, leaving both the mine and his dance band behind him. His first year was less than successful and, just twelve months later, Boro put him on the transfer list. Luckily as it turned out for Boro, no clubs expressed an interest. McWilliam instead persisted with Baxter and in October 1932 he made his first-team debut, at inside-left, in a match at Birmingham. In the next few seasons Baxter's versatility was used to fill gaps throughout the team: he ended up playing in nine different out-field positions. In 1935 Boro's regular centre-half Tom Griffiths left the club. Baxter took over the role and made it his own. He was also elevated to the position of captain, again taking over from the departing Griffiths. Baxter was to go on to make 266 League and Cup appearances for the club before the outbreak of war in 1939.

Middlesbrough started the 1930s in the First Division, having been promoted in 1928/9 under McWilliam's managership. McWilliam continued as manager until 1934, when he left to become chief scout for Arsenal. (He was eventually to become a club manager once again, returning in 1938 to Tottenham, the club that had given him his first managerial appointment in 1912.) While McWilliam was never the most popular manager among the Ayresome Park faithful, he at least created some stability within the club and helped to establish it in the First Division.

McWilliam's role at Middlesbrough was taken up in 1934 by Wilf Gillow, then 51 years old. Boro remained in the First Division throughout the 1930s. This was an improvement on the previous decade, when they had experienced both promotion and relegation, but neither League nor Cup success came its way. Having flirted with relegation in both 1931/2 and 1932/3, the club then managed to miss the drop by just one point in 1934/5, being humiliated by the all-conquering Arsenal 8–0, and ending up in twentieth place, their lowest position in the 1930s. The season, however, did see the purchase of the highly rated Ralph Birkett from Arsenal.

The following season, 1935/6, saw an improvement both in Boro's League position, to fourteenth, and in their players' ability to score goals. Led by the centre-forward George Camsell, with 28 goals, Boro managed to put a total of 84 past their opponents. The wingers Birkett and Cunliffe played particularly well, as did the half-back line of Brown, Martin and Baxter. The team's Cup form also improved and they reached the quarter-finals for the first time since 1904, before being beaten 3–1 by Grimsby. The season's high point was the remarkable 6–0 victory in front of a crowd of 30,000 at Ayresome Park over the champions elect, Boro's local rival, Sunderland. (Sunderland, however, recovered from this embarrassment and ran out as First Division champions by eight points.) The match was a notable one for Baxter, as his own outstanding performance was witnessed by the Scottish international scouts, who were there to run their eyes over Sunderland's Scottish players. The match ended on a sour note with two Sunderland players being sent off, including the team's star, Raich Carter.

Baxter and his team-mates maintained their steady improvement in 1936/7, and finished the season in seventh position. Until the very last match they had managed to keep an unbeaten record at Ayresome Park, but they then went down 3–1 to Derby County. A review of the season noted that Camsell, in his thirteenth season with the club, 'is still a successful, keen and interesting centre forward'.[4] Unfortunately for Boro, Camsell pulled a leg muscle towards the end of March and played no further games in the season. Birkett's injuries also hampered Boro's wing play, although he managed 7 goals in the early part of the season. Mickey Fenton led the goal-scoring with 22 goals, fulfilling the promise that he had shown in the previous few seasons with the club. The club also found itself 'a really sound goalkeeper for the first time in a number of years',[5] in the form of Dave Cumming, who was bought from Arbroath.

The 1936/7 season saw Baxter being joined by two players who were soon to become giants of the game: Wilf Mannion and George Hardwick. Mannion, then 17 years old, played only twice during the season, but his 'no nonsense' style of forward play made an immediate impact. Hardwick, a full-back who had been courted by Arsenal's manager George Allison, signed for Boro mainly because his mother felt that he was too young, at just 14, to go too far from home. Hardwick's own account gives an illuminating insight into the social background from which many of the professional players came at this time:

> My father had found employment as an electrician at Smith's Dock shipyard. . . . My mother was also working in the local council offices. . . . Everything was rosy for the Hardwick family, especially as we were all now achieving. It was a very happy time because there was a lot of pressure removed from the family due to the fact that three regular wages were coming into the household.[6]

Hardwick eventually made his first-team debut in December 1937, against Bolton Wanderers. Playing alongside Baxter, Hardwick did not get off to the best of starts, managing to score an own goal in the very first minute.

Boro's fifth and fourth positions in 1937/8 and 1938/9 respectively signalled their rising status as one of the strongest and most consistent teams in the First Division. In 1937/8 Boro looked in the first three months of the season as if they might even take the championship, but then their performance fell away, only to improve once again with a challenge in the early weeks of 1938. Seven consecutive victories saw the team once again moving up the division, but a further lapse in April saw them winning only one of its last seven games. Fenton maintained his goal-scoring form from the previous season and went on to be leading goal-scorer, with 23 goals, including 4 in the last match of the season, against West Bromwich Albion. He also played centre-forward for England. The goalkeeper Cumming and the winger Milne both received call-ups from Scotland during this most successful of seasons for Boro.

In 1938/9 Boro went one better, as mentioned above, and became the First Division's top-scoring side, with 93 goals. Fenton excelled himself with a total of 34 goals. Camsell, now ageing, appeared only 11 times during the season but still managed to score 10 goals. Mannion was also getting onto the score-sheet: he slotted 14, including 4 in a 9–2 thrashing of Blackpool in December 1938. Baxter was the pivot of a 'respectable half-back line'.

Baxter's success with Middlesbrough was eventually recognised at the international level. In November 1938 he made his debut for Scotland, alongside Bill Shankly, in a match against Wales. He made just two further appearances for Scotland, winning caps against Hungary and England during the 1938/9 season. Although Boro achieved their best League position since their return to the First Division some 10 years before, a review of the season suggested that Boro lacked 'grit'[7] and that it was this that was keeping the team from reaching the very highest level. The anonymous writer of the review expressed his reservations with some eloquence (while displaying indecisiveness, as so many writers on football still do, about whether a team is a singular entity or a plural one):

> The Boro are a club with a long tradition of graceful play behind it and this is maintained today. They give the vague impression that is often exuded by a man of excellent family with talents above the ordinary which have been developed in comfortable circumstances. The natural ability is all there, as are the personality of breeding and the assurance of good standing, but there is missing just that strength that a rougher schooling in the past would have added.[8]

Playing for the Boro in the 1930s

Duncan McKenzie, Boro's right-half, gave an insight into the club and its ways in a piece published in the *Topical Times* in 1939. He claimed that 'a quiet handful talking together or watching a game of billiards is the Middlesbrough way of whiling away the time' after training. He also stated that training itself had changed under Wilf Gillow's management, with the traditional 'Swedish drill' being replaced by three-a-side games of head-tennis. This novel approach, introduced by the club's trainer Charlie Cole in 1938, proved popular with Boro's players, and Jackie Milne and McKenzie himself are said to have formed 'a supreme partnership'.[9] However, jogging was still a mainstay of training sessions. Having no dedicated training ground, the players had to lap the Ayresome Park ground twelve times in the morning and then repeat the feat in the afternoon. George Hardwick, writing in 1998, has described Gillow and Cole's approach to training and tactical management at this time:

> There was very little time allocated to skills practice. To be given a ball was considered a treat in those days and tactical discussions were kept to a minimum. Games were won and lost by the individual ability of the 11 men on the pitch. We always concentrated on our own strengths and were never immersed in the quality of the opposition.[10]

The players also tended to socialise outside the club. Many became involved in local charity events, where their appearances added to the occasion and to the takings. Other sports were also pursued, especially in the summer months. Bob Baxter specialised in golf.

Wilf Gillow was a quiet pipe-smoking man who had played for Preston and Grimsby Town (the 'Mariners') before leading the latter team, as manager, to promotion to the First Division, just behind the champions, Middlesbrough. He was successful in bringing through up-and-coming stars such as Hardwick and

Mannion, as well as managing more experienced professionals such as Camsell and Bobby Stuart. Describing Gillow's approach to the management of Boro, McKenzie commented (in the article already cited) that: 'There are meetings, but they are irregular. Manager Gillow feels that these are only necessary every two or three weeks. I think this helps the team's confidence, because criticism, even the friendliest, can knock some players right off their game. Mr Gillow is quiet, makes careful decisions and watches games as a student.'[11] McKenzie, who had played for Brentford before joining Boro, also drew a contrast between the ways in which the two clubs dealt with their players:

> Strangely, Middlesbrough of the quiet tastes has less [*sic*] restrictions than Brentford. Thinking it over, I cannot recall any restriction that Boro makes. They trust the player, and argue that any sensible man will take care of himself when he knows his career depends on it. Brentford, on the other hand, play for safety, and impose restrictions because they believe that some players have to be saved from themselves. Brentford forbid any player to have a car or motorcycle and compel him to be home by ten o'clock every Friday night. But when it comes to the social life, Brentford have the advantage. Their players get regular trips to shows and round the bright lights. The Boro don't go in for things like that except when they have a game in London. But that is probably explained by the fact that there is only one theatre in the town. Still, Brentford go in more for the all-boys-together idea.[12]

George Hardwick has recalled the need for the players to conform to certain standards set by the club: 'you were expected to be well-groomed, clean-shaven, wear a tie and represent the club with a certain amount of decorum on away trips. Failure to comply with the regulations would lead to severe reprimands and in extreme cases you were dropped for the next match.'[13]

Boro's approach at this time is also illustrated by the requirement that all younger players had to call their older team-mates 'Sir' or address them as 'Mister' followed by their surname. George Hardwick describes how Mannion, soon after he had joined the club, attempted to take a stand against this rule and started to call Baxter 'Bob' instead of 'Sir'. Mannion ended up being thrown fully clothed into a cold dressing-room bath. This anecdote illuminates the hierarchy operating in the club (but not unique to it) and indicates how younger players, even potential stars such as Mannion, were expected to show respect to their elders, whether they were their betters or not. Hardwick also comments on the club's 'strict established pecking order'.[14] Recalling his time as a newly signed young professional, he remembers being involved in sweeping out the changing rooms and cleaning the senior players' boots: 'The latter task I actually enjoyed and made sure that the footwear of the club skipper, Bob Baxter, always received an extra polish. It was an honour to clean the boots of the great man.'[15] Baxter was the young George Hardwick's favourite player and his mentor.

Like all the other clubs, Middlesbrough was restricted by the maximum-wage regulations. After Hardwick, for example, signed professional terms with the club in 1937 he was initially paid £6 a week during the season and just £4 a week as a summer retainer. These sums were increased to £8 and £6, respectively, a year later. Players were also awarded winning bonuses of £2 and draw bonuses of £1. Hardwick has recalled that 'in those days, with so many people out of work, it was a real privilege to play football for a living. Even skilled tradesmen were only earning two pounds ten shillings.'[16] He also gives an insight into the social status of professional footballers in the 1930s: 'Football was a profession which was well-respected. The most famous players were lauded, and for me to be given the opportunity to play for my home town club filled me with enormous pride.'[17] (It was not for nothing, perhaps, that Hardwick was known as 'Gentleman George'.)

War, Scotland and retirement

At the outbreak of war in 1939 Baxter was a 28-year-old Scottish international and the captain of an increasingly successful English First Division team. Although football was briefly disrupted by the outbreak of hostilities, Baxter stayed with Boro at first. However, after making an appearance for Boro in 1940 against a rival local team, Newcastle United, he decided to return to his roots. He spent the rest of the war years guesting for the two Edinburgh clubs, Hibernian and Hearts. He also went back to coalmining, and then opened a newsagent's and tobacconist's. Baxter achieved further personal accolades during the war, being picked to play for Scotland in four internationals, including one against England in October 1944 in which his Boro team-mates Hardwick and Cumming also played, and which ended with England, inspired by Tommy Lawton, winning 6–2.

During the early war years Wilf Gillow remained in post as manager of Boro, but could afford to do so only by taking on an additional job with Middlesbrough Council. He died in 1944, following medical complications during an operation.

With peace returning and Gillow gone, Baxter found himself surplus to requirements at Ayresome Park. He was transferred to Hearts on 17 August 1945. Although the Scottish League recommenced in 1945, with teams being located in the same divisions as in 1939, no promotion or relegation was conducted, in order to enable clubs to get themselves re-established as their players gradually returned from the armed forces. Hearts managed only seventh position in the Scottish League in this first post-war season, well behind the champions, Rangers. Baxter became captain of Hearts and led the team into the 1946/7 season in front of a crowd of 18,000 at Falkirk, achieving a 3–3 draw. While Hearts' league form varied, finishing eventually in fourth position, the team managed to reach the semi-final of the Scottish League Cup before going down 6–2 to Aberdeen. Baxter appeared in 25 League games, as well as in 10 Scottish and League Cup matches, scoring a total of 3 goals from his centre-half position.

The following season, 1947/8, saw Baxter dropping out of the first team and taking on coaching duties, before being released by the club during the close season.

Baxter's next career move was to try his hand at football management, at another Scottish club, Leith Athletic. Always one for trying new things, he then left football and took on the job of managing the Edinburgh Monarchs speedway team.

Baxter eventually returned to Teesside to spend his last years near what had been his primary footballing home. He spent much of his retirement improving his golf handicap and performing with some accomplishment on his accordion. His son, also called Bob, went on to pursue a career in professional football, playing for Darlington, Brighton and Torquay.

Bob Baxter, the inspirational captain and resident comedian of Middlesbrough FC, died in Middleton St George in April 1991, aged 80.

HARRY BETMEAD,
Grimsby Town F.C.

9 Harry Betmead – Grimsby Town

Harry Betmead was very much a local boy made good. For many he has strong claims to be the finest player ever to have been born in Grimsby and to have played for his home-town team, fondly known as the Mariners. Born on 11 April 1912, the son of a former Grimsby Town player and trainer, Betmead started his career by playing schoolboy football in the town and then joined a local club, Haycroft Rovers, playing in the Grimsby League. In October 1930, while working as a railway porter, he was signed on professional terms by Grimsby Town. This marked the start of his 17-year association with the Mariners, during which he made 296 League and 19 Cup appearances, but scored just 10 goals. He also managed to pursue a summer cricketing career and represented Lincolnshire, his home county, on a number of occasions.

Betmead and the Mariners, 1931–8

Having established himself initially in the reserves playing in the Midlands League, Betmead made his debut in the Grimsby first team almost a year after signing for the club, when he helped the club to a 2–0 home victory over Bolton Wanderers in a First Division match early in the 1931/2 season. The season ended unhappily with relegation, alongside West Ham United. Betmead got 'a fair blooding' during the season, making 17 League appearances and scoring twice. While Grimsby maintained a respectable home record, losing only 6 out of 21 matches, the team's away record was appalling, with just 2 victories and 2 draws. Their run in the Cup also reflected this tendency, with 2 home victories being followed by a 1–0 defeat away to Liverpool in the fifth round. The champion team in 1932 was Everton: the great Bill 'Dixie' Dean contributed a remarkable 45 goals, in contrast to Grimsby's joint leading scorers, Tim Coleman and Pat Glover, who each scored just 13 times. Grimsby's management was also suffering at this time. The club's secretary, H.N. Hickson, died in 1932, aged 75, after 34 years in the post, and the manager, Wilf Gillow, resigned in early April that year. Frank Womack, who had been a player at Birmingham City, took over as manager. He was to become, for many, the most successful manager the club has ever had.

A six-footer, Betmead soon made the position of centre-half his own and became known for his skill, both on the ground and in the air. His particular talents lay in his heading ability and in his sure, crisp, uncompromising tackling. During his career Grimsby had to beat off approaches from other bigger clubs for Betmead, including one from Arsenal. In fact Arsenal made a 'blank cheque' offer for the famous Grimsby trio of 'Hall, Betmead and Buck', Hall being Alec 'Ginger' Hall and Buck being Ted Buck. Grimsby turned down the Gunners' offer, which was rumoured to be about £25,000, although this must have been a difficult decision for what was then a Second Division club to make. (Hall remained a part-time player throughout his career with Grimsby, combining his tough tackling mid-field play with a job in the local docks.)

Betmead has been described as an 'elegant' centre-half, although he was also known for his 'maddening lapses', such as dribbling the ball into his own net. Ted Buck summed up his character, when writing Betmead's obituary, as follows: 'It would be impossible to find another man like him, and he was, without doubt, one of the best.'

Having been in the team that was relegated to the Second Division in 1931/2, Betmead was also a key figure in the Mariners' Championship-winning team just 2 years later. So successful was it that the Championship was won a month before the season's end. With 103 goals scored and a 7-point lead over the runners-up, Preston North End, it had been a remarkable season for the Mariners. Betmead was one of the 7 Grimsby players who appeared in every match and the club managed to play the whole season using just 18 players. Glover, centre-forward and Welsh international, led Grimsby's attack with aplomb, scoring a record 42 goals in 39 matches, which is still a club record. The club's chairman at the time was the burly George Pearce, known for his black Homburg hat and his rolling gait. He was a fish merchant, like several others among Grimsby's directors at the time. He always made sure that visiting teams went home with a parcel of locally caught fish, even if, in this season, only 3 of those teams went home with a victory.

Grimsby's manager, Frank Womack, summed up his team in an article in the *News of the World* in April 1934: 'They had the ways, the punch and bite of a promotion side almost from the start, and I am not with those who fear [that] they will find it hard to keep pace with all the demands of the First League.' Womack has been described as a 'system' manager. Drawing on his careful analysis of the opposition's players, he gave each Grimsby player specific responsibilities in each game. He developed strategies on the dressing-room blackboard before testing them out in practice matches, which he saw as being the best kind of training.

The Football League's own survey of the 1933/4 season makes interesting reading in relation to Grimsby's achievement:

> Grimsby Town were a sound side, and their clear success was thoroughly deserved. But, as was the case in the First Division, the general standard was not high, and even a pronounced pre-eminence like that of Grimsby is

not sufficient this season to win any greater name than for being a very capable lot. Their surprising success in keeping the same side together was a great factor in their success. This immunity to change, which reflects great credit alike upon their training methods, and upon the players' keenness and physique, was really remarkable. Throughout the season there was no change in either the full-back or the half-back lines. Kelly and Jacobson in the former, and Hall, Betmead and Buck in the latter, did not miss a game, while the two inside forwards, Bestall and Craven, also appeared in every game. In addition, Jennings, the wing player, was absent only once, and Glover, the centre forward, missed only three games. The latter was a ready and consistent goal-scorer, who may attain some fame now that he will be moving in the highest circle. The regularity with which this club finds notable centre forwards is remarkable, and Glover, the latest of the series, is certainly far from the least of the band which comprises, besides himself, Carmichael, Robson and Coleman. It seems churlish to cavil at such a successful record, but it is to be doubted whether Grimsby will achieve greatness in the higher competition. There is more than a suspicion of age about Jacobson and Bestall, not to mention Read; Buck, Jennings and Glover have been tried in the First Division before, and, without being found wanting, they did not then display conspicuous merit; while the remainder is mostly talent untried in the stronger fire. But for the moment the future must take care of itself, and Mr Frank Womack, the old Birmingham full-back, must be congratulated on having so capably guided his club to unquestioned success.[1]

The Football League's rather dismissive view of Grimsby's prospects for the forthcoming season in the First Division proved to be unfounded: the team went on to finish fifth, the highest position ever achieved in the club's history. To give the League its due, in its survey of 1934/5 it did make a point of complimenting Grimsby on its achievement: 'especial credit must be given to Grimsby Town, who, in the first season after promotion, finished fifth. It was probably the best team ever enjoyed by the Lincolnshire club, and, had they been stronger away from home, their challenge for honours would have been quite formidable.'[2] Whether the team would have been strong enough to beat the invincible Arsenal, which picked up the First Division Championship for the third consecutive season and for the fourth time in 5 years, is another matter. Grimsby maintained continuity in team selection from the previous season, with only 19 players being used in the 42 League matches that were played. This contrasts with teams such as Tottenham Hotspur (36 players), Wolverhampton Wanderers (33) or Huddersfield Town (32). Glover also maintained his goal-scoring feats of the previous year, scoring 34 times. Betmead chipped in with one goal in a 2–2 draw at home to Middlesbrough.

An interesting comment on the progress that Grimsby had made since their return to the First Division in the 1934/5 season appeared in the 'Arbiter' column in the *Daily Mail* on 2 January 1935: 'Other teams are building their

fortunes on the same lines. This is especially notable in the complete trans-
formation which has been brought about in the football of Grimsby. I warmly
congratulate Mr Frank Womack, the manager, on the way he has modelled the
team and trained them to play in the best style.'[3] The writer went on to point to
Betmead and the inside-left, Craven, as future England players.

Having reached fifth place in 1934/5, Grimsby were unable to maintain their
form in 1935/6, although, as the Football League's review noted, they were
'always a pleasing side'.[4] It went on to say:

> The forward line was good even if too much of the execution depended
> upon Glover (scoring 31 of the team's 65 league goals, including four in one
> match, in addition to two hat-tricks), and [George] Tweedy and Betmead
> were the mainstay of the other ranks . . . Inability to avoid defeat with any
> regularity away from home kept them down to seventeenth place.

Grimsby's record shows that, while 16 out of 21 away matches ended in defeat,
they lost only 4 matches at home. In the FA Cup Grimsby did much better and
reached the semi-final, for the first time in the club's history, playing against
Arsenal. Betmead was unable to play in this landmark match, as in the previous
round, against Middlesbrough, he had been sent off after a physical and verbal
clash with Tim Coleman, who had left Grimsby for the Boro; Coleman was also
dismissed. Whether Betmead's absence influenced Grimsby's performance against
Arsenal is open to debate, although losing the established defensive pivot against
a team with the might of Arsenal was hardly likely to have helped matters.
Grimsby lost 1–0 with a breakaway goal from Arsenal's goal-scoring star Cliff
Bastin. (Jack Crayston, the subject of the next chapter, was also playing for the
Gunners that day, as well as in the Final, when the Gunners won the Cup by
beating Sheffield United 1–0.)

In October 1936 Grimsby suffered the resignation of Frank Womack, who
was appointed manager of the Second Division team Leicester City. George
Pearce took over as manager while the club sought a full-time replacement. It
was not until the end of March 1937 that Charlie Spencer, the manager of
Wigan Athletic, was appointed. Spencer, who had himself been an English
international centre-half, had been a member of the Newcastle United team
that won the Championship in 1927.

The 1936/7 season proved very similar to the previous one, with home performances outshining away ones. Glover hit 30 goals to keep up his impressive
record. This total included 5 against Sunderland and 4 against Middlesbrough.
The Football League's review of the season recognised his achievement,
commenting that 'this club possesses probably the best centre-forward in the
Kingdom in Glover, and the Welshman was uniformly as good as ever'.
The review noted that Glover 'was ably assisted in the front line by a fellow-
countryman in Lewis at outside-left, who unluckily had, through injury, only
two League games after February'. Lewis managed to score 18 times, including 4
goals in one match and 3 in another. The Football League's review also noted

that 'Tweedy in goal won international recognition, as also did Betmead in the Continental tour in May. Both the latter player and Craven at inside-left continued to be good, but neither have quite fulfilled early promise.' Overall, 'the side was workmanlike without winning higher praise'.[5] Grimsby maintained their continuity during the season, calling upon only 20 players for the 42 fixtures played. Manchester United, by comparison, had to use 31 players to get through the season.

Betmead's finest personal achievement was to gain an international cap for England when he played against Finland in Helsinki in May 1937. England won the match 8–0. Betmead never made another appearance for his country; instead the legendary Wolves centre-half Stan Cullis became the automatic choice in the years leading up to the war. Betmead does, however, remain the only Grimsby-born player ever to have played for England while also playing for his home-town club.

The 1937/8 season saw Grimsby narrowly escape relegation, finishing just two points above West Bromwich Albion and Manchester City, the previous year's League champions (despite outscoring every other club Manchester City had still managed to lose twenty matches). Grimsby's plight can be put down to one factor: the loss of Glover to injury for a large part of the season. Having regularly scored thirty or more goals each season, Glover suffered a serious knee injury in the very first match of the season, at Preston, and was not to play again until early April. This loss of goal-scoring power was not adequately covered by Grimsby's other forwards; although the reserve centre-forward, Reg Tomlinson, was tried for some time he managed to score only two goals. In order to address this sudden decline in goals Charlie Spencer entered the transfer market. Hearing that a now ageing Hughie Gallacher, a former colleague and star player at Newcastle, had put in for a transfer at Notts County, following the departure of that team's manager Jimmy McMullan to a post at Sheffield Wednesday, Spencer beat off competition from Bradford City and Stockport to sign Gallacher for £1,000 in January 1938. While Gallacher never replaced Glover's firepower, he did manage to give Grimsby a boost and helped the team to steer clear of relegation on the very last day of the season. Spencer also managed to add two further signings alongside Gallacher: Everton's Irish international outside-left Jackie Coulter and the experienced inside right Jock Beattie, who had played previously for Huddersfield, Birmingham and Wolverhampton.

A twist to the story of Gallacher's arrival came in the final week of the season. With six clubs, including Grimsby, all on 36 points, the Mariners had a home fixture against Chelsea, one of Gallacher's previous teams. Spencer, however, took the tough decision to go with Glover, his tried and tested goal-scorer, who had only recently returned from injury. Glover duly obliged and Grimsby won 2–0. Gallacher was pleased for the club but was apparently less pleased with his former team-mate, now his manager.

Gallacher's biographer indicates that he enjoyed his early weeks at Grimsby: 'The club were good to their players, to the extent of having a crate of beer in the dressing room for refreshment after the match, as well as giving each man a box of local fish to take home.'[6] However, finding that even a half-fit Glover was getting precedence over him in team selection, Gallacher started to have dressing-room disagreements with Charlie Spencer. He also got into trouble with the police during his short time at the club, being found to have driven while under the influence of alcohol: he was banned from driving for a year and fined £12. Grimsby had had enough of Gallacher by the time he went to court and welcomed the opportunity to sell him on to Gateshead for a mere £500. The team had achieved safety in the First Division and Glover the goal-scoring machine was back in action. Gallacher had served his purpose. However, with or without a goal-scoring centre-forward, Grimsby's survival was also due to their defensive strengths. As the Football League's review noted: 'The old half-back line of Hall, Betmead and Buck formed a sound stand-by, while Tweedy and Hodgson behind them were dependable all through the season.'[7]

Grimsby's relative success during the 1930s has been put down to the club's ability to field consistent sides, drawing on relatively few players in any one season. Betmead was very much a central part of this success, alongside Hall and Buck. Grimsby's reserve team, playing in the Midlands League, was also outstanding throughout the decade, winning the championship 3 times and establishing a reputation for consistent high-scoring performances. In 1932/3, for example, the reserves scored 189 goals in 42 games.

Football in the shadow of war: the 1938/9 season

The 1938/9 season started under the cloud of growing international tension that was to culminate in the Second World War. As the Football League review noted at the end of the season:

> Perhaps the most surprising thing about the 1938/39 season was that it was ever concluded. The international sky was lowering when the first games were played on August 27th, and by September 10th, the third Saturday, the situation was even more menacing as the world waited for the German Leader's speech at Nuremburg. The fourth and fifth Saturdays went by to the accompaniment of the Prime Minister's visits to Berchtesgaden and to Godesburg, and then the position had to be faced that we might not see the next Saturday in a state of peace. On the Wednesday (September 28th) the League announced that the fixtures of the following Saturday would be fulfilled unless the worst had happened by that date . . . the crisis passed. Peace for Britain still existed and the fixtures for October 1st were played. But if the critical moment had gone, the period of tension continued all the way through the season, and Easter itself had been reached before it could be postulated that the season would be brought to a safe conclusion.[8]

While Neville Chamberlain went off to meet Adolf Hitler Grimsby Town continued much as before, although their results early in the season were of a higher order than in 1937/8. The major problem still facing the club was a lack of goals from Glover. At the start of October 1938 Grimsby went into the transfer market, a relatively rare event for the club during the 1930s, and purchased Fred Howe from Manchester City who were then offloading several players as part of a rebuilding programme following relegation. Howe had only recently moved to Manchester City from Liverpool, where he had been the leading goal-scorer. Although he did not achieve the heights that Glover had, Howe went on to become Grimsby's leading scorer that season, with 15 goals, including 4 in a 6–1 home victory against Leicester. Glover continued to suffer from illness and mishaps during the season, and eventually scored just 4 times before moving to Plymouth Argyle just after the close of the season.

Grimsby's success in 1938/9 was primarily in the FA Cup (as discussed below). In the League the team ended up in a creditable tenth place, while Everton, led by their centre-forward Tommy Lawton, took the Championship. The League's review once again commented on Grimsby's approach to the game at this time:

> Grimsby were always gay adventurers. About them too, there is a distinct atmosphere. While they play hard and with all seriousness they avoid that habit of regarding a defeat as a catastrophe which makes present-day football so grim a business. It is just this hint of not being afraid to lose that gives Grimsby an attractive and rakish air. In the League they had one of their best seasons. They began not too well, but from October 22nd they had a run of ten games without defeat. This was followed by four consecutive reverses, but after that they were always giving as good as they took . . . most of the club's personnel were as usual . . . the stout half-back line of Hall, Betmead and Buck again being the basis of all.[9]

Betmead contributed three goals during the season, including the single-goal winner against Manchester United. It was also during 1939 that he was selected for the end-of-season FA tour to South Africa: he played twice against the national team there.

Betmead and Grimsby had another opportunity to reach Wembley in March 1939, just six months before the outbreak of the war in Europe. The Mariners were once more in the FA Cup semi-final, this time against Major Frank Buckley's Wolverhampton Wanderers, a team that was widely expected to win, at Old Trafford. The match programme notes described Betmead as 'generally acknowledged to be one of the outstanding pivots in the League . . . has done much to enhance the side's defensive reputation'.[10] While 1936 had seen the 'defensive colossus' Harry Betmead missing through suspension, there was also a significant absentee in 1939: George Tweedy, regarded by many as Grimsby's best-ever goalkeeper, had succumbed to flu. He was replaced by the untried George Moulson, the reserve keeper. Little did he or his team-mates know what was to ensue. Watched by a crowd of 76,962 (a record for Old Trafford), the match went well for Grimsby for the first 20 minutes. Then Moulson was suddenly injured by a kick on the head in a challenge with Wolves' forward, Dickie Dorsett. Moulson was taken to hospital and, with no substitutes allowed, the full-back, Jack Hodgson, put on the goalie's jersey. Grimsby played on with just 10 men, including Betmead. Wolves took full advantage of the situation and quickly put 2 goals past Hodgson. With 3 more second-half goals, Wolves drove on to Wembley, where their forward, Wescott, scored 4. Yet again Grimsby and Betmead had been denied their day of glory.

Betmead's later years

Following the outbreak of war and the suspension of normal League football, Grimsby participated in the regional competitions organised by the Football League. In 1940, suffering from uneconomical crowd sizes, Grimsby transferred all their home matches to the nearby town of Scunthorpe and continued to play there until 1944, when the team returned to their home ground, Blundell Park. As at most clubs at this time, Grimsby made use of guest players. Charlie Spencer continued as manager and at times found himself also acting as head groundsman. Betmead made a few appearances in the 1939/40 and 1940/1 seasons, but then spent the rest of the war serving in the armed forces. He rejoined the club for the 1945/6 season and made twenty appearances in the Football League North.

With the resumption of normal peace-time football in 1946/7, Grimsby once again played in the First Division and Betmead was still at the heart of the defence. By this time the players in the first-team squad were ageing and many expected that Grimsby would be relegated. However, the team managed to avoid the drop with an unbeaten run of seven games in October and November 1946, and some useful victories towards the end of the season, enabling sixteenth position to be achieved. Betmead played his last game for Grimsby at the end of this season, helping to achieve a rare victory, 4–1 at home against Leeds United.

While Betmead was still on Grimsby's books in the opening weeks of the 1947/8 season, he was not to play again and he retired from the game that December. Sadly, for the club and for Betmead, this season ended with relegation. Gaining just 22 points, with 45 goals scored and 111 conceded, Grimsby ended up in twenty-second position, with the prospect of once more rejoining the Second Division.

The *Grimsby Evening Telegraph*, reviewing the best players to have appeared at Blundell Park in the history of Grimsby Town, included Betmead in the list, commenting that, as 'those who watched him will tell you, Harry Betmead was one of the best centre backs in England. The fulcrum of the famous Hall, Betmead and Buck half-back line, he took on the Dixie Deans and Tommy Lawtons, and usually kept them quiet.'[11]

After concluding his career in professional football Betmead left the game and went on to pursue a business career in Hertfordshire and North Yorkshire. He died in Middlesbrough, aged 62, on 26 August 1984.

W. J. CRAYSTON,
Arsenal F.C.

10 Jack Crayston – Arsenal

'Gentleman Jack' Crayston, a true and loyal servant of Arsenal, the dominant team of the 1930s, typified every manager's dream of the genuine professional both on and off the field. Described by another long-serving Arsenal icon, Tom Whittaker, as 'that elegant gentleman of the football field',[1] Crayston was a teetotaller, a non-smoker, a fitness fanatic and a smart dresser. He is reputed to have taken a Bible with him on away trips, so that he could read his favourite psalms on the journey, yet he was also known for his dry sense of humour.

Crayston's style of play was also a model for both his contemporaries and the players whom he managed later in his career, when he took over the managerial reins of Arsenal in the mid-1950s. He was described variously as a 'quietly spoken, quick-thinking half-back, who fitted so well into the Arsenal scheme, and who would sooner cut off his leg than go over the ball at a man';[2] 'a graceful performer, height giving dominance in the air, and systematic in his approach to the game';[3] 'tall and powerful';[4] 'the long-striding immaculate Crayston';[5] and 'wily and strong'.[6] Crayston made 312 appearances during his lengthy career with the Gunners before moving onto the backroom staff, first as a coach, then as assistant manager and eventually in the manager's hot seat itself.

Crayston's career in the 1930s

Born William John Crayston on 9 October 1910, in the small town of Grange over Sands (then in Lancashire, now in Cumbria), Jack commenced his football career playing centre-forward in schoolboy football in Barrow and Ulverston. League football came at the age of 18, when he joined the local team, Barrow. He went on to make seventy-seven League appearances for Barrow, again as a goal-scoring forward, before moving onwards and upwards by joining Bradford. Having established himself at his new club, he went on to play at centre-forward and in each of the half-back positions before settling as the regular centre-half. Following a lay-off due to injury, he returned to the first team, but this time at right-half. It was in this position that he established himself as one of the best players outside of the First Division. He also became known as something of a long-throw expert. During the 1933/4 season he suffered both a broken leg and a broken wrist, and it was thought that he probably had brittle bones.

It was therefore somewhat surprising that the all-conquering Arsenal came for him, eventually paying £5,250, which was then a record fee for Bradford, in May 1934. Arsenal had just defended the First Division Championship, so the move to Highbury gave Crayston the opportunity to gain the glory and financial rewards of playing at the very highest level. Arsenal's legendary manager, Herbert Chapman, had been negotiating with Bradford for Crayston's signature when he suddenly died of pneumonia. His replacement, George Allison, took up the negotiations and signed both Crayston and a fellow wing-half, the former miner Wilf Copping, who moved from Leeds United for a fee of £8,000.

George Allison recalled Crayston's transfer from Bradford as 'one of the most extraordinary in the history of the game'.[7] Allison had been warned by colleagues that Crayston suffered from brittle bones and therefore would be too great a risk, but he still believed that Crayston was the man for Arsenal. Allison took a prudent approach, however, and eventually signed a transfer agreement based on payment in instalments. He paid £4,000 down and agreed to pay a further £250 after Crayston's first match; he also agreed to pay a further £500 after Crayston had played ten more games. Crayston successfully came through all these matches without any sign of brittle bones. Arsenal then paid a further £50 for each of a further ten League and Cup matches, eventually bringing the total transfer fee to £5,250. Allison clearly regarded Crayston's signature as a worthwhile one, regarding him as 'one of the greatest half-backs who ever gained an England cap and one of the grandest fellows I ever met in football'.[8]

'Gentleman Jack' Crayston and 'Ironman' Wilf Copping formed an unlikely alliance, both on and off the pitch. Whittaker recalls that 'although very dissimilar . . . they were inseparable. They trained together, always insisting that a fast runner (Crayston) should train together with a slow mover (Copping) so as to help him increase his pace . . . and on all journeys they were to be seen together, inevitably playing a peculiar form of Chinese whist.'[9]

Crayston made his Arsenal debut at the start of the 1934/5 season, scoring in an 8–1 thrashing of Liverpool at Highbury. Although he faced competition from his fellow half-back Frank Hill, Crayston made thirty-seven appearances in what was yet another Championship-winning season for Arsenal, the third in just three seasons. As Whittaker recalls, the team was 'led by the fearless Ted Drake, and with the side reinforced by the grace of Jack Crayston and the dour determination of Wilf Copping on either side of the towering Herbie Roberts'.[10] Crayston and Copping 'fitted in perfectly to the Arsenal machine'.[11] Crayston also started to achieve recognition outside the club, playing for England against a team of Anglo-Scots and also for the Football League XI.

Crayston's career continued to flourish with Arsenal. In 1935/6 the team went on to win the FA Cup, beating a Second Division side, Sheffield United, 1–0, in what the *News of the World* called 'one of the most colourless and uninspiring Cup Finals Wembley has known'.[12] The reporter commented that 'all three half-backs were brilliant in their different ways, with Crayston, perhaps, outstanding'.[13] The Sheffield United side at Wembley included the young Jock Dodds, who was to become one of that team's greatest goal-scorers (see Chapter 12). Another goal-scoring legend, Ted Drake, playing with a strapped knee, came out on top, scoring with a left-foot drive with just sixteen minutes to go, to give Arsenal yet another trophy. Crayston and Arsenal then had to wait until 1937/8 before they added to their haul, winning yet another First Division Championship, their fifth in just eight seasons.

Crayston's prominence in Arsenal's success story was becoming increasingly recognised. His picture adorned the cover of the *Topical Times Sporting Annual* for 1936/7, as one of six leading sportsmen of the year and the only footballer to be chosen. Arsenal's domination of the decade brought recognition to many of the players, including Crayston. As Bernard Joy commented:

> The honours showered on Arsenal were due not only to the floodtide of success which reached its heights in the 1930s. They reflected the club's reputation for disciplined, reliable, wholehearted and clean football. The selectors knew that an Arsenal man would not be a worry before a match or on tour. He would be conscientious in training, early to bed and a model of behaviour on and off the field.[14]

Having made his international debut in a 3–0 victory over Germany in December 1935, Crayston went on to play a further seven times for England. His last cap came after a 5–4 victory over Czechoslovakia in December 1937. He scored his sole England goal in this match, but he was also injured and had to play much of the match on the wing. He was never selected to play for England again.

Arsenal in the 1930s

Crayston joined the Arsenal 'machine' at a time when the team had captured the football public's imagination and become the most talked-about team in the country. Herbert Chapman's 'modern' game, nobly followed by his successor, George Allison, was far ahead of its time and goes a long way to explain Arsenal's domination of the First Division throughout the 1930s. Luring oppositions further and further up field with a clever covering system worked by the full- and half-backs, Arsenal relied on speedy break-outs to achieve success. One piece of testimony to the effectiveness of this approach is that Arsenal's forwards scored all but 28 of the 683 goals taken between 1930 and 1937.[15]

Arsenal relied heavily on continuity throughout the decade, both on and off the pitch. Players were replaced by skilful management of the transfer system, money being made available to buy the very best players from rival teams, including Bryn Jones from Wolves for a then record fee of £14,000. Under Chapman Arsenal had unsuccessfully attempted to set up a nursery team by trying to buy and run Clapton Orient. They later went on to acquire a Southern League club, Margate, which was to fulfil the same function. As Tom Whittaker observed: 'You cannot expect a boy to be ready for top-class football under a period of five years, unless he is an "infant prodigy". It was expensive, but then Arsenal have never quibbled on the grounds of expense.'[16] Chapman's methods and values were carried forward after his untimely death by the Highbury 'boot room' of Whittaker, Joe Shaw, Peters and Wall.

Arsenal's financial strength during this period is illustrated by Allison's record in the transfer market. Between 1934 and 1939 the club spent £81,000 on new players while receiving £51,000 in transfer fees, a net expenditure of just £30,000. During the six seasons from 1933/4 to 1938/9 the club's total profits amounted to £136,000, a massive sum for any football club of the period. In the 1934/5 season Arsenal became the first club ever to gross more than £100,000 from gate receipts in a single season, while also making a profit of £35,000. With financial reserves of £60,000, even match programme sales brought in £2,500. Arsenal, the 'Bank of England' club of English football, had a significant edge over all their First Division rivals, which they exploited as they strove to dominate the game both on and off the field.

During the 1930s the Highbury ground was significantly redeveloped, with new stands being built. Yet despite the club's financial acumen in managing the football side of things, they got into serious financial difficulties by the time that football was suspended at the outbreak of war in September 1939. Luckily, the post-war boom in attendances solved Arsenal's debt problems and created the financial base for continued success in the late 1940s and the early 1950s.

Almost inevitably, Arsenal's success also attracted envious criticism, especially as other clubs, striving for the same success, adopted the Highbury model. Criticised for playing 'safety first' football, Arsenal came to be blamed for the decade's increasingly mechanistic approach to the game, both at the club level and at the international level. However, as Bernard Joy, Arsenal's amateur centre-half in the late 1930s, has commented:

> Critical although footballers were, they could not argue with the hard facts of success. Most hastened to copy Arsenal. Practically everywhere, centre-halves were changing from the traditional role of supplementary forward to a third back. The forwards sought were those who could put their heads down and run fast, irrespective of personal safety and often of football skill. Most clubs, unfortunately, did not perceive the subtlety in the Arsenal attack. [Alex] James's strategic ability, positional sense and passing skill enabled him to knit the eleven men into a co-ordinated team, in which all had a part in defence and all a share in attack. Too often now, the imitators bridged the mid-field gap with a hefty kick, usually in the air, and we see the beginning of the 'negative football' era which lasted until after the war.[17]

Much of the criticism emanated from the North and can be seen as, to some extent, a symptom of the resentment felt in many parts of England towards the increasingly prosperous Southeast. As Alex James's biographer has put it,

'Arsenal in their bright expensive-looking new red shirts, stepping from their private railway carriage, parading expensive stars – good-looking [Eddie] Hapgood, debonair Crayston, aristocratic [David] Jack and jazzy little James – were the perfect targets.'[18] Hapgood himself commented that Arsenal were 'the most publicised football team the world had ever known . . . everything happened at Arsenal. Rarely a day passed that we didn't read something about ourselves.'[19] In fact, newspaper coverage of the day was less about the players, and more about the facilities and methods being adopted. To quote Hapgood again: 'all of the time the papers were writing about our luxury stand, our cocktail bar, new club colours, special training methods, cotton-wool diet, our private train, etc.'[20]

Resentment of the Arsenal team as privileged southerners is reflected in the response when they visited Middlesbrough (albeit according to an account published in 1988 rather than at the time):

> The enmity of the Middlesbrough crowd was given complete unity and its greatest power when the visitors to Ayresome Park were Arsenal. This team of remarkable talents represented wealth and privilege. They came from the soft South, from London, from the city of government where, it was imagined, all social evil was plotted and directed against places like Teesside. The Arsenal club could afford to pay large sums in transfer fees to buy the best players. The players themselves enjoyed comforts and amenities such as no other club could afford to provide. They carried themselves with pride and played with a stylistic beauty. They were fine footballers and had a long history of victory.[21]

The Arsenal players were well aware of how they were viewed by their fellow professionals and by the crowds. George Male recalled years later that 'we were hated all right. They came in their thousands to watch us get hammered – that was all the enjoyment they got out of it.'[22]

Arsenal's approach to preparing players for the rigours of the First Division ran like clockwork, initially under Chapman's guidance and then later under Allison's. All the players were expected to conform. Eddie Hapgood has described their working week:

> Sunday – normally a busy day at the ground, treatment day. Monday – was a day off initially, then became light training and a 'chinwag', a couple of loosening-up laps around the track and then head-tennis, then home for lunch. Tuesday – training was slightly heavier, eight to 12 laps, skipping exercises and kicking into goal with special soft shoes invented by Chapman, golf in the afternoon or a spell in the 'shooting box' to practise shooting at goal when the ball came back at the player at awkward angles, thereby speeding up reactions. Wednesday – less track work and more on the field, goalkeepers were put through their paces, work on skeleton plans which might be used in matches, heading exercises and head-tennis. Thursday

– much like Wednesday. Friday – the big day, first thing we got our spikes on and did short bursts, stops and starts, plus gym exercises, punch ball and skipping, then a bath. Shortly before midday, the teams would go up on the notice-board. The first team and 12th man would go to the board room with the manager [Allison] and Whittaker, very serious affairs, every little detail of the last week's game and the match on the following day were discussed, decisions were made on who would take penalties and free kicks in certain parts of the field. Saturday – players arrived an hour to 90 minutes before the game, and chatted to friends and team-mates until about 30 minutes before kick-off, then the usual pep talk was held, with everyone apart from the team, 12th man and trainer being thrown out, including the directors.[23]

Several of the Arsenal players, and in particular Hapgood, the captain, had uneasy relationships with Allison, regarding him as unsuited to replace the legendary Chapman. In his autobiography Hapgood recounts one incident involving Crayston. Allison was attempting to give a Friday team talk in preparation for the following day's match. He told Crayston: 'The danger man for Wednesday is Charlie Napier, and you have the job of marking him and not letting him have the ball.' Crayston tried to interrupt, but Allison stopped him: 'Wait a moment, let me finish and then give me your views.' When Allison had finished he asked what Crayston wanted to say. The half-back simply remarked: 'Napier does play well for Wednesday, Mr Allison, but we're playing Blackpool tomorrow.' Hapgood notes that at least Allison also saw the funny side of this exchange.[24]

The lifestyle of Arsenal players such as Crayston was essentially a matter of using their football success and the consequent financial rewards to build better lives for themselves and their families, to raise their standard of living, and to achieve a social status well beyond their mainly working-class roots. Arsenal actively encouraged players to save their wages, bonuses and benefits, and (as mentioned in Chapter 2) the club even went as far as opening a special savings scheme that offered additional interest payments. Once a player had saved £1,000 the club would place it in the player's name in a trust fund and guarantee a 6 per cent return on it. Many first-team regulars purchased new houses in the North London suburbs of Hendon, Barnet and Finchley, often drawing on financial assistance from the club. David Jack, who had trained originally in the Civil Service, invested in insurance policies to ensure security in retirement. As one of the more literate members of the team he also managed to secure a regular newspaper column, which he actually wrote himself, rather than relying on the services of a ghostwriter, as other stars did (and still do today).

Crayston too was well known for his frugal habits, despite his regular first-team wages. Looking back from the 1980s, he recalled:

I was rather mean with myself. My father was a strict man and had always said to me, do what you like but don't spend your money carelessly. Save it.

I had five shillings a week spending money and invested the rest in a building society. I led a strict life really; I criticise myself sometimes, but when I went to London I was a bit of a loner. I went to the cinema and the theatres; I didn't isolate myself from the rest of the players, but I preferred to have a walk around London and a cup of tea at a Lyons Corner House. Wilf Copping and I were good mates. We used to wander about in the evenings but generally after a match I'd just walk to the Tube and catch a train to Harrow on the Hill, where I had digs. I was lucky there. A family who knew my family from Grange over Sands saw that I was coming to London and they wrote to my parents offering to put me up. I stayed with them right up until the war.[25]

Arsenal recruited many young players who, like Crayston, were reluctant to engage in the 'bright lights' culture of the capital. Unmarried players, such as Joe Hulme, Wilf Copping or George Male led relatively simple lives by today's standards. Hulme played billiards, Copping liked a quiet pint and, of course, Crayston had his Bible. Golf was also widely played by Arsenal players, as it was by many professional players of the time. Newspaper reports of the 'special training' trips to seaside resorts or to spa towns before important Cup matches tended to feature golf as an important ingredient. Crayston himself played off a 14 handicap.

Crayston also recalled, perhaps through rose-tinted glasses, how Arsenal insisted on the very highest standards of behaviour from its players, and sought to act as their guardian and confidant:

The manager expected you to behave yourself. We were always told that we would be confronted by the press, journalists and so on, and that we were to try and help but not to be controversial. The press could help us and hurt us, we were told. We were also encouraged to confide in the management if we had problems, financial, social, girls; we were like a family.[26]

While Arsenal actively encouraged this somewhat simple life for many of their players, they was not above using them in schemes that would enhance the image and glamour of the club. One example is the involvement of both Allison and a number of Arsenal's star players in Thorold Dickinson's comedy thriller *The Arsenal Stadium Mystery*, filmed in the summer of 1939 (as already mentioned in Chapter 5). Described as Britain's most lavish soccer production to date, the story centres on a murder investigation set against the background of a match day at Highbury. Crayston, Cliff Bastin, Ted Drake, Hapgood, Swindin, Male and Kirchen all appeared in this venture, receiving £50 a week each, while Allison collected £500 for participating both as a bit-part actor, playing himself, and as technical adviser. The film's scenes from a fictional match between Arsenal and the Trojans incorporate superb action footage from a match that was actually played against Brentford on the last day of the season. The Brentford players wore white shirts and black shorts to make things easier for the black-and-white cameras. In total, fourteen cameras were used to film the match, which Arsenal won 2–0. With subsequent filming taking much longer than anticipated, the Arsenal players who appeared were put on a daily fee of 10 guineas (£10, 10s.), quite a sum when their normal summer wages were £6 a week. Student players from Oxford and Cambridge were used alongside the Arsenal team for close-ups, but they were paid significantly less for their services, at just 3 guineas (£3, 3s.) a day. One scene in the film shows the Arsenal players engaged in one of their favourite training activities, head-tennis.

Arsenal's involvement with the changing mass media also extended to the new medium of television. Since the team's manager, George Allison, had been a journalist and a football commentator for the BBC, this is not surprising. The world's first live television broadcast of a football match took place from Highbury in September 1937, when excerpts from a practice match between the Arsenal first team and the reserves were shown on the BBC's fledgling station.

War-time and after

Crayston's career as a full-time professional footballer was brought to an abrupt halt, along with the careers of all his contemporaries, at the outbreak of war, which coincided with the start of the 1939/40 season. Crayston joined the RAF, but he managed to make nearly 100 war-time appearances for Arsenal; collected three Football League South Championship medals, and another medal for being a member of the team that won the War Cup; and made one war-time appearance for England. His playing career was then permanently halted after he sustained a serious knee injury playing against West Ham United in December 1943.

Two stories about Crayston's war-time playing career both feature the legendary Bill Shankly. Crayston was captaining a team from an RAF base at Hanforth when he came up against Shankly in a match against the Manchester Barrage Balloon Depot's team. As Crayston's son recalls, 'my father said it was like tackling a brick wall': Shankly was 'very terse and single-minded, interested only in winning and saying very little throughout'.[27] Later in the war Shankly guested for Arsenal, covering for players such as Crayston who could not gain release from the armed forces. Having played in every round of the Football League South Cup to reach the Final, Shankly found himself being usurped as Crayston and other regulars returned. While the press coverage of the day suggested that Shankly had no problem with this, Crayston himself recalled events somewhat differently: 'You can imagine what he thought of it! Ever after, if you spoke about Arsenal he got upset, he just fell out with them. He was straight and wanted everyone else to be. If they weren't, he was upset. If you didn't do things right, he didn't like it, wouldn't tolerate it.'[28] When Arsenal offered Shankly tickets for the Final and some money as compensation, he rejected the offer and made his contempt for the club very clear. Crayston noted that Shankly always stressed the importance of integrity and honesty. There was so much sleaziness going on around then. He told me of many instances where he'd been offered money for certain things but he refused it. He didn't agree with it and he didn't want anyone to be able to point the finger at him. He was very protective of his own reputation. When Arsenal had behaved badly towards him, as he saw it, and then had offered him money, he was finished with them. He wouldn't play for them any longer and he went to Luton.[29]

After his demobilisation at the end of the war Crayston returned to Highbury to join the coaching staff. In May 1947, still only 36 years old, he became assistant manager under the newly appointed manager Tom Whittaker. Crayston's main job was to groom Arsenal's reserve team, but one of his other jobs was to maintain Arsenal's extensive system of files on players throughout the country, an indication that Arsenal was even then a buying club. Because he had also received some training in accountancy Crayston was occasionally asked to help out with some of the book-keeping duties at the club.

Under Whittaker and Crayston Arsenal continued their winning ways. The team ran out as First Division Champions in 1947/8, FA Cup winners in 1949/50 and League Champions again in 1952/3. By then Arsenal had also recruited Joe Mercer, rescuing him from imminent retirement at Everton, the team he had played for before and during the war (see Chapter 14).

Jack Crayston eventually crowned his long career at Arsenal by becoming manager, following the death of his fellow stalwart and friend Tom Whittaker in 1956. His appointment was perhaps a sign of the times at the club: it was the first time in more than thirty years that Arsenal had appointed a manager rather than a secretary–manager. Bob Wall became the club's secretary, handling the administrative side of things at Highbury. Wall recalls his time working alongside Crayston with some reservations: 'he had learned a great deal about management under Tom Whittaker but I never felt he was really at ease as team manager. I know he disliked having to put people on the spot and telling them they were not good enough or that they must play it this way or that way.'[30]

While Crayston's first season as manager, 1956/7, saw Arsenal achieve a respectable fifth place in the League and reach the quarter-finals of the Cup, management did not prove to be his forte. It was at this time that Arsenal sought the advice of the Football Association's director of coaching, Walter Winterbottom, on finding a manager who could communicate the new thinking on tactics and technique. Winterbottom recommended Ron Greenwood, then manager of a non-League team, Eastbourne United. The following season saw Arsenal drop to twelfth place, which would not have been too bad for many other clubs but represented Arsenal's worst performance on points since 1930. Disillusioned by the approach being taken by the directors, especially their reluctance to provide sufficient money to buy their way out of problems, Crayston resigned in May 1958. He had been with Arsenal for a total of twenty-four years, proving himself a truly loyal 'terrace hero'.

Crayston tried his hand at management just one more time, at Doncaster Rovers, first as manager and then as secretary–manager, before retiring from the game in 1961, aged 50. He then moved to Streetly, near Birmingham, where he ran a newsagent's and general store until 1972, when he retired. Looking back in 1985 on his life in football and reflecting on how things had changed since the 1930s, he commented: 'In my time, players had short hair, wore long shorts and played in hob-nailed boots. Now they have long hair, short shorts and play in slippers.' Jack Crayston died in his home town, Grange over Sands, in December 1992, aged 82.

Jack Crayston, the 'first gentleman of soccer', as Tom Whittaker called him, made professional football his life. He won glory for himself with Arsenal and made his own distinctive contribution to Arsenal's 'glory years' in the 1930s, and then on into the 1940s and 1950s. He was a true 'terrace hero' who upheld the 'Corinthian' spirit of days gone by.

W. DALE.
Manchester City F.C.

11 Billy Dale – Manchester City

William or 'Bill' or 'Billy' Dale, known to many as 'Old Surefoot', was widely regarded as one of the best uncapped full-backs of his era, an era when English football was dominated by Arsenal and its star full-back Eddie Hapgood. Having joined Manchester City in December 1931 from Manchester United, Dale quickly became a regular in what was to be one of City's most successful sides until the time of Joe Mercer and Malcolm Allison some thirty years later. Dale was in the side that won both the FA Cup, in 1934, and the First Division Championship, in 1937; he was also a member of the team that lost 3–0 to Everton in the Cup Final 1933 and of the team that was relegated from Division One in 1938. While other players in the City team of the 1930s are probably better known today, Billy Dale was what most full-backs have been: the solid reliable rock upon which the more creative mid-field and forward players could build, thereby justifying his nickname. Before the Cup Final in 1933 the *Bolton Evening News* described Dale as 'clever and studious, quick and sure in anticipation, a sound tackler who volleys the ball beautifully in his clearances'.[1] His contemporaries included Matt Busby, Peter Doherty and Frank Swift; Dale was one of the unsung heroes of the club. By the time he left to pursue his career with Ipswich in 1938 he had accumulated 237 League and 32 FA Cup appearances with City.

Dale had the distinction of being the only Manchester-born player in the City team, a relatively unusual situation in an era when players often stayed close to their roots. Born on 17 February 1905, Dale started his football career with the Hugh Oldham Boys Club before moving on to Sandbach Ramblers and Marple. At the age of 20 he signed amateur forms with Manchester United, becoming a full-time professional a year later. He stayed with United for 6 years and made 64 appearances before making the switch to Maine Road on 23 December 1931. Dale and his team-mate Rowley joined City in exchange for Harry Ridding and a sum of £2,000.

Dale quickly made his first-team debut in a Boxing Day match at Portsmouth, playing at left back. He went on to become a first-team regular under the supervision of City's manager, Wilf Wild. In the 1934/5 season City signed Sam Barkas, a left-back and future team captain, from Bradford City, and Dale made the switch to right-back, where he continued to hold down a first-team place until 1938, when City achieved the notable feat of being relegated despite having scored more goals than any team in the entire First Division and being the previous year's League Champions, playing with virtually the same team of players.

Winning the Cup Final in 1934

Manchester City reached Wembley in 1934 having played seven matches in front of a total of 399,874 people who had paid £28,554 for the privilege. The Wembley trail had started before a home gate of 54,000, the largest in the third round, who saw City beat Blackburn Rovers 3–1. The next game was against Hull City: after drawing 2–2, it took a 4–1 replay victory at Maine Road to put Manchester City through. The team had been leading 2–1 in the first tie, with just five minutes to go, when Hull equalised after Manchester City's goalkeeper, Frank Swift, and the full-back, Dale, had created sufficient confusion in the defence to allow a tap-in goal. The fifth-round match, against Sheffield Wednesday, also needed to be replayed. Playing at Hillsborough before another record crowd of 72,841, City drew 2–2. Sadly, the match was notable for the death of a supporter, who was crushed against railings on the Spion Kop in the minutes leading up to the kick-off. Many others were also injured at the match. The mid-week replay, again before a large crowd of 68,614, many of whom had taken the afternoon off work, saw Dale involved in the 2–0 victory for City: the winning goal came from his 40-yard free kick, which was headed in by the forward, Bobby Marshall. City's sixth-round 1–0 home victory against Stoke City, then dominated by Stanley Matthews, drew an even larger gate of 84,568. Again, safety became an issue after a barrier collapsed and several fans were injured.

City reached the semi-final for the third consecutive season. Playing before 65,000 in appalling conditions at Leeds Road, Huddersfield, City swept aside Aston Villa 6–1, setting a semi-final record, with a three-goal burst in five minutes just before half-time. City had reached Wembley for the second successive year. In the previous year Dale and City had been beaten 3–0 by Everton, captained by its star goal-scorer Bill 'Dixie' Dean.

Despite having one more match to play before the Final, City adjourned to the team's usual preparatory haunt, the Palace Hotel in Southport, a full two weeks before the big day at Wembley. Portsmouth, soon to be City's opponents in the Final, had also made a booking at the Palace Hotel, but, after hearing that the City players were not going to move, the Portsmouth players decided to do their preparations elsewhere. City took the First XI players and a number of reserves to Southport. As Frank Swift recalled: 'It was there that I really learned of the magnificent team spirit, coupled with [the players'] schoolboyish sense of humour.'[2] Golf was a very important part of City's training regime. According to the *Manchester Evening News*, 'Both sides will play a good deal of golf in the next fortnight and it is a safe guess that not much will be seen of the football.'[3] The paper's regular columnist, 'The Captain', commented that 'this is the modern plan, however absurd it may appear to those not inside the game, and the trainers must be given credit for knowing their jobs'.[4] Led by Sam Cowan, Eric Brook and Ernie Tosland, the City players, including Dale, played 'cowboys and Indians' in the bunkers. Swift recalled:

> Tosey used to come prancing up, with a 'Whoa there, Silver', pull his imaginary horse to a halt, and then tie it up to the flag pole in the middle of the green! Then the other lads would, in dumb pantomime, shoo and drive his horse from the green, using guns, lariats and anything else their fertile imaginations could think of. It was great fun, and helped me more than ever to knit into the happy comradeship which made up this great team.[5]

In his autobiography Swift summed up some of his team-mates: 'Merry-faced Sam Barkas, dry-as-dust Fred Tilson, little "Tosey", the prankish Jackie Bray, whimsical Brookie and Bobby Marshall . . . the Crazy Gang had nothing on them.'[6]

Another aspect of City's preparations was featured in the sports column of the *Manchester Guardian* (the sister paper of the *Manchester Evening News*) on the day before the Final. In a move that would now be referred to as 'community relations', the players paid a visit to the Sunshine Home for Blind Babies in Birkdale, near Southport. The children there presented Sam Cowan, City's captain, with a horseshoe decorated with maroon and white carnations, and with a kitten. Cowan was reported to have been 'delighted with the gifts, and told the little ones that he and his team would do their best to win the Cup'.[7] The *Guardian*'s columnist concluded his piece with a reassurance that 'as the players left the home the babies gave them a cheer and shouted, "We hope you'll win the Cup"'.[8] In itself this incident was not unusual, since over the decades football clubs and their players have always sought to foster links with local communities, preferably in the presence of reporters and, better still, photographers. What is remarkable, perhaps, is that this story was regarded as worth covering in a sports column on the day before the biggest match in the football calendar.

City's directors spent the days leading up to the Final not only selecting the eleven men who would play at Wembley but also considering which players were to be retained for the following season and which were to be made available for transfer. At this time City employed thirty-four full-time professionals; it was suggested in the press that not all the members of this sizeable squad would be retained. The names of the eleven players chosen for the Final were in doubt right up to the Friday before the match, when the team was officially announced just before it set off for London. Injuries to both left-halves, Jackie Bray and Jimmy McLuckie, had been the primary causes of concern, although Bray eventually got the nod. While the directors appeared to have no concerns regarding the defence, in his column in the *Manchester Evening News* 'The Captain' raised doubts as to their ability: 'in recent games the backs have not convinced, either separately or as a pair . . . The tackling is keen and good, but the kicking [is] not as hearty as I would like.'[9] However, if only to reassure the paper's readers in Manchester, he commented: 'Portsmouth are not a fast side, and Barnett and Dale, given the big occasion, should be equal to it.'[10] Dale had been picked out for special mention in a report of a recent game against Tottenham Hotspurs: 'it was only Dale's due that he should be paid a tribute for the skill he showed . . . at times, so poor was the play of the City half-backs and inside forwards, he seemed to be facing the quick and clever Tottenham raiders on his own, and his tackling and kicking were alike remarkable'.[11]

Wilf Wild was still the manager, or more accurately the secretary–manager, of Manchester City. Like many other secretary–managers (see Chapter 4), Wild was restricted to performing mainly administrative tasks, while powers over team selection and continued employment rested with the directors of the club. Nevertheless, Wild's role in the club's affairs was reflected later in a tribute in the *Manchester Evening News*, which complimented him on his 'tact, ability and judgment', and then went on to state that 'the distribution of tickets and the other work consequent on the semi-final and final of the FA Cup have imposed a big strain on him, but it had all been accomplished with the normal staff at Maine Road'.[12]

Sam Cowan, who was about to appear in his third Cup Final for City, was the primary motivator among the players. In the 1930s captains generally tended to carry out many responsibilities that later came to be the remit of managers and coaches. Cowan spent much of his time during the run-up to the Final calming the nerves of some of his less experienced team-mates, in particular the young Frank Swift, who would be making his first appearance at Wembley. Sam Barkas, who was later to take over as club captain under Cowan's managership, emphasised the captain's motivating role when reminiscing about Cowan: 'Wilfred Wild held the title [of manager] but he was the secretary and never got involved with team tactics. We were professional enough to know what was needed to keep fit and we worked hard in training without supervision. But Sam was a wonderful motivator.'[13]

On Friday 27 April, as the team set off for London, the *Manchester Evening News* ran the headline 'City's Speed Should Win the Cup' over its reporter's assertion that 'When the half-backs and the forwards are in their best attacking mood there is not only no side in the country that can be sure of holding them, but there is no side can play in such an attractive, and at the same time such a devastating style. Their speed can dazzle spectators and opponents alike.'[14]

City's supporters from Manchester and across the Northwest swarmed southwards in droves. Special trains left towns such as Blackburn, Colne, Clitheroe and Blackpool as well as Manchester. More than 9,000 fans were expected to travel by train, while many more made the journey in what were then called charabancs or motor-coaches. Local newspapers reported that demand was being inhibited by ticket touts in Manchester: 'Half-Crown Cup Final Tickets Sold in Manchester for 16 Shillings' was one of the *Evening News*'s headlines in the days before the Final, and the paper also ran an interview with a local 'ticket queen' who was openly selling tickets at various prices at a shop in the city centre. So strong was the concern that the Home Secretary was asked in the House of Commons if he would introduce legislation to 'prohibit the re-sale at increased prices of tickets for any entertainment'. His answer was brief: 'No, sir.' Others were pressing for the adoption of a policy of paying at the gate instead of prior allocation, as at League matches, but they too were rebuffed.

The supporters' experiences of going down to the capital for the Final were reflected by the London correspondent of the *Manchester Evening News* in his report:

> Train after train arrived from Lancashire at Euston and St Pancras today, and brought the quietest and most sedate crowd to London for a cup final. I walked for an hour or two among the arriving fans and I did not hear a snatch of song or a whoop of enthusiasm. In Southampton Row I found 20 youths standing round a dairyman's cart. They were drinking bottles of milk. That characterised the early crowds. It was not until I penetrated into a tea-shop that I heard a burst of music and I knew that Lancashire had not lost its soul. While their friends were having breakfast, four members of a concertina band played to them a selection of tunes which included a hymn.[15]

His report continued:

> Scores of charabancs were parked in Leicester Square and Piccadilly at an early hour while their 'loads' visited nearby restaurants for what was being advertised as 'a real Lancashire breakfast'. Many visited the Cenotaph, and by eight o'clock, many bunches of flowers and wreaths had been laid at its base. Later in the morning, the crowds began to waken up. A sailor was seized and carried shoulder-high around Trafalgar Square and deposited on the plinth of Nelson's Column by a score of Manchester City supporters who demanded a speech! The sailor was obviously regarded as a symbol of the Portsmouth team and the Manchester City supporters were expressing their admiration for their opponents. The blue-jacket shouted 'Pompey will win' and jumped from the plinth into the crowd. After some good-humoured banter, the whole crowd set off to see the Changing of the Guard.[16]

One sad incident occurred on Cup Final day: a Manchester supporter, Joseph McGuinness, was knocked down and killed by a coach bringing other City supporters to the match.

The supporters' experiences just before the match were described in the *News of the World* the next day:

> The great Stadium began to fill up as early as 12 o'clock. Martial music and community songs whiled away the intervening hours, and a big cheer went up when the Australian cricketers walked on the ground. Spontaneously

the crowd rose and sang 'For they are jolly good fellows', and Woodfull and his men appeared overwhelmed by the warmth of the welcome as they manoeuvred their way to seats near the Royal Box. . . . Then, as one man, the multitude were on their feet again cheering madly. King George [V], in a long brown overcoat, decorated with a white gardenia, was standing at the entrance gangway, ready to go out and meet the rival teams.[17]

The City team and the club's officials had travelled down to London, in a special saloon car on the Liverpool to London express, the day before the Final. They had then been taken to a hotel on the edge of Epping Forest in Essex. Frank Swift was experiencing pre-match nerves and Sam Cowan had to spend many hours talking to him about anything and everything but football. Cowan himself was bathing a septic toe, which he had hidden from the club's officials. Swift was allowed to sleep in until 11 a.m. on the Saturday and was then taken by Cowan for a walk in the hotel grounds, well away from loitering newspaper reporters and interested members of the public. The team had lunch at midday and then 'took a charabanc' to Wembley, stopping on the way so that Swift, at 20 the youngest member of the team, could buy chewing gum for himself and his team-mates, thus keeping up what had become a City tradition before away matches.

Having arrived at Wembley the players were allowed to walk on the hallowed turf (a practice that was subsequently banned for many years). Swift recalled later that the 'pitch was rough'.[18] After returning to the dressing room the players sat around waiting for the order to get stripped from trainer, Alec Bell. Swift remembered being so nervous that Bell gave him a tot of whisky. Alec Herd quietly read a thriller by Edgar Wallace, others cracked jokes, and Eric Brook sang his favourite song, 'Trees', on request. The Portsmouth players, meanwhile, were being entertained by the comedians Bud Flanagan and George Doonan.

City played in the Final wearing specially designed maroon shirts in order to avoid a colour clash with the Portsmouth players, who appeared in white shirts and blue shorts. The Wembley crowd of 93,000 included not only the king (as mentioned above) but also the prime minister, Ramsay MacDonald; they sat together in a brand-new royal box that was much closer to the pitch than ever before. Unlike on Cup Final days in recent years, a full programme of League fixtures was also played that Saturday, including matches at Tottenham and Chelsea, the latter in a local derby with the League Champions, Arsenal.

The first half of the Cup Final match saw Portsmouth take the lead in the twenty-eighth minute through Rutherford, against the general run of play. As the *Manchester Evening News* reported:

> Weddle put Rutherford away and he easily beat Barnett, and then had to face a challenge from Dale, who dashed across. Dale, however, half-slipped on the turf which had been made greasy by the recent showers and there was outside-left, Rutherford, clear of everyone and standing by the penalty

spot. He shot wretchedly but it counted [as] a goal. The ball was a shade to Swift's right and the goalkeeper dived full length instead of stooping. He went down, moreover, too late for a comparatively simple ground shot and the ball passed under his body.[19]

Swift later blamed his decision not to wear gloves, despite the wet conditions. He had observed that his opposite number, Gilfillan, was not wearing gloves and had decided to put them on only when Gilfillan did. Portsmouth was still 1–0 ahead at half-time. The *Manchester Evening News* commented that 'Bray and Dale had shut out the more dangerous of the Portsmouth wings', and also noted that 'there was more hard tackling than one normally sees in a Cup Final, but after some early fouls the game had been clean'.[20]

Reports on City's dressing-room discussions at half-time suggest that Swift was still upset at what he regarded as having been primarily his error over Portsmouth's goal. City's centre-forward, the Yorkshireman Fred Tilson, is said to have told Swift, 'Tha doesn't need to worry. I'll plonk two in the next half.'[21]

While City had lost the services of Herd, because of injury, for a time in the first half, but with no real disadvantage, Portsmouth's players did not have so much luck with their injuries in the second half. The centre-half, Allen, had to leave the field to receive treatment after a collision and it was during this spell that City, through the efforts of Tilson, equalised in the seventy-fifth minute. With five minutes to go both teams were exerting pressure and the game was swinging from end to end. Then Tilson fulfilled the promise he had made to Swift at half-time. Picking up a cross-field pass from Ernie Tosland, Tilson hit the winning goal high into Portsmouth's net. The *News of the World* described what happened: 'For one fleeting fatal second they faltered and left unshadowed and unmarked Tilson, the demon shot. Like a flash the Manchester wizard broke through and beat Gilfillan, whose goalkeeping had been faultless and heroic. Three minutes later the match was over and the Cup [was] safe for the North.'[22]

Frank Swift then unwittingly became a newspaperman's dream: hearing the final whistle, he promptly fainted. Reports suggest that the photographers behind City's goal had added to Swift's nervousness by audibly counting down the number of minutes left in the game after Tilson's goal. With the aid of the trainer's wet sponge Swift recovered and just about made it up the steps to receive his medal, and a concerned enquiry, from the King. Swift was quoted as saying: 'Fancy a great strapping fellow like me fainting in front of all those people and the King.'[23] The *News of the World* headlined its match report 'Player Faints as Cup is Won', pointed to Swift's relative youth, and explained that he had been just a spectator at the previous year's Final, that he spent his summers working as a boatman in Blackpool and that he had come from virtually nowhere to become a member of a Cup-winning team in just a few months. (Swift eventually joined the press corps after his retirement from football; it was as a reporter that he died in the Munich air disaster that also killed several players from Manchester United.)

The *News of the World* summed up the Final in the following terms: 'To call it a game of thrills does not do justice to a football epic.'[24] A less emotional but no less positive view of the game was given by the *Manchester Guardian* in an editorial on the following Monday: 'The detached observer of our social life, who sometimes wonders why "soccer" steadily extends its spell through Europe, even to the tropical lands, would find much to enlighten him in such a game as Wembley saw on Saturday.'[25]

Having won the FA Cup for the first time and at the third time of trying, City's players were wined and dined at a London hotel on the Saturday evening and then taken down to Brighton on the Sunday, with the Cup. After their return to Manchester on the Tuesday they were taken on a tour of the city centre by coach and then welcomed by the lord mayor at a civic reception. The team then took tea with him and other city dignitaries.

Local businesses were predictably quick to take advantage of the victory. Sam Cowan was featured in a large press advertisement for 'Chefex, a meat and yeast preparation' on the day the team returned to the city, with the following endorsement: 'As captain of Manchester City football team I want to thank you for persuading me to try Chefex, your new beverage. We have found the vitaminic properties of Chefex invaluable during our training and in my opinion it is the finest beverage of its kind.'[26] Lewis's, one of the city's department stores, offered the public the opportunity to 'come and shake hands with the conquering heroes' by visiting its men's department on the Thursday, Friday and Saturday following the Final.

Even before the match another local company, Wilson's Brewers, had also taken advantage of the commercial opportunity and the fact that many supporters would be unable to travel to London by taking a half-page in the *Manchester Evening News* to advertise its Wembley Ale, under the headline 'If you can't go to Wembley – let Wembley come to you! Enjoy listening to the Wembley broadcast with Wembley Ale at your side.'[27] The advertisement showed two besuited men, one with a cigarette and the other with a pipe, sitting next to a radio with their glasses of ale. The tobacco industry was also active in relation to football during the 1930s. A typical press advertisement of the time, linking the Final to the popular Players' brand, was headlined 'The captains and twenty popular players' and included photographs of all twenty-two Finalists.[28]

Apart from the clash of matches within London on Cup Final day (mentioned above), there was concern in some quarters about the experimental televising of the Final itself. For example, Joe Smith, a columnist in the *Bolton Evening News*, declared: 'The broadcasting of last week's FA Final proved once again what a serious loss it means to other clubs.'[29] The five First Division matches played that day attracted only 23,000, while only 43,000 attended the eight Second Division matches. Smith concluded: 'And remember, it was a fine day. I dare not think what would happen if television is ever perfected and adopted. I venture to say people would not go to matches at all.'[30]

For most football supporters radio was the most accessible means of following the Final, providing an important opportunity for fans to socialise, and have a smoke and a beer. Newsreel companies also covered the Final but their coverage was limited because the Football Association attempted to charge each of them a £700 fee for the rights to film the match. The *Manchester Evening News*'s correspondent reported that he had seen one newsreel crew attempting to hide a camera inside a dummy figure of a sailor, 'ostensibly a Portsmouth mascot, one of the less subtle subterfuges!'[31]

From the Final to retirement

Like many other leading clubs, Manchester City customarily completed the season by engaging in an overseas tour. Having won the Cup, the team left in early May for a trip that took in matches against Rapid Club of Paris, Florence and Milan, Nice and Marseille Olympic, before the players returned to Manchester at the end of the month. These tours were a lucrative feature of club life and were regarded by the players as a reward for a season's hard work. For most of them such tours offered the only opportunity they would ever have to travel abroad and stay in hotels for any length of time.

Billy Dale continued to play for City in the 1934/5 season, despite the signing of a new left-back, Sam Barkas from Bradford City, for £5,000. Dale and Barkas became a fixture as City's full-backs, ahead of the previous incumbent and Cup Finalist Barnett. While expectations were high, the City team failed to maintain its trophy-winning ways, although a final League placing of fourth was a respectable return from yet another long, hard season.

The 1935/6 season saw City lose one of their 'greats', Matt Busby, who was sold to Liverpool for £8,000, but it also saw the recruitment of another player who was soon to become great, the Irish international Peter Doherty, who was bought for the then massive sum of £10,000. Despite Doherty's presence in the latter months of the season, it turned out to be a disappointing one for City, which achieved only a ninth place in the League and a 3–2 defeat at Grimsby in the fifth round of the FA Cup.

The 1936/7 season brought City their second and final major achievement of the decade. Billy Dale was still a first-team regular, alongside Barkas, who was now club captain. By Christmas 1936 City had gained just 20 points from 20 games and the season was looking as if it was over as far as winning the Championship was concerned. However, a remarkable upturn in form saw City go on an unbeaten 22-game run, with 15 victories and 7 draws. Goals flowed from every quarter: in those 22 games Doherty scored 18, Tilson 14, Brook 13 and Herd 11, as City swept all before them. In his autobiography Doherty recalled what happened after the 4–0 home victory over Sheffield Wednesday: 'amazing scenes at the end of the game, thousands of people rushing on to the playing pitch'.[32] Sam Barkas expressed the view that the players' success had been down to their all pulling together: 'We have been a happy family and that is one of the secrets of our success.'[33] Taking 57 points from the 42 games and scoring 107 goals against 61 won City the First Division Championship for the first time. Billy Dale played in all but one of the 42 games in this most successful of seasons. Doherty, summing up the team that achieved this remarkable feat, commented that Dale was 'a model of all full-backs in the precision of his tackling and the cleanliness of his kicking'.[34] Dale had added a League Championship medal to the Cup Final medal he had gained in 1934.

City then undertook an end-of-season overseas tour, this time in Germany. A notable event occurred in a match against a German representative side in the Olympic Stadium in Berlin: not for the first time, English players were expected to give the Nazi salute during the playing of the German national anthem. However, City's players, including Dale, refused to do so and instead just stood to attention.

Having won the Championship in 1937 and outscored every other team, City managed to get relegated in the very next season, despite once again scoring more goals than any other club in the Division. The 1937/8 season also included two seven-goal victories and one six-goal victory. The club was using virtually the same players as in the previous, Championship-winning season, although it had signed another full-back, Bert Sproston, for £10,000 (see Chapter 16). Doherty, who was still leading City's attack, later summed up the season as follows: 'There was a crop of injuries, of course, and any amount of bad luck; but, excuses apart, we failed by a long way to show the sparkling form which had made us the first team in the country. Many games were lost by scrappy, indifferent displays, and the occasions when we looked like champions were few and far between.'[35] Doherty specifically recalled the last game of the season, when City was seventh from bottom and playing at Huddersfield, who were bottom, having just lost to Preston in the FA Cup Final:

> It might appear that City's position was fairly safe. But the relegation issue was a very open one that year, and several clubs were in dire peril on that last Saturday of the season. With ordinary luck, we would have escaped; but Dame Fortune, who hadn't smiled too often on us during the preceding months, dealt us a wretched blow at the end.[36]

With fifteen minutes to go Huddersfield scored and saved themselves while relegating City. Even then City had to wait for news from matches involving other strugglers: Grimsby, Portsmouth, Birmingham and Stoke. Defeat for any one of them would have saved City on goal average, but unfortunately they all won and City went down.

Dale, now aged 33, became one of the City players 'released' from the team as the club started to rebuild the line-up in an attempt to reach the top once again (it eventually achieved that aim in 1947). A. Scott Duncan, the manager of Ipswich Town, which had been elected to the Football League in 1938, came in for Dale in an attempt to build a squad with significant League experience. He was eventually transferred in May 1938. His signing was considered quite a coup at the time. Making his debut in Ipswich Town's first League match, Dale helped the team to a 2–1 home victory against Southend United. He then went on to play forty-six more games before the outbreak of war.

During the war years Dale lived in East Anglia and made a number of guest appearances for Norwich City, alongside another former City favourite, Jimmy McLuckie. After the war he retired from professional football and took up plumbing as a career. He died in Manchester, the city where he had been born and brought up, and had played most of his football, on 30 May 1987, aged 82.

Billy Dale's contribution to the success of Manchester City during the 1930s was perhaps summed up best in a tribute paid to him by City's chairman, one R. Smith, in March 1937, when Dale was awarded a club benefit cheque for £650 (as reported in the *Manchester Evening News*): 'No player connected with the club had ever deserved this reward more than Dale. He had never given the club a single moment's anxiety and had never failed to pull his weight. And Dale is the only Manchester-born player in the City team.'[37]

JOCK (EPHRAIM) DODDS,
Sheffield United F.C.

12 'Jock' Dodds – Sheffield United and Blackpool

'Jock' Dodds, who was typical of many centre-forwards of the 1930s and 1940s, has been described as a 'heavyweight amongst players',[1] referring both to his physique and to his significance as one of England's leading goal-scorers during these years. His sustained popularity and his status as a terrace hero also owed much to his outgoing, joking demeanour, typified by such comments as this, from the *Topical Times*: 'a fine fellow without an ounce of venom or unfriendliness in his whole make-up. A credit to the game and a pal to everyone who knows him.'[2] Later in his career, however, he earned a different epithet, becoming known as a 'rebel' because of his assertive attitude to club directors and football authorities alike, as he strove to protect his income and his contractual freedom. His assertiveness only helped to enhance his status as a hero among his supporters and as one of the real 'characters' in the English game of his time.

Dodds's career up to the Second World War

Born Ephraim Dodds on 7 September 1915, in Grangemouth, Fifeshire, Dodds soon moved to Kuilhill, near Glasgow, where, at the age of 9, he made a hat-trick-scoring debut for his school team. Trials for Lanarkshire Schoolboys followed, but at the age of 12 he moved with his family to Leadgate in County Durham. His successful playing career continued at his new school, which he helped to win both league and cup in his first season. Recognition quickly followed and he became captain of Durham Schoolboys, playing in a variety of positions from full-back to centre-forward. He left school at 14, like all but a very small minority of his contemporaries in Britain, and took a job in a local foundry. Finding the heat and the dust from the ovens too much to bear, he moved to a job with Shell–Mex, helping to deliver fuel to farms in the area. He also started to play for the company's football team. Again his skills were quickly spotted and a local team, Medomsley Juniors, offered him a trial when he was still just 14. Medomsley had a track record of grooming youngsters for League clubs and at the age of 16 Dodds was taken onto the ground staff at Huddersfield and started to play in that club's Central League team. His arrival at Huddersfield also saw him being given the lasting if not very imaginative nickname 'Jock'. Having scored four goals in just three games, he was offered a professional contract by the First Division club when he turned 17. He was now a fully fledged professional footballer and on the first rung of the ladder to stardom – or so he thought. In a newspaper article published later he described how his life had been then: 'I used to walk four miles to the ground every day and then four miles back home for my lunch, and return in the afternoon to cut the grass and undertake other tasks that the ground staff were expected to do in those days.'[3]

During his time as a member of Huddersfield reserves Dodds came up against another goal-scoring legend in the making, Bill 'Dixie' Dean, then in Everton reserves, which Dodds's team defeated 6–1. His career at Huddersfield did not last much longer. Despite scoring ten times in twenty-seven reserves matches as an inside-right, he was let go at the end of the 1933/4 season, which had seen the club finish as runners-up to the champions, Arsenal. As Dodds has recalled: 'They gave me a free transfer because they could only sign on 34 professionals and I hadn't come through as well as some of the others.'[4]

Dodds was quickly snapped up for the 1934/5 season by Sheffield United, then managed by Teddy Davison. The team had just been relegated from the First Division and were looking to bring in new blood. Dodds infused the team with much-needed firepower. After playing just four times for the reserves he made his first-team debut against Burnley, replacing the regular forward, Pickering, who had been injured. A further game followed for the 18-year-old Dodds, this time against Oldham, and then it was back to the reserves as soon as Pickering recovered. Later in the season United sold their regular centre-forward, Bill Boyd, to Manchester United and Dodds seized his chance, going on to become the club's leading scorer with nineteen goals in twenty-eight games, in a season that saw the team achieve a mid-table eleventh position.

While much has been made of players having to labour under the maximum-wage restrictions of £8 a week during the season and £6 a week in the summer months, in fact most clubs, including Sheffield United, used a sliding scale to determine the pay of their players. United's club records show, for example, that only four players were guaranteed the maximum wage during the 1934/5 season, while others received it only if they played in the first team. Dodds himself was offered a basic weekly wage of £4, plus a £3 first-team bonus, when he signed for the club in 1934, although his basic wage rose to £5 in the following season.

Dodds's lifestyle at this time was relatively simple and home-based. In 1936, for example, it was reported that he was interested in going to the cinema, collecting gramophone records by Bing Crosby and Nat Gonella, and dancing. In the same year a Sheffield newspaper reported that he had bought himself an accordion and was intending to take lessons. Two years later the *Topical Times* reported that he was spending much of his spare time at home, and that he had 'a car with which he potters about. He plays an accordion, reads a thriller or does a picture show when he fancies it or when his mother wants an evening out.'[5] He was also regarded as one of the best-dressed players at United. The same article commented:

he's always neat in appearance, and has a mop of inky-black hair, worn rather long and always brushed until it glistens. In his off-time, he goes in a great deal for flannels and sweaters. He has a collection of pullovers and slip-ons in all colours and degrees of woolliness. When he comes to the ground, he is usually in blue suit and heavy coat, and never wears a hat.[6]

Dodds was also ribbed about his accent, especially when he was overheard speaking in 'Scots' to players from his native Scotland. Yet others regarded him as a Geordie, since he had spent his teens in the Northeast of England.

Dodds went on to score 113 goals for the 'Blades' in just 178 League matches and a further 10 goals in 17 Cup games. His goal-scoring reached record heights for the club and in 1935/6 he was the division's joint leading scorer, with 36 League goals and 4 Cup goals. The local press was starting to eulogise him for his talent for hitting the back of the net: one paper claimed that 'he is beginning to be mentioned in the same breath as [Ted] Drake, the Arsenal centre-forward'.[7] Given Arsenal's status as the premier club at the time and Drake's standing as England's centre-forward, this was high praise indeed, albeit it was probably also an expression of Sheffield patriotism rather than an objective assessment.

The 1935/6 season proved to be a 'nearly' one for United, finishing in third place in the Second Division and as runners-up to Arsenal in the FA Cup. United had been in top position in the League until the day of their victory in the Cup semi-final against Fulham, having put together an unbeaten run of fifteen games from December 1935 up to that point. However, with two defeats and three draws during the run-in Sheffield United was overtaken by both Manchester United and Charlton Athletic. In the Cup tournament Dodds and his team-mates outshone two First Division teams, Preston and Leeds, before beating another Second-Division team, Fulham, in a 2–1 victory to set up a Final against all-conquering Arsenal at Wembley. United had had a hard route to the Final, beating Preston in a replay with only ten men after the right half, Stacey, had gone off injured. In an earlier round the team had also had to beat Burnley, again in a replay and again with virtually ten men, as the centre-half, Johnson, had had to play most of the game with his injured arm tucked in the front of his shirt following a heavy fall. With the Final coming up Dodds, still only 21, was reported as saying: 'if I do win a medal, it'll be 50 per cent of my life's ambition realised. The other 50 per cent is to grade a Scottish cap.'[8] It was not to be, although he was later to see his second ambition realised with caps and goals for Scotland.

Dodds was the youngest player on the field in the Final. Jack Crayston (see Chapter 10) was among the glittering stars in the Arsenal team. Reflecting on the game many years later, Dodds recalled that glory was nearly his, with a header hitting the crossbar after 'Ironman' Wilf Copping accidentally punched him in the back as he went up for the ball. According to a contemporary match report, this incident came just after Ted Drake had scored what turned out to be the only goal of the game: 'The cheers had not died away before we were in the throes of further excitement. Quickly United responded. Barton sprinted clear, centred perfectly, and Dodds, running in, headed against the corner of the bar with Wilson beaten to the wide.'[9] While recognising Dodds's 'atrocious luck', the writer of this match report went on to criticise him for a 'lack of finesse and judgment'.[10]

Dodds explained his approach to the role of centre-forward in a newspaper article published in 1938:

> My method has often been questioned, but I find it profitable. I hang back, more or less lying at the bottom point of a V, with the two wingers making the topmost extremities. This enables me to pick up loose balls which a full-back may mis-kick, and to draw the opposing centre-half and allow my inside partners to get through. I can immediately take up their position. It is easier also to dash forward to a centre than to try to gather a ball which may be going behind my back.[11]

Despite his bulk and his powerful physique, which made him a hard man to stop, Dodds was far from slow and covered the ground with short, quick strides. He also had a deceptive body swerve, along with fine shooting and heading abilities. Early in his career he had been essentially right-footed, but at Sheffield United he undertook special training to develop his weaker foot, a sign of how seriously he took his task of scoring goals.

The following season, 1936/7, proved unremarkable for United, which finished in seventh place in the Second Division and lost to Wolverhampton Wanderers, after a replay, in the fourth round of the FA Cup. Dodds, however, maintained his goal-scoring prowess, ending up once again as the club's top scorer, with 23 League goals and 4 Cup goals. The only feature of the season that seems noteworthy is that United had the best home record in the entire Second Division, losing only once and scoring 48 goals against only 14 in 21 games. However, the team's away record was almost the complete reverse, with only two victories, 18 goals for and 40 goals against.

The 1937/8 season again saw Dodds as United's leading scorer, with twenty-one League goals. The team continued to perform well at home, with only two defeats, and as their away performances showed some improvement, with only nine defeats, they ended up in a creditable but frustrating third place, losing out on promotion on goal averages to Manchester United after a disappointing run-in in the latter stages of the season.

Building on the steady development of the previous season, Sheffield United eventually made it back into the First Division, gaining promotion in the 1938/9 season as runners-up to the champions, Blackburn Rovers. Wise investment in new players such as Hagan, Reid, Henson and Sandford strengthened United's push for promotion, although it was not until the very last day of the season that the team clinched it over the local rivals Sheffield Wednesday. The players achieved this feat without the leading scorer, Dodds.

In March 1939 Dodds asked the club to let him leave. He told a local newspaper that he sought the move for 'personal reasons and because of the ill-health of my mother. Sometimes you can stay too long in one place and I thought the time had arrived when it would be beneficial for me to make a move.'[12] The reporter who interviewed him added that 'too much was being expected of Dodds, who had become a marked man, a player whom all the "stoppers" set out their stalls to check'.[13] Dodds, who lived with his mother and two step-sisters, was granted his request by United and put on the transfer list. Although several clubs wanted his goal-scoring services, including Sheffield Wednesday, he was eventually sold to the First Division team Blackpool for a reported fee of £10,000. Dodds received only £600 out of this money, instead of the expected £650, as United held back £50 on the grounds that he had not completed the entire season. The record fee no doubt also helped to cover the cost of the various players the club had bought during the season. The supporters' club regarded Dodds's transfer as a sad loss. A mass meeting was held to pass a resolution saying how sorry they were that he had left the club. These supporters stated that, while they appreciated the reasons for his departure, they would watch his future with interest. Dodds ended his Sheffield career with 123 goals in just 195 League and Cup games.

The move to Blackpool, where Dodds was to receive a weekly wage of £6 and a further £2 when playing in the first team, turned out to be very successful. Although he did not join the club until March 1939, he still ended the season as its top goal-scorer. His 10 goals in just 12 League games, including all 4 scored in a match against Middlesbrough, helped his new team to secure their place in the First Division for yet another season. Dodds was one of 5 forwards signed by the club during the season, but was clearly the most significant, both in this season and for many seasons to come. He had the unique distinction of ending the 1938/9 season as the top goal-scorer for two clubs.

Blackpool started the 1939/40 season on the highest note, winning all three of the matches they played, with Dodds up front as centre-forward. At the outbreak of war, when all League football was suspended, Blackpool was sitting at the top of the First Division, the only club with a 100 per cent record. Dodds had already scored three goals.

A goal-scoring hero in war-time

Dodds and his new club both experienced a 'good war', at least in the limited sense that they both reached the pinnacle of success on the field of play. The town of Blackpool became one of the country's major training centres for the RAF, and as a result many leading players spent some time in the town and with the club, turning out in the reconstituted regional League and Cup competitions. Stanley Matthews, for example, made appearances well ahead of his better-known post-war stint with the club. Dodds himself joined the RAF and became a physical training instructor, based in the town and responsible for training air crews. This posting allowed him to continue his playing career with his new club, with considerable success. He also represented the RAF in many matches against the other armed forces.

Blackpool went from strength to strength, winning the 1941/2 Northern League championship, the 1942/3 War Cup and, in 1943, 'the Championship of England', beating the southern champions, Arsenal, 4–2 in an outstanding match played before a crowd of 67,000 at Stamford Bridge. The match was broadcast live across the country, a vital service to supporters, who had few opportunities to travel because of the war-time restrictions. There are some reports that Blackpool's streets were deserted while the match was being broadcast (although, as usual with such reports, it is not clear which streets were meant, or whether this familiar claim was ever tested). From Blackpool's perspective this match was also outstanding in that the team included only Dodds and three other regular players, alongside Stanley Matthews of Stoke City, Burbanks of Sunderland, Dix of Tottenham Hotspurs, Hubbick of Bolton, Pope of Hearts and Savage of Leeds, all of whom were serving locally in the RAF. Arsenal, on the other hand, drew on many of its first-team regulars, including Ted Drake, Cliff Bastin, Bernard Joy, Kirchen, the Compton brothers and Jack Crayston. Dodds himself played as a guest during the war for several other teams, including Manchester United, Fulham and West Ham United.

Dodds's international career took off during these years as he achieved his lifetime's ambition of being capped for Scotland, nine times in all. The most famous of his games for Scotland was its 5–4 victory over England, in which he scored a hat-trick, as did the English centre-forward, Tommy Lawton. Dodds has recalled that 'it was a gloriously sunny day and there were many thousands locked out of the ground. Those who saw the game say it was the best international ever played, with Bill Shankly scoring the winning goal.'[14] Joe Mercer (see Chapter 14) was also in the England team that day and is remembered for having to play with one eye closed after being hit in the face by the ball. Dodds scored a total of nine goals for Scotland.

In 1944 England managed to beat Scotland three times in one year. One match played at Hampden Park, which England won 3–2, was described by Tommy Lawton as 'the toughest game I ever played in'.[15] Dodds, Matt Busby as captain and Bob Baxter of Middlesbrough (see Chapter 8) were among the players on the home side. Having been presented to Field Marshal Bernard Montgomery in front of a Hampden crowd of 133,000, England reached half-time 3–1 to the good. Dodds managed to score a goal in the second half, beating Stan Cullis to a cross to head past the England goalkeeper, Frank Swift, but it was not enough. What Tommy Lawton called this 'hot-blooded, all-out struggle'[16] ended in yet another war-time victory for England. The fact that the England team included such star players as Lawton, Swift, Matthews, Carter and Cullis suggests that the English football authorities took this match seriously, treating it as more than just another morale-boosting occasion for a nation (or, perhaps more appropriately in this context, two nations) at war.

Dodds later recalled that one of his Scottish team-mates had his £5 expenses queried after the game. When this player explained that he had brought his wife to watch the match, the riposte was 'We picked you, we didn't pick your wife.' As Dodds remarks, 'On that day we had played England before 133,000 people at Hampden Park. How much money did that crowd generate? That was how ridiculous it was in those days, that they could quibble over a player's expenses when it was such a small amount involved.'[17]

Dodds is recorded as having scored an amazing 223 war-time goals in 161 games, including an 8, a 7, two 5s and 3 or 4 goals on 20 occasions. In the 1941/2 season alone he scored a record 66 goals, including at least one in every game up to Christmas 1941. His 8-goal haul came in a 9–2 victory over Stockport County. He even managed to miss a penalty in that match, although he has always claimed, in his inimitable style, that in fact the ball hit the back stanchion in the net and rebounded so fast that the referee missed it. His 7 goals came in a match against Tranmere Rovers; they included the country's fastest ever hat-trick, achieved in just two and a half minutes.

Dodds in the late 1940s

With hostilities at an end professional football started to return to normal. Once the 1945/6 transitional season was over Dodds fell into a dispute with his club over wages and was placed on the transfer list. As he recalled later, 'Blackpool's problem was [that] they earned big money, but they didn't like to part with any of it.'[18] An offer then arrived for him to go to the Irish Republic to play for Shamrock Rovers while remaining on Blackpool's books. Irish clubs were not then governed by FIFA's rules and could pay players whatever they wished. Dodds allegedly received £20 a week, as compared to the weekly maximum of £8 at Blackpool, as well as a signing-on fee of £1,500. He played for Shamrock Rovers for a few weeks but, after the Irish Football Association came under pressure from FIFA, the club had to let him go. The authorities at Blackpool believed that Dodds had seen the error of his ways and now wanted to return to the club. Shamrock Rovers, which had easily covered its costs because large crowds had turned up to see the British star, agreed to release him from his contract and he returned to Blackpool, but the club insisted that he remain on the transfer list.

Several leading clubs, including Everton, Arsenal and Sheffield Wednesday, expressed interest in signing Dodds. Eventually he signed for Everton, for a reported fee of £8,250, although his new club claimed that this figure was excessive. Dodds went on to play 56 matches for Everton, scoring 36 times. At the time he was described as 'an enormous, no-nonsense centre-forward who led the line with his own distinctive brand of robust football'.[19] One particular local derby match against Liverpool, played in September 1948 and watched by a club record crowd of 78,299 at Goodison, stands out from the 56 that Dodds played: in 2000 it was nominated by Everton themselves as one of their 'Matches of the Millennium'. Dodds scored an equalising penalty just 6 minutes from time, ensuring that an earlier goal by the Liverpool star Joe Fagan would not give the Reds the spoils on this day at least.

The very next month Dodds was on the move again, joining Lincoln City for a then club record fee of £6,000. His star status was reflected in the fact that 7,000 Lincoln fans travelled to see him make his debut at Grimsby. He did not disappoint them, scoring twice to bring his new club back from being 2–0 down. He made 60 appearances for Lincoln in the 1948/9 and 1949/50 seasons, and, remarkably, kept up his goal-scoring tally, hitting the net a further 38 times. In one match against West Ham United he scored a hat-trick against 3 different goalkeepers, including a former colleague from his Blackpool days, George Dick. Dodds's time at Lincoln brought him back into contact with a childhood friend, the club's manager, Bill Anderson, who had also started his playing career with Medomsley Juniors. Anderson had subsequently moved on to play for Sheffield United, where he and Dodds had already met again after Dodds too joined the Blades. Dodds eventually ended his remarkable playing career in June 1950.

Dodds the rebel

Dodds's post-war football career included two incidents that gave him something of a reputation as a rebel, for which he has no regrets. They also say something about the wider context in which professional footballers had to earn their living.

When Dodds moved to Shamrock Rovers on £20 a week he became 'Britain's highest paid player'.[20] As reported many years later, this 'sent shock waves through the Football Association',[21] for, while players in England were still labouring under the rigid maximum-wage restrictions, one of the country's greatest stars was cocking a snook at one of the longest-lasting traditions of the professional game. Dodds had effectively taken control of his working conditions and shown what opportunities were available to players who were willing to test themselves in the wider labour market. Whether that makes him a hero or, however unwittingly, something of a villain depends on what view one takes of the state of football now that the maximum wage is long gone.

Dodds's reputation as a rebel was further enhanced a year or two later when he became involved in the 'Colombian scandal'. In an attempt to establish professional football in Colombia a number of rich businessmen had formed their own clubs, such as Millionarios and Santa Fe, and then set out to recruit some of the best European players. Using established players such as Charlie Mitten of Manchester United and Dodds, then still at Lincoln, as their representatives, they managed to attract Neil Franklin, George Mountford, Bobby Flavell, Billy Hogg, Roy Paul and Trevor Ford from England. Mitten himself was recruited as a player, and was apparently offered a salary of £5,000, a further £5,000 as a signing-on fee, a house, a car, a maid and a chauffeur. Dodds, appearing before the Football League to face a charge of bringing the game into disrepute, admitted to offering players signing-on fees of £4,000 and monthly pay of £100. Franklin, then England's centre-half, was probably the most famous of the English recruits. However, he stayed in Colombia for only a relatively short time. According to Mitten's biographer: 'Sadly for Franklin and his family, the culture shock had proved too great: they had been unable to adapt to local customs and found the language too great a barrier to overcome.'[22] On his return to England the FA imposed a suspension on him. He was never to appear in an England shirt again. Nevertheless, the incident had a significant impact on the globalisation of the game and gave impetus to the notion that a professional footballer's career does not have to be limited to the country of his birth, a view that today is taken for granted. Jimmy Guthrie, the chairman of the Players Union at the time, said that the players who had gone to Colombia had 'struck a blow for players' freedom'.[23] Dodds himself also received a suspension. By his own account, 'it was very quickly lifted, but by that time I had decided to retire and concentrate on my business interests in Blackpool'.[24]

Dodds turned down offers to become manager at Port Vale and at Stoke City, and continued to build a business career which over the years has included hotel management, the manufacturing of sweets, and the ownership of betting shops, night clubs and gaming machines. He also turned out in charity football matches. In 1959, aged 44, he was offered the chance to play for a local team, Lytham, in the Lancashire Combination League, but, probably wisely, he turned them down. In 1982 the *Sheffield Star* reported that he was 'urging people, notably sportsmen and sportswomen, to improve their lifestyles'. He had become a 'hot gospeller of natural health foods', acting as a distributor for an international health foods company. His own lifestyle reflected this new business venture: he was now a non-smoking vegetarian, running 3 miles a day before breakfast and still playing in charity matches despite being in his sixties.[25]

Speaking in 1995, at the age of 80, Dodds recalled his days in the game as 'happy, happy days . . . I enjoyed every minute of it. I'm pleased to say that I have left my memory on quite a number of people in a good way.'[26] At the time of writing Dodds remains the only one of the terrace heroes profiled in this book who is still alive, remaining to this day in his football heaven, Blackpool.

HAROLD HOBBIS,
Charlton Ath. F.C.

13 Harold Hobbis – Charlton Athletic

Harold Hobbis, an outside-left who could score goals, started his career with Bromley, an amateur club in Kent, but the team he stayed with throughout his professional career was Charlton Athletic, which he joined at the start of the 1930s, initially as an amateur and then, from March 1931, as a full-time professional. During the 1930s Hobbis saw his own career advance in line with the growing and remarkable success of the club. Under their manager, Jimmy Seed, the 'Addicks' rose from the depths of the Third Division to the upper reaches of the First, challenging the likes of Arsenal for the League Championship. Hobbis's career similarly blossomed, eventually leading to international recognition as a player for England. As a key element in the 'Seed revolution', Hobbis can be regarded as an Addicks hero.

Before the 'Seed revolution'

Charlton Athletic did not become a professional team until 1921. They started the 1930s as a mid-table Second Division team, having gained promotion in 1929. They were then relegated back to the Third Division (South) in 1933. From that point, however, they went on one of the most remarkable journeys of any club in the whole Football League, winning promotion from the Third Division to the Second, and then to the First Division, and then becoming runner-up to the champion team in three consecutive seasons, 1934/5 to 1936/7. They remained in the First Division until the outbreak of war, achieving great success as the fourth- and third-placed club in the following two seasons.

Harold Hobbis, an outside-left, played a key role in this success story, which led to his eventually being capped for England. Alongside Hobbis was the team's legendary manager, Jimmy Seed, who masterminded this rise from the ashes and went on to establish himself as one of the country's most successful managers, staying with Charlton for a total of twenty-three years. He eventually managed Charlton for 727 games before moving on for a short spell as manager at Millwall.

Hobbis arrived at Charlton before Seed did. In 1931, when Charlton achieved a respectable but uninspiring fifteenth place at the end of the 1930/1 season, Hobbis was at the start of his career, playing on amateur terms in Charlton's reserves. In March 1931 he was offered a professional contract by the secretary–manager, Alex MacFarlane, who was in his second spell with the club. MacFarlane had had a successful career as a player with Newcastle and Scotland.

The 1931/2 season saw Charlton maintaining their mid-table place in the Second Division, eventually reaching tenth, well behind the champions, Wolverhampton Wanderers. Hobbis scored just twice, in the last month of the season.

Having gained Second Division status at the end of the 1928/9 season, Charlton was soon to return to the Third Division (South): the 1932/3 season saw the team come bottom. As the Football League's review of the season noted: 'nobody was surprised. Starting the season with high hopes, they were consistently disappointing and throughout looked the weakest side in the Division.'[1] Charlton had the worst home record of any team in the whole Football League, with just nine victories. Hobbis scored four times, including two goals in a remarkable 5–5 draw at Grimsby. Charlton also lost MacFarlane in December 1932. Following his resignation, Albert Lindon, who had been goalkeeper for Merthyr Town, took over as temporary manager while the club searched for a replacement. This took some time and it was not until after the team had been relegated that the club appointed the manager who would turn out to be their saviour: Jimmy Seed.

Before turning to management Seed had had some success as a player. Having been signed by Sunderland just before war broke out in 1914, he joined up, was gassed and then, after his return to Roker Park in 1918, found that he had been sold to the non-League club Mid-Rhondda. Seed eventually moved to Tottenham Hotspurs and helped them to win the FA Cup in 1921. Six years on Spurs sold Seed to Sheffield Wednesday after a dispute about a proposed wage cut. Wednesday, then facing the drop from the First Division, made Seed team captain and, with 17 points from the last 20 games won, he managed to lead the team to mid-table safety. (Spurs were relegated.) Wednesday went on to win the First Division Championship the very next season, again with Seed as captain.

Seed then became secretary–manager at a Third Division (South) club, Clapton Orient (later to become Leyton Orient), working initially under the guidance of Arsenal's manager, Herbert Chapman. In the late 1920s Arsenal had bought into Clapton in the hope that they could serve as a nursery club for the Gunners and Chapman had approached Seed to act as secretary–manager under his direction. Chapman still handled the business side of the club, including buying and selling players. The FA then ruled that clubs could not have nursery relationships with other professional clubs and Arsenal was forced to pull out. This left Seed on his own in charge of the team's affairs. Having just missed the need to seek re-election by finishing twentieth, Clapton also had to suffer suspension by the FA at the end of the season on the grounds of 'lack of order in its finances'. By the time the suspension was lifted Seed had moved to Charlton.

The key year in Charlton's development was 1932. Two local timber merchants, Albert and Stanley Gliksten, joined the club's board, and put a total of £105,000 into its coffers, partly to gain control and partly to fund the purchase of players. May 1933 saw Charlton's relegation to the Third Division (South): the Glikstens' investment started to look somewhat misjudged. However, a pure piece of good fortune came their way. At a banquet organised by Arsenal to celebrate their winning of the First Division Championship Albert Gliksten ended up sitting next to one Jimmy Seed. Their conversation got round to Charlton's dilemma and the need for a new manager. Seed halfheartedly put his own name forward. A few days later Albert Gliksten made contact and, having asked Seed if he 'had always been lucky in football' and received a positive reply, offered him the job that was to keep him at Charlton until 1956. Seed's initial salary was £12 a week. At first the Gliksten brothers were prepared to fund the development of the club, but they took the view that they wanted their money repaid as quickly as possible and they did not intend to put any further money in, leaving Seed to build a team by careful management of the transfer market. Throughout Seed's long career at Charlton it was never to be a 'buying' club.

Charlton's rise to the top

One of Seed's first tasks when preparing for the 1933/4 season in the basement of the Football League was to establish a comprehensive scouting system, especially in the Northeast of England, the region in which he himself had been born. Using five scouts, including his own brother Antony, Seed was able over the years to recruit some thirty players from the region, often at little or no cost. Sam Bartram, Charlton's legendary goalkeeper, was one such player. Seed also hired men from the local labour exchange to carry sandwich-boards around the streets to advertise home matches. Charlton maintained a fairly useful level of performance throughout the season and even reached the top spot for a week in October 1933. However, the Football League's review described the team as a 'sound, if uninspiring side'.[2] In a comment on Seed's approach to his task, the review noted that 'the management would appear to have shrewdly recognised the side's limitations, and, while a good place was always preserved, building for the future was their real aim'.[3]

Hobbis played in all but one League game during the 1933/4 season and scored 8 times. Cyril Pearce was the side's leading goal-scorer and, although he broke his leg in a match at the end of March 1934, he still managed to end the season with 26 goals. Charlton's challenge for honours could well have been damaged by this injury, as the team won just one game of the 7 that it played without Pearce. Norwich City eventually ran out as champions, 9 points ahead of Charlton, which was in fifth place.

During the season Seed had started to build his team, combining the experienced players he inherited on his arrival, such as Hobbis, with new players such as Harris, bought from Cardiff for £450; Turner, who came from Welsh football for no fee; Butt, transferred from Bath City for £160; and Green, for whom Seed paid £250. Seed managed to increase attendances and ran the club with a reduced loss of £9,000.

The 1934/5 season marked the start of Charlton's magical rise to the very top of the English game. Seed essentially kept on all the players from the previous season, augmenting them with Stephenson from Preston North End, bought for £660, and Bill Dodgin from Lincoln. By the end of December 1934, after the leadership of the Division had see-sawed between a number of clubs in the first half of the season, Charlton had established a 4-point lead. They were never displaced for the rest of the season, which they ended with an 8-point advantage over the runners-up, Reading. Charlton also had the best away record of any club in the Football League and won the largest number of matches. Their players also scored a total of 103 League goals. Hobbis played in 36 League matches and ended up as the second highest goal-scorer, with 15 goals. Seed described him as 'one of our key men in our promotion'.[4] The Football League's review of the season rated Charlton the best team in the Division, deserving to be promoted back into the Second Division.

However, Charlton were not without misfortunes during this season. The centre-forward, Cyril Pearce, who had broken his leg towards the end of the previous season, was unable to play at all during 1934/5. However, Ralph Allen was signed for £650 in late October 1934, from neighbouring Brentford, and went on to set a club record of 32 goals, a remarkable feat given that he had missed 2 months of the season and played in only 28 games. Charlton also suffered from the sad loss of the goalkeeper Alexander Wright, who died after sustaining a spinal injury diving off a raft into shallow water.

Seed had strong views on the game at this time. In an article published in the *Daily Mail* on 3 January 1935 he argued for a revision of the rules to bar players from charging goalkeepers, pointing out that there was a strictly enforced 'no charging' rule on the continent. In the year when he was leading his team out of the Third Division he asserted that his club's success, and that of others, was being inhibited by injuries caused to goalies by overzealous forwards. However, he saw the idea of having 'substitute' goalkeepers as 'too revolutionary a change'.[5]

Having suffered the sad loss of Alexander Wright, Seed went back to his roots in the Northeast in search of a long-term replacement. He found one in the form of 'a young, carroty-haired out-of-work coal miner from Bolden Colliery'[6] named Sam Bartram. Seed also convinced the Gliksteens to finance his biggest signing up to that point, Torquay's centre-half, Don Welsh, who cost the club £3,250. Welsh went on to become the bedrock of Charlton's defence in the years to come and was duly capped by England.

Having made the return trip to the Second Division after just two seasons in the Third, Charlton maintained the good form they had shown and gained instant promotion to the First, finishing as runner-up to Manchester United. As Seed recalled in his autobiography: 'Harold Hobbis, our left-winger, had a wonderful season and was to finish top scorer with 23 goals.'[7] He had appeared in every League match, the only player to do so. Seed also commented that 'The effective left-winger is the most difficult player to come by.'[8] In Hobbis he had found his man. Once again Seed stuck with his tried and tested team, bringing in only the full-back Syd Cann from Manchester City, for £400. The more significant recruit, however, was Jimmy Trotter, the new club trainer, who also dealt with the players' injuries and supervised their fitness regimes. Trotter had been a team-mate of Seed's at Sheffield Wednesday; he was to work alongside him at Charlton for twenty years. (After Seed's departure, in 1956, Trotter was appointed as his replacement; he also served as trainer to the England team under Walter Winterbottom.) Charlton's other new development in the 1935/6 season was a 'nursery club' arrangement with a local amateur club, Bexleyheath and Welling, which was to groom young players for the future, reflecting Charlton's policy of developing talent rather than buying established stars.

During 1935/6 the Second Division was characterised by almost continual change at the top, with seven different teams holding the position at various times. Charlton first took over at the head of the Division at the start of January 1936, lost it, then took it again as the season neared its end. Manchester United closed up at the vital time, however, taking over at the top on Easter Monday and then again, and for the final time, just three days before the last fixtures. Charlton ended up unbeaten at home but just one point behind United. Seed's own assessment of the season was as follows:

> the team was not too consistent and we had been hit by injuries. With six matches to go to the end of the season, we were still in the running . . . few of our supporters gave us a real chance of finishing in the first two, but the boys pulled out something extra over Easter and collected five out of a possible six points. When we defeated West Ham 3–1 at Upton Park the following Saturday we required three points from our last two games to be sure of beating Sheffield United in the promotion race.[9]

Both of the last two games were at home. Having beaten Bradford 3–1, Charlton needed just a draw against Port Vale. In front of a crowd of 30,000 Hobbis put Charlton ahead in the first half and, although Vale equalised later, through Caldwell, Charlton got the point and the promotion.

As the Football League's review of the 1935/6 season noted, Charlton were 'never overawed by their superior quarters. They took to the Second Division quite easily and were always one of the most noticeable sides. Strength at home was their strong suit.'[10] In relation to Charlton's players the review commented:

> If Allen, the centre-forward who had shot in so deadly a style in the lower Division, was not quite so successful this season, there was compensation in the advance of the already promising Hobbis, who had a fine season. He took on the role of leading goal-scorer and performed it well. He thoroughly deserved the international honour which came his way at the end of the season.[11]

It also commented that 'in the closing weeks when that decisive spurt had to be made a good addition was made to their ranks in the person of John Oakes from

Aldershot Town, a versatile player who can play both as forward or half-back'.[12] It concluded by congratulating Jimmy Seed on 'a fine two consecutives seasons' and observed that 'there is no reason to suppose that the club's membership of the First Division will not be a long one'.[13]

Approaching the First Division for the first time, Seed summed up his tactics and the views of at least some of the national newspapers:

> Once again, I pledged myself to stick to the boys who had made promotion possible, and once again we were scoffed at. Some football scribes declared [that] we were lucky to have survived some bad lapses during our promotion bid, and certainly we could never hope to hold our own consistently in the First Division, unless we spent a fortune.[14]

The Football League's rather more optimistic expectations of Charlton under Seed's managership proved to be well-founded.

The results of the 1936/7 season must have exceeded even Seed's expectations and aspirations. Having spent £5,000 on additional terracing and turnstiles over the summer, in anticipation of the larger crowds to be expected in the First Division, Charlton started the season with broadly the same set of stalwarts that had brought about their rise from the depths of the Third Division, including the outside-left, Hobbis. The investment in ground improvements proved to have been a sound decision as, just a few weeks later, a home match against Arsenal attracted a club record crowd of 77,000, almost 30,000 higher than the previous record attendance. Over the season home gates averaged 30,000.

Although Manchester City, which included Billy Dale (see Chapter 11), were generally seen as the most brilliant team in the Division and, after an unbeaten run of twenty-two games in the second half of the season, won the Championship for the first time in their history, Charlton were nonetheless, as the Football League's review of the season commented, 'the most remarkable team',[15] finishing as runner-up to City, just three points behind. The League's review went on to note: 'In the First Division it was felt that they would do quite adequately if they retained their new classification and would be doing really well if they finished in the first half. Charlton soon showed that they had other ideas.'[16] Charlton were in ninth position by the end of September 1936, in eighth position by the end of October and in sixth position at the end of November. On 12 December the team went to the top of the First Division. Although they were knocked off after just one week, they were soon back in the top slot and remained there from 30 January 1937 to 10 March, when Arsenal took over, only to be overtaken by the fast-improving Manchester City team, which reached the top on 10 April and stayed there for the few remaining weeks of the season. Charlton's players maintained their good form throughout and were seen as worthy runners-up. A match report in the *News of the World* on Charlton's 2–1 home victory against Brentford, which clinched second place, commented: 'Their amazing keenness plus their rapid advance work and grand placing of low passes, when going at top speed, characterised their victorious display in this, their last game, as it has so often during this, their first season in the top class.'[17]

One of the most remarkable features of Charlton's success was the comparatively low number of goals scored, just 58 in 42 games, as compared to the champion team, Manchester City, which scored 109. Only 5 other teams in the whole of the First Division scored fewer goals than Charlton and 3 of them finished at the bottom of the League table. Charlton also achieved the distinction of having the equal-best defensive record in the division, with just 49 goals conceded, the same as Arsenal, which was in third place: Manchester City let in 61. Charlton's goalkeeper, Bartram, and the defenders, John Oakes, Turner and James Oakes, played well throughout the season. Charlton had problems, however, in finding a centre-forward who could score regularly. Seed had judged Ralph Allen, the team's previous goal-scorer, as unlikely to prosper at the higher level and had sold him to Reading for £800 over the summer. Seed then tried 6 different players in this position, including the previously successful Cyril Pearce. Only George Tadman, normally an outside-right and the only player signed by the club upon promotion, for £1,000 from Gillingham, made any success of the role. He ended up as the club's leading scorer, with just 11 goals. Harold Hobbis, still playing on the left wing, was the next most prolific, scoring 8 goals across the season. The Football League's review concluded its discussion of Charlton with the statement: 'theirs was a notable performance, and taking their record over a term of four years, Mr James Seed's period of management has been one of outstanding success'.[18] In his autobiography Seed himself commented: 'We had failed by only three points to achieve a remarkable record – from Third Division to League Champions in three seasons. Still, we had done well, and made a £7,000 profit compared with £3,000 the previous year.'[19] Ever the shrewd manager, Seed also noted that 'I reckon our playing staff to be worth every bit of £100,000, although it had cost less than a quarter of this sum to buy.'[20]

Reflecting on this greatest of times, Seed also offered some barbed comments on the newspaper reporting of the day: 'In spite of all this, still we were not given a good Press. Some football writers seemed dazzled by the Arsenal's earlier success, and our remarkable performance was rather dismissed as a lucky phase. Charlton Athletic were still regarded as the ragamuffin team!'[21] As for tactics, Seed pointed out:

> you need luck in football but our performance has been mainly brought about by ability and team-spirit. Our success was not any flash in the pan, even though many did not like our style, which they classed as negative football. I am prepared to take the blame for this. As captain of Sheffield Wednesday, I had developed into a tactician, and it is my firm belief that the inside-forward really worth his salt is the man prepared to drop back to pull his weight in defence. Indeed, I would go further and say that the defence of any successful side starts with the inside-forwards.[22]

Seed and Charlton were now faced with the challenge confronting all successful new boys. Could they sustain their initial burst, or would it be, as some in the press predicted, just another freak of football? In the 1937/8 season, which was characterised by the lowest number of goals scored in any First Division since the change in the offside law in 1925, Charlton managed to improve their own tally, with 65 goals. The defensive strength was also in evidence from the previous season and, with just 51 goals conceded, Charlton ended up third best in the Division. This performance resulted in another fine year, with a final position of fourth, 6 points behind the all-conquering team of the 1930s, Arsenal, which had Jack Crayston (see Chapter 10) at right-half. Two of the highest-scoring teams in the division were relegated: Manchester City, with 80 goals, and West Bromwich Albion, with 74. Arsenal scored only 77.

Charlton's workmanlike side, with their emphasis on defence, continued to perform well at home. Losing only two matches at the Valley, they had the second-best home record in the division. Sadly, this was not matched away from home, where Charlton won only two matches all season. While goal-scoring was better than in the previous season, the search continued for a centre-forward who could score goals. Four different players took on the role at various times. Charlton's real discovery during the season was brought about after the unfortunate Harold Hobbis broke his leg in the third playing of the fifth-round tie in the FA Cup against Aston Villa. His replacement for the rest of the season was Brown, a young player signed from Yarmouth in late January 1938, who went on to score 9 times in just 13 games. Hobbis had managed to score 6 times before he sustained his season-ending injury. Charlton's first attempt at this fixture with Aston Villa at the Valley had drawn the day's highest attendance, as more than 76,000 people crowded in to see the match.

The Football League's review of the 1937/8 season concluded that Charlton lacked what the anonymous writer referred to as 'personality'. Presumably this meant that Charlton's style of play was too negative, a view that Seed was aware of and disagreed with (as mentioned above). The review commented: 'When this elusive element can be supplied without the solidity of the main structure being weakened the Londoners may carry all before them.'[23]

What turned out to be the final full season before the outbreak of war, 1938/9, saw Charlton once again maintain their successful run in the top drawer of the League and finish in a very creditable third position behind the champions, Everton, and the runners-up, Wolverhampton Wanderers. Yet again goal-scoring improved: Tadman at last got back to a decent total for the season of 24. One of Charlton's achievements in the season was doing the 'double' on Everton, especially a 4–1 victory at Everton's Goodison Park ground in mid-December 1938. The Football League's review highlighted the 'daring' of Sam Bartram, the 'invaluable consistency' of John and James Oakes, the 'dash' of George Tadman at centre-forward and the 'all-round capacity' of Don Welsh, both as half-back and as forward. Special reference was made to Harold Hobbis's return after he had broken his leg: 'the renewal of his confidence was open to doubt, but having returned to the side on December 31 he scored nine goals in 20 games'.[24] Seed's own view of Hobbis after his return was that 'he was never the same force as before his injury'.[25]

Charlton's players were now being regarded as established First Division class. This final season before the war saw Welsh being selected for the Football League XI against the Irish League in Belfast in September 1938. Welsh scored in the English team's 8–2 victory, which also featured four goals from Tommy Lawton of Everton. Welsh was then selected for the England tour to Italy, Yugoslavia and Romania at the end of the season, and played in the 2–0 victory over Romania. At the same time the FA took a party to South Africa and, for the first time, three Charlton players, Bartram, John Oakes and Brown, were included. Charlton was now being recognised as a source of talent. The outbreak of war brought an end to the prospective international careers of these and, possibly, other players, including Hobbis.

Hobbis's brief international career had taken place at the end of the 1935/6 season with matches against Austria, in Vienna, and Belgium, in Brussels. England lost 2–1 against the Austrians, who were, at the time, probably the best team on the continent. Hobbis himself was injured in the match and rushed to hospital. Luckily he was not as badly hurt as was first thought and he made such a rapid recovery that he was able to take his place in the team against Belgium. England's luck did not change, however: in pouring rain the team lost 3–2, having missed many scoring chances. A former Arsenal star, Charles Buchan, who was a newspaper reporter on the tour, wrote: 'It was a sad party that made the journey home. I don't think I have ever enjoyed a Continental trip less.'[26] Hobbis never had the chance to play for England again, partly because of his long lay-off.

An interesting insight into Jimmy Seed's approach to his task, and the thoroughness and 'professionalism' that he adopted, is revealed in a piece published in the *Topical Times* in 1939. Seed describes a 'bible'[27] that he had kept ever since becoming a manager, in which he recorded the playing performance of every team played against, the conditions of the ground and other factors that, in his view, upset known form. Seed also carefully studied every member of each opposing team, noting their peculiarities of play and their weak spots. In an era when having a 'manager' rather than a 'secretary–manager' was still a matter of preference among the different clubs, Seed was clearly at the vanguard of team management, alongside Herbert Chapman and Major Frank Buckley (see Chapter 4).

Seed also attempted to break into the big time once Charlton had become established as a First Division club, making an offer of £13,000 to Stoke City, in November 1938, to bring the great Stanley Matthews to the Valley. Seed admitted that the bid was made 'on the spur of the moment' after he watched Matthews play outstandingly for England in a 7–0 trashing of Ireland. While Seed and Stoke's manager, Bob McGrory, agreed the fee, Stoke's directors refused to sell, apparently much to the relief of Charlton's chairman, Albert Gliksten. This was just a few months after the cash-rich directors at Arsenal had broken the current transfer record to bring Bryn Jones from Wolverhampton to Highbury for a fee of £14,000. In his autobiography, written after he had left Charlton, Seed still insisted that Charlton should have persisted with their interest in Matthews: 'Charlton would have had the glamour that the team had always lacked in spite of their many splendid achievements.'[28]

In the autobiography Seed also recalled his experiences of the business end of football management and what, in his view, was the 'shady' side of the game:

> on the few occasions I had gone all out to sign some of the big boys of the game, negotiations broke down because some of the Glamour Boys think [that] their box-office quality should be rewarded. I lost chances of signing an English, a Scottish and a Welsh international because we would not make the under-the-counter payment [that they] asked for and, presumably, received from the clubs for whom they eventually signed.[29]

Seed described the terms that the Scottish international in question had demanded in order to come to Charlton: 'if I gave him £1,000 in his left hand then he would sign with his right.'[30] Payments of this kind were illegal but they were undoubtedly being made. Such cases of corruption may, arguably, be seen as yet another sign of the changing nature of the game at the highest level. In contrast to this evidence of 'professionalism' and under-the-counter payments in the transfer market, the public face of English football was still old-fashioned even by the standards of the 1930s, when paternalism was already being questioned in other quarters. In 1939, for example, the *Topical Times* described how Charlton's chairman Albert Gliksten ensured that every member of staff at the Valley went home from training every Christmas with a turkey 'tucked 'neath their arms'.[31]

Seed's later years

During the Second World War Charlton Athletic engaged in regular football, with some success. Harold Hobbis had joined the RAF, but still managed to turn out for the club on a regular basis. Towards the end of the war Charlton twice reached the Final of the Football League Cup (South), losing 7–1 to Arsenal in 1943 but beating Chelsea 3–1 in 1944; the team then drew 1–1 in the resulting match with the Northern Cup winners, Aston Villa.

Following the return of peace in 1945 Charlton maintained their form and had continued success, although in the FA Cup rather than in the League. In the 1945/6 season, when League football was still being run on a regional basis and Cup matches were played over two legs, Charlton reached the Final only to be beaten by Derby County 4–1 after extra time. The following season saw Charlton go one better, beating Burnley in the Final with a goal seven minutes from the end of extra time from the Scottish outside-left Chris Duffy. Duffy, who had played as a guest during war-time matches for Charlton, had been signed from Leith Athletic after the war for a mere £330, primarily as a replacement for the ageing Hobbis. Charlton maintained their First Division status, although with little success, through to 1957, when they managed to let in 120 goals in the season and, not surprisingly, were relegated back to the Second Division. Jimmy Seed had left Charlton in 1956, as had the goalkeeper Sam Bartram, who by then had made 583 appearances since he had joined the club in 1934. Jimmy Trotter, Seed's trainer at the club since the mid-1930s, took over as manager and led the team until 1961.

Charlton Athletic, with Seed, Trotter and Hobbis, had experienced one of the most remarkable periods of on-the-field success in the 1930s. Hobbis, having played throughout this professional career with the 'Addicts', had experienced the game at all levels, from amateur and professional, from Third Division to the upper reaches of the First Division, and then at international level. As a goal-scoring left winger, he had been central to manager Jimmy Seed's plans throughout this period and is clearly remembered as one of the club's loyal servants at this key time in the history of the club.

JAMES MERCER,
Everton F.C.

14 Joe Mercer – Everton

Of all the terrace heroes of the 1930s Joe Mercer is probably the best known to contemporary football supporters and observers of the game, although more because of his post-war exploits, both as an inspirational player and later as a manager, than for his contribution at Everton during the 1930s. Both his autobiography and the 'authorised' biography published after his death[1] display a similar focus on his post-war experiences and achievements. Accordingly, this chapter draws less on these more recently published sources and more on materials that appeared in the 1930s, as well as on standard reference texts and the memories of those who knew Mercer in the earlier part of his career.

Mercer's status as one of English football's true heroes is indicated in descriptions of him as having 'the heart of a lion';[2] being 'a master of interception and distribution, a shrewd cultured tactician with the ability to lift the spirits of the men around him';[3] possessing a 'superb tactical brain and outstanding ability',[4] as well as 'spirit, courage and determination';[5] and being 'a man whose warm personality shone through even the game's greyest days'.[6] His Everton team-mate Bill 'Dixie' Dean rated Mercer 'one of the greatest players of all time';[7] the Liverpool and Scotland star Billy Liddell saw him as 'a real gentleman – on the field and off it';[8] and John King, the former manager of Tranmere Rovers, saw him as 'one of the true cavaliers'.[9]

Mercer in the 1930s

Joe Mercer was one of several star footballers of the 1930s, including Stan Cullis and Frank Soo, who emerged from Ellesmere Port in Cheshire. Mercer was born on 9 August 1914. His father played centre-half for Tranmere Rovers and Nottingham Forest but, as a young child living in a poor district of the town, Mercer was brought up on back-alley football, learning his craft with a bundle of newspapers tied up with string or, on good days, with a tennis ball. As he commented later: 'If you could control a small ball with certainty, you found later that bringing down a normal ball came more easily. It was wonderful training for the eye.'[10]

At that time schoolboys in Ellesmere Port who were interested in football were divided into two distinct camps: the 'Portites', who were local boys, and the 'Wafflers', boys from families that had members working for the Wolver-hampton Corrugated Iron Company, which had been transferred lock, stock and barrel from the West Midlands. Mercer was a Portite and his friend Stan Cullis was a Waffler. Many fierce games were played out in the alleys and fields between the two of them and their mates. Both were also selected to play for Ellesmere Port schools, demonstrating that their footballing prowess was already being recognised.

At the age of 14 Mercer joined the village team of Elton Green. He is said to have received both his bus fare and a bag of vegetables after every game. He then moved on to play for his employers, Shell–Mex, while holding down a variety of jobs in the company, including petrol delivery. Eventually he joined the main local team, Ellesmere Port, and it was while he was playing there that he was first spotted by the local First Division club Everton, then under the control of Tom McIntosh as secretary and Harry Cooke as trainer. Mercer signed for Everton, initially on amateur terms, in 1931, but fulfilled his boyhood dream of becoming a full-time professional when he signed his first contract in September 1932. He was paid £5 a week, which, as he later commented, 'was a lot of money then – twice what the average working man got – and I was only a lad'.[11]

Everton had won the First Division Championship at the end of the 1931/2 season and were about to build on this success by winning the FA Cup, beating one of Mercer's future clubs, Manchester City, in 1933. Bill 'Dixie' Dean was Everton's captain and goal-scoring maestro, scoring 45 goals in 42 League games in 1931/2 and a further 24 in 1932/3, with another 5 in the team's successful Cup run, including one of their 3 goals in the Final. Mercer, however, played virtually no part in the 1932/3 season, appearing just once, as a replacement for a resting Cliff Britton, in the match immediately before the Final, a 1–1 draw with Leeds United. The following two seasons saw him continuing to play mainly in the reserves, with only an occasional promotion to the first team. In 1934/5, for example, he made just 8 appearances in the first team. Meanwhile, he was already becoming known for his smile, described as 'natural, humorous and warm',[12] and for his legs, usually described as spindly. Dixie Dean reportedly commented, when seeing Mercer getting changed as an apprentice, 'Look at them, they wouldn't last the postman for a morning.'[13]

It was not until the 1935/6 season that Mercer made a breakthrough into the first team on a regular basis, replacing Jock Thompson, the regular half-back. Having established himself, Mercer then went on to represent Everton in 149 League and 12 Cup matches up to the outbreak of war in September 1939. However, he scored only one goal, in a 4–0 home win over Blackburn Rovers in March 1936, in a period of sustained top-level football for his skilful First Division side, which culminated in a further First Division Championship in 1938/9. Everton, which had become known as the 'School of Science', boasted not only Mercer and Dean among their players but also other 'greats' such as Tommy Lawton, Ted Sagar and T.G. Jones.

The 1935/6 season saw Everton achieve relatively little, especially away from home. Winning just one away match, at Grimsby, the team managed to have the third worst goals-against record in the Division that season, surpassed only by the two teams that ended up being relegated, Aston Villa and Blackburn Rovers. Everton did, however, manage to reach the safety of sixteenth position on the basis of their good home record and their prolific goal-scoring achievements. Led by Cunliffe and Dean, with 40 goals between them, Everton amassed a total of 89 in the season, bettered only by the 109 scored by the champion team, Sunderland.

The season was also marked by the death in October 1935 of Tom McIntosh, who had been Everton's secretary since 1919. Theo Kelly, the assistant secretary, was appointed as his successor in February 1936. One of Kelly's significant early signings was T.G. Jones, from Wrexham, who was destined to become an Everton legend. Having played just six matches for Wrexham, Jones was snapped up for a modest £3,000. As one of his team-mates, Gordon Watson, commented later: 'T.G. Jones was the best signing that Everton ever made.'[14]

Mercer's own success in his first full season was starting to be recognised nationally and he was featured as one of the twelve 'best discoveries of the 1935/6 season' in the *Topical Times*, which commented: 'The boy from Ellesmere Port had to wait for his chance, but obviously came right to his game last season. Strong all round. Takes the ball through well to his attack. Gives the long cross pass with a suddenness very upsetting to his opponents. Is a strong tackler and covers the ball well with his body when he himself is being tackled.'[15]

Everton's first full season under Kelly as manager, 1936/7, proved less than successful and the team finished in seventeenth position. Their record at Goodison Park was excellent, with only two home matches being lost, but their away performances were the complete opposite: they won just two and lost seventeen. Goal-scoring, however, did not prove to be a problem, since Dean and Stevenson hit the net more than forty times between them. Another key signing during the season was the Burnley centre-forward, Tommy Lawton, then aged 17, who was regarded as likely to replace Dean some day, although Dean was then only 30 and still as lethal in front of goal as ever. The £6,500 paid for Lawton set a record for a player of his age. By this time Mercer was established in the team's half-back line, alongside Britton and Gee, both of whom joined Dean in representing the Football League in a 2–0 victory over the Scottish League. Britton also made his international debut for England during the season.

The 1937/8 season again proved unremarkable for Everton, which finished at fourteenth position in the League. However, the season was significant in that it saw the emergence of the new Goodison Park goal-machine, Lawton, and the eventual sale of his predecessor, Dixie Dean, to the Third Division (North) club Notts County. This ended an era, dating back to 1925, that had seen Dean emerge as the first national football superhero. Sadly, after just three games for his new club, he received an injury that kept him out of the side for the remainder of the season. Lawton, meanwhile, blossomed as the new leader of Everton's forward line and ended the season as the First Division's top goal-scorer, with 28 goals. Everton also ended up as the Division's second-highest goal-scoring team, with just one goal fewer than Manchester City, which, remarkably, managed to be relegated having scored 80 goals. Everton also received further national recognition when Geldard played for the League in a 3–0 win over the Irish League at Blackpool.

With growing disquiet over the international developments that seemed to presage war, the 1938/9 season hardly got off to an optimistic start. At Goodison Park, however, things were looking up, with six straight victories, a record at the time. Everton never looked back. Taking over at the top of the Division for the last time in February 1939, after a 3–0 victory at Anfield, the team clinched the Championship by 22 April, despite losing on the day to Charlton Athletic. The runners-up, Wolverhampton Wanderers, managed no more than a draw. Everton's fifth championship victory was acclaimed as 'exceptionally pleasing' by the Football League and its review of the year commented that Everton had 'solved the problem of producing a style which was at once effective and pleasing to the eye, a combination of merits which it has often been beyond the Champions to achieve'.[16] The *Liverpool Echo* summed up the team's achievement in a similar vein: 'They have succeeded by sound, skilful football and polished artistry, without glands or doctored grounds [as at Wolves], on sheer merit, based upon a true scientific exposition of the game as opposed to the modern craze for speed, hard-hitting and first-time tactics.'[17]

Playing with essentially the same team as in the previous season, Everton managed to provide Lawton with greater all-round support. The international wingers Gillick and Boyes provided excellent service to the head of Lawton. The normally frail defence was bolstered by the developing Jones at centre-half and the introduction of Bentham brought 'added brains into the attack'.[18] Mercer, at right half-back, remained rock-steady and as consistent as ever, playing in all but one League game. Lawton, as lethal as in the previous season, scored 33 times, just one goal fewer than Micky Fenton of Middlesbrough, the Division's leading goal-scorer. The Goodison Park fortress remained as strong as ever, with just one defeat all season and 60 goals being scored in just 21 matches. Although Everton lost 9 matches away from home, they won the greatest number of away points. They were not to add to their championship haul for another 24 years, an interval that has been described as the 'most ignominious period in their history'.[19]

As England's most successful club Everton achieved further recognition both on and off the field. Ten players received international caps during the 1938/9 season, helping the club to a total of thirty-two. Lawton continued to play regularly for England, collecting eight caps, and he was now joined by his team-mate Joe Mercer. They made successful appearances for England, initially against Ireland and then against Scotland in a 2–1 victory in front of 150,000 spectators at Hampden Park, only the third such victory on Scottish soil since the start of the twentieth century. Mercer's performance on the day was described as 'all legs and wings. Joe certainly brought off the encircling of the enemy . . . [and was] the inspiration behind England's ultimate success.'[20] Both players were then selected for the end-of-season continental tour, and made appearances against Italy, Yugoslavia and Romania. Stan Cullis recalls that in the match against Romania Mercer played a 'storming game' despite having the sole of one of his boots torn off after a strong tackle. According to Cullis, 'he refused to leave the field. With his toes hanging out, Joe kept going until Tom Whittaker, the trainer, could patch up the damage with a roll of sticking plaster.'[21] Cullis clearly rated Mercer highly: 'In addition to his tremendous ability, the bow-legged Joe possessed the heart of a lion. Together these two qualities combined to make him just about the most effective left half-back whom I ever saw.'[22] Lawton also valued Mercer's contribution to this tour. In his view the drawn match against Italy, which was then holding the World Cup, was Mercer's best-ever match for England. Lawton himself marked his growing national status by making his debut for the Football League's team in an 8–2 victory against the Irish League and scoring four times. Lawton and Greenhalgh were also in the League's team in a match against the Scottish League that ended in a 3–1 victory.

The 1938/9 season also saw the death of Charles Sutcliffe, the president of the Football League. Will Cuff of Everton, who was already vice-president, was elected unopposed as Sutcliffe's successor in June 1939. That summer Everton faced the future with some optimism. The team was well established and had won the Championship; the players were gaining greater international recognition; the club's chairman was leading the national game as president of the League: things were at their most positive for years. Little did they or the rest of the football world realise what was to come just weeks later.

Everton's methods and attitudes

Everton's reputation as the 'School of Science' reflected the team's attacking approach to the game. Led initially by Dean and then by Lawton, Everton had always found goals easy to come by, although their lack of success in the middle years of the 1930s proved that goals were not enough if the opposition was also scoring them. While Arsenal were using their third-back formation, coupled with break-away attacks, to devastating effect, Everton attempted to maintain the traditions of the game with the strong encouragement of Will Cuff, the club's chairman. T.G. Jones, recalling the successful 1938/9 season, has commented, 'Believe me when I tell you there were games I went on the field and didn't break sweat. It was that good.'[23]

Playing for Everton at this time was, not surprisingly, a pleasure for Mercer, Lawton and the rest of the team. Lawton recalled that 'there were no splits or rows or arguments, we were a very happy family. Everybody was friends with everyone else. You used to look forward to training because we just loved going to the club.'[24] During a bus strike in Liverpool in 1938, for example, Gordon Watson, who lived in a club-owned house in Huyton, walked 5 miles to the training ground and then walked back again. Lawton, recalling his time with Everton, noted that 'we were paid £8 a week, but nobody moaned, we didn't know any better. When they put a contract in front of us, we just signed it. Never read it, we were just happy to be playing.'[25] He added that 'it was a grand life, we just couldn't believe that we were getting paid for doing exactly what we wanted to do. Other lads of our age were working shifts down the pits or in factories. We got up every morning and it was football, football, football.'[26]

Training at Everton consisted of the traditional lapping the ground and sprinting, with some ball-work. Under the club's trainer, Harry Cooke, the younger players were often sent on long runs with an assistant trainer following them on a bicycle to ensure they did not shirk, while the more experienced professionals stayed with Cooke to undertake less arduous exercises. During Dixie Dean's final years with the club, and especially under Theo Kelly, then called a 'secretary–manager' but later to be the club's first 'manager', there were regular disputes over Everton's approach to training and match tactics. Dean, who tended to regard himself as the 'boss' of the younger players, resisted any attempts to devise tactical plans. His advice was often as simple as 'make sure you pass it to a man in the same shirt'. Mercer recalled a meeting in 1936 when it was decided, against Dean's wishes, to adopt the third-back tactic used so successfully by Arsenal. The next match resulted in a 6–0 trouncing by Middlesbrough. Mercer added: 'Perhaps Dixie thought that proved his point!'[27] Everton persisted with the third-back tactic, but with limited success. Eventually Will Cuff intervened and gave the team a pre-match lecture in which, according to Mercer's later recollection, he stated: 'Thrills and excitement are what they want. This bloody third-back game will bankrupt us. Now, I don't care if you are beaten 6–0. Get out there and start to play as Everton are expected to play!'[28] The players did what they were told and were promptly beaten 6–5 by Preston North End, having taken the lead five times.

While Kelly was regarded as a good administrator, he was not well liked by many of the players. He eventually imposed his will on the team nonetheless, dropping Dean and replacing him with Lawton, and then letting him go to Notts County for just £3,000. Dean had made 399 League appearances for Everton, scoring 349 goals along the way, but sadly for him and for much of Merseyside he was allowed to leave the club with no ceremony, thanks or tribute.

One innovation introduced at this time by Will Cuff was the use of 'special training' at a location well away from Goodison Park. During a week at, for example, Harrogate, Harry Cooke provided an intensive programme of shooting and heading practice, along with, for the first time, a series of six-a-side games. One-touch football with no dribbling allowed became the order of the day.

Everton believed in building a 'family' spirit among the players, most of whom were still relatively young and inexperienced in the ways of the world. Kelly used away matches to encourage his players to discuss the game while relaxing in their hotel. He required them to stay indoors before each match, avoiding the temptations even of casual shopping in the local town. This rule was relaxed only to allow the players to attend the post-match social normally organised by the home club.

Mercer and Everton in war-time

Along with all the other professional clubs, Everton suspended all their players' contracts when the Second World War began. However, Everton was one of the very few clubs that agreed to pay players their accrued share of any benefits. Mercer initially went to work at the local shipyard, Cammell Laird. Then Stanley Rous, secretary of the FA, issued a plea for players to join the armed forces, coupled with a promise that if they applied to join the army's Physical Training Corps they would automatically become sergeant instructors. Mercer was one of the first to respond. Having been sent to Reading for training, he soon found that Rous's promise was not all that it had seemed. Mercer and other professional footballers in the Corps reacted by refusing to take orders. Rous, realising his error, managed to negotiate a compromise, so that Mercer and others became 'temporary sergeant instructors', much to the annoyance of the Corps's regulars, who had spent years earning promotion with little recognition or reward.

Representative football was an important feature of life in the armed forces. Very early on in the war a British army side was formed and sent to play against a French army team as an entertainment for the troops of the British Expeditionary Force. Mercer and Bert Sproston (see Chapter 16) were involved in this venture, as were other star players such as Tommy Lawton, Stan Cullis and Matt Busby. The team played three games, in Rheims, Lille and Paris.

Back in England Everton joined the quickly established regional competition, playing in the Northern League with teams such as Liverpool, Manchester United, Wrexham and New Brighton, and finishing the 1939/40 season in fifth position. Mercer was selected to play for England against Wales, but he was not allowed to play as the match clashed with his club's appearance in the Liverpool Senior Cup Final against Liverpool. Everton played Mercer in the team, which won the match 4–1. Mercer himself did not attract any blame for this early example of the 'club versus country' dilemma being resolved in the club's favour, but the FA suspended two of Everton's directors for a short time.

The following seasons proved to be significant only in the numbers of goals scored. During the 1940/1 season Everton defeated Tranmere Rovers 9–0 and 8–2, but during the 1941/2 season the team were beaten by Stoke 8–3 and by Wolves 11–1. These untypical results continued throughout the remaining war-time seasons, partly because many major clubs put up relatively weak teams, having lost key players to the armed forces, and partly because normally modest clubs used star players as guests. Everton did, however, manage to hang on to the goal-scoring services of Tommy Lawton, who scored more than 60 goals in the 1944/5 and 1945/6 seasons, and achieved a remarkable total of 301 war-time goals.

Everton players such as Mercer and the rejuvenated Britton made major contributions to the successful England side during the war years. Mercer played twenty-seven times for England in these 'unofficial' internationals. Combining with Britton and Stan Cullis of Wolverhampton Wanderers, he formed one of

England's best-ever half-back lines. He looked back on these years as his 'peak' period, taking the view that army life made him fitter than he had ever been before. The high point of his war-time career came in 1943, when he was chosen to replace Cullis as captain of England for a match against Wales in Liverpool. Mercer and his fellow players started to do something which apparently had not occurred in relation to previous internationals: they held meetings on the evenings before matches to discuss how they could best play as a team. Before the war players generally met only on the day of an international and then returned quickly to their own clubs. International teams were selected on the basis of the best individual players available. Little or no thought was given to the resulting blend and victory was typically expected to depend on the genius of individual players rather than effective teamwork. With so many England footballers playing and mixing together in the armed forces at this time, a more collaborative spirit was being engendered. The new meetings were for the players themselves, although Stanley Rous occasionally dropped in to listen. This pre-match innovation gradually became normal practice for international matches, reflecting changing perceptions of what was needed to succeed at the highest level.

Mercer and post-war football

With the return of peace and the maintenance of a low level of unemployment, many people found themselves with money to spend but little to spend it on, and football boomed. For Everton, however, this was a time of disappointment. Lawton sought a transfer and was sold to Chelsea in November 1945 for £11,500. Sergeant-Major Mercer, now aged 31, returned to Everton only to find that, despite having captained England during the war, he was no longer Everton's captain. Finding that Theo Kelly regarded him as an ageing and injured has-been, Mercer too put in for a transfer. He also threatened to give up the game for good if Everton did not grant him his request.

In 1946 Mercer played in his last international match, a game against Scotland at Hampden Park that England lost by the only goal in the very last minute. The knee injury that Mercer sustained in this match spelled the end not only of his international career but also of his career with Everton. His form deteriorated and eventually he was dropped from the first team. The club had come to the conclusion that his career was at an end. As we shall see, Arsenal and England believed otherwise.

Mercer then entered the wholesale grocery business, with the assistance of his father-in-law, who had been in the trade since childhood. While Everton and, in particular, Kelly refused to either play him or place him on the transfer list, Mercer immersed himself in his new job. A few weeks passed and then he received a phone call from Kelly, who told him that George Allison of Arsenal wanted to meet him to discuss a possible transfer. Mercer jumped at the chance to continue his playing career, although he persuaded Allison to agree to his continuing to live on the Wirral so that he could go on supervising his grocery business. Allison also agreed that Mercer could train in Liverpool, reducing the need to travel regularly to London. Mercer later recalled that Kelly brought his boots to the meeting with Allison, clearly anticipating that the transfer was going to happen. Arsenal paid a £7,000 transfer fee and Mercer became a Gunner.

Arsenal, the dominant team of the 1930s, were struggling to recover their leading position. Mercer was regarded, to some extent, as a stop-gap, bringing experience and solidity to a team that was tending to run out of spirit in the latter stages of games. Arsenal duly went on to win the Championship in the 1947/8 season, the FA Cup in 1950 and the Championship again in 1952/3, all with Mercer at the helm. Interestingly, Theo Kelly, the man responsible for selling both Lawton and Mercer, and previously alienating Dean, soon returned to his administrative role at Everton, with the former Everton star Cliff Britton taking over as manager.

Unlike many stars of his generation, Mercer managed to make the transition from player to manager, and his career culminated with the ultimate accolade of managing the national team. As a result Mercer is now better known for his managerial achievements, especially with Manchester City, than for his time as a player. Yet his playing career straddled three decades and brought him the highest honours in the game, as well as the opportunity to lead the England team as captain. It was during his playing career and, in particular, his career with Everton in the 1930s that his reputation was established, both as a player of the highest calibre and as a person who attracted the utmost respect and loyalty, both from his peers and from the football-going public.

Joe Mercer died on his birthday, 9 August, in 1990, at his home in Hoylake. The next day the *Liverpool Echo* published the following tribute on its front page: 'Soccer legend Joe is dead. Joe Mercer, who won League championship medals with Everton and Arsenal before going on to plot an outstanding managerial career, was Mr Football, in every sense. Loved and respected by everyone who knew him, genial Joe was one of the game's great characters.'[29] With more than a touch of local patriotism it also declared: 'He will be remembered first and foremost as a Merseyside giant who never forgot his roots.'[30]

CLIFFORD PARKER,
Portsmouth F.C.

15 Cliff Parker – Portsmouth

Cliff Parker was the player who did most to bring the FA Cup to Portsmouth for a record period of six years. His double strike at the Wembley Final in 1939, against the hot favourites Wolverhampton Wanderers, helped Portsmouth to achieve a remarkable and unexpected victory, and the outbreak of the Second World War just months later did the rest, as Portsmouth held onto the Cup until the resumption of peace-time football in 1945. Portsmouth's supporters, however, still regard Parker as 'without doubt, one of their most famous wingers',[1] a man who served the club for nearly twenty years, both as a player and then as a scout. He was very much a terrace hero, 'remembered . . . by many supporters with great fondness . . . he was a very popular figure among the team and players, supporters alike'.[2]

Parker's career up to 1938

Parker was born in Denaby in Yorkshire on 6 September 1913. Having represented Mexborough and District Schools, he joined the local team, Mexborough Athletic, then in the Midlands League. He started his goal-scoring exploits with Mexborough, scoring against Denaby United at the age of 17. After he was spotted by the local professional club, Doncaster Rovers, he signed on amateur terms in August 1931 and then professionally in 1932. Parker then helped Rovers to reach sixth place in the Third Division (North) by scoring seven goals in his first season as a professional.

The following season, 1933/4, brought personal triumph for Parker. Having started the season at Doncaster and scored four times in the early months, he was suddenly sold to the First Division club Portsmouth as part of Rovers' attempt to balance the books. He was signed on 11 December 1933 by Portsmouth's manager, Jack Tinn. Parker made an immediate impact, for his debut Boxing Day goal at Anfield proved to be enough to bring Portsmouth a valuable victory against Liverpool. He quickly followed this up with a further goal on 30 December in a 2–0 home win against Newcastle United. Unfortunately, he then failed to maintain this good start and drifted into the ranks of the reserves for the rest of the season. Portsmouth ended the season in tenth place, well behind all-conquering Arsenal, who took the Championship for the second year in succession. Portsmouth used only twenty players throughout their League programme and were 'distinguished by their capacity to field the same 11 with surprising regularity'.[3]

However, Portsmouth's main achievement in this season was to reach the FA Cup Final. Although the team eventually lost 2–1 to Manchester City, Portsmouth came very close to victory, since City scored only in the last fifteen minutes of the match, the first goal coming while Portsmouth's key defender, Jimmy Allen, was off the pitch being tended for an injury. Billy Dale (see Chapter 11) was full-back in the City team.

Cliff Parker did not feature in the Final side and was to wait five more years for his day of glory to come. The season had seen him leap from the relative obscurity of the Third Division (North) to the First Division and to a club that had, in his very first season, made what was only their second appearance at Wembley. Parker had arrived on the big stage.

Portsmouth began the 1934/5 season with a lucrative home match against Arsenal. In front of a club record crowd of 39,700 Portsmouth fought out a creditable 3–3 draw. However, the team failed to maintain this good start over the season and finished in fourteenth position. Arsenal fared much better, going on to seal a third consecutive Championship. Cliff Parker eventually made his breakthrough into Portsmouth's first team during the season and ended up scoring five times in the closing weeks. He was gradually taking the place of the ageing Sep Rutherford, who had worn the No. 11 shirt for many years and had scored the goal in the Cup Final in 1934. Although the centre-forward, Weddle, scored twenty-five goals, Portsmouth was unable to build on the Cup exploits of the previous season. As the Football League's review put it, this was 'a club of modest achievements'.[4]

'Modest' might also be used to describe Portsmouth's overall approach to the game. In 1934 the *News of the World* quoted the club's trainer, Jack Warner, as saying that Portsmouth put its success down to 'having the right club spirit'.[5] He went on to say that 'we may not hit the front page with ballyhoo about training methods, but we get there just the same. No special dieting or fancy gymnastics for [the manager] Jack [Tinn]. His training system produces footballers, not matinee idols.'[6] Warner emphasised that

> our aim is to make every player a club player. We encourage him to think of himself as first, last and all of the time a Pompey man. More than that, we try to make our club activity a family affair. Every Friday we take the players and their wives for a jaunt. We go out into the country somewhere. A lunch is arranged, then we go sight-seeing, and in the evening the whole party go to an entertainment of some sort. The truth is that our players' wives become wholeheartedly Pompey fans. No need for me to play policeman. The wives see to it that my players toe the line, fit and keen.[7]

During 1935/6 Portsmouth maintained their mid-table position, but their home record was much better than their away form. Parker scored 9 times, becoming the club's second-highest goal-scorer behind Weddle, who scored 16, an indication of Portsmouth's general lack of firepower. The team eventually ended up in tenth position, while Sunderland broke Arsenal's run by taking the Championship. Portsmouth Reserves also became the first team to win the newly formed Football Combination League for reserve sides. More than 12,000 people turned out on Boxing Day 1935 to see a reserve game against Charlton Athletic.

Mid-table performances continued to distinguish Portsmouth in 1936/7, although the team started the season well and were at the top of the First Division for a brief period in September 1936. Goal-scoring continued to be a problem, the more so as Weddle, now ageing, could no longer match the form he had shown in previous years as centre-forward. Portsmouth bought Beattie from the Scottish club St Johnstone as an eventual replacement, but he had little time to settle down with his new team-mates. Jimmy Guthrie also arrived, from Dundee, and soon became captain, taking over from Bob Salmon, who was sold to Chelsea. Guthrie, who was to become one of the key figures in the fight for players' rights and conditions as chairman of the Professional Footballers Union, also took over from Salmon as the club's union delegate. Parker continued to score regularly during the season and his 12 goals made him the club's leading goal-scorer, indicating once again the absence from the side of a first-class central striker. Parker distinguished himself in another way during this season: he appeared in every one of the 42 League matches, being the only player in the club to do so and one of only 13 in the whole First Division. Portsmouth ended the season in ninth place, while Manchester City took the Championship after an unbeaten run in the second half of the season.

The following season, 1937/8, saw the emergence of Beattie as the club's new centre-forward. Despite his 22 goals and Parker's 15, Portsmouth suffered one of its worst seasons for many years. The team had no victories at all until mid-November 1937, won only two away games throughout the season and ended up with the worst away record in the Division. On the other hand, they suffered only 4 defeats at home. On the last Saturday of the season they was one of 6 clubs facing the possibility of relegation, but a 4–0 home victory over Leeds United saved them. Parker was once again a constant presence in the Portsmouth side, along with the full-backs Morgan and Rochford. These three were among the 15 players in the entire First Division who played in every League game.

Up for the Cup

In the final season before the outbreak of war and the suspension of League football Portsmouth achieved the greatest and most surprising result in their history: they won the FA Cup. Since 1934, when they appeared in the Final, the club had been knocked out in the third or fourth round every year. Their League form in 1938/9 also continued to be modest, leaving them in seventeenth position as the First Division's lowest-scoring side. Parker added just

8 goals to the club's total of 47, but he maintained his remarkable record of consecutive appearances and played in every one of the 42 matches for a third season. Since 29 August 1936 he had played in 126 successive League matches, a reflection of both his form and his ability to avoid injury.

Portsmouth's season was turned round with the signing of a new inside-right, McAlinden, who came over from Belfast Celtic in December 1938, and a new inside-left, Bert Barlow, who was transferred from Wolverhampton Wanderers in late February 1939. Both contributed goals and Barlow in particular started to create goals for others, including Anderson and Parker. Anderson ended up as the team's leading goal-scorer, with just 10 goals, while Parker scored a further 8 times. As the Football League's review commented: '[Freddie] Worrall and Parker worked regularly on the wings, and Anderson toiled nobly as leader. The half-backs were clever and the rear defenders sound, but the side never had a hint of greatness in its League games. But in the Cup all was different!'[8]

Captained by the half-back Guthrie and still managed by Jack Tinn, Portsmouth's players were 'no respecters of persons'[9] in their Cup campaign. Having the luck of a home draw in all the rounds leading up to what was to be the team's third semi-final, they beat Lincoln City 4–0, West Bromwich Albion 2–0, West Ham United 2–0 and Preston North End 1–0. In the semi-final, played at Highbury in front of 60,000 spectators, Portsmouth reportedly showed 'persistence and courage' in coming from a goal down, with fifteen minutes to go, to beat Huddersfield Town 2–1. The team had reached Wembley for the second time in the 1930s and were to face the hot favourites Wolverhampton Wanderers. The Wolves, managed by Major Frank Buckley (see Chapter 4) and captained by an England international, Stan Cullis, were challenging for the 'Double' of League and Cup. They, too, had had the benefit of a run of home matches in the early rounds of the Cup and had beaten the eventual League Champions, Everton, 2–0 in the sixth round before trouncing a First Division side, Grimsby Town, 5–0 in a semi-final match at Old Trafford in which Wescott had scored four times.

Wolverhampton attracted most of the publicity in the days leading up to the Final. One of the best-known stories of the day was that the players had all been put on a special course of injections and capsules, involving 'monkey glands', to improve their strength. The treatment, organised by Buckley from the start of the 1937/8 season, caught the imagination of many. Questions were asked in the House of Commons and the British Medical Association was asked to comment. So great was the concern that the Football League found it necessary to advise all players that the taking of such treatment was entirely voluntary. Portsmouth also decided to put their players on what was supposedly the same treatment. Although it was later reported that the Portsmouth version had mainly involved water, the players were not informed at the time, so they apparently felt as well-treated as their opponents in the preparations for Wembley. The Wolves' captain, Stan Cullis, claimed later that the whole 'monkey glands' story had been no more than a stunt in the psychological warfare between the clubs. Billy Wright, then playing in the junior ranks at Wolves, also recalled taking the half-inch-long light-brown capsules and, while he disliked the taste, he found no cause to condemn the treatment. Buckley seems to have been genuinely convinced that the treatment did have a beneficial effect, sharpening up the minds and movements of his players. Others have commented that the treatment was no more than a way of fighting the common cold, much like the Vapex endorsed by the Wolves' trainer, J.H. Davies (see Chapter 3).

The Portsmouth players prepared for the Final by moving to a training camp in Bognor Regis. Tactical preparation was under the control of the trainer Jimmy Stewart. As Guthrie later recalled, 'years before soccer became a mathematical formula'[10] Portsmouth adopted a 4–2–4 formation, using a table-tennis table to display team formations and tactics. According to Guthrie, he and his team-mates were well aware of Wolves' reputation for rough play, but 'we had little fear of being kicked. If we were, we had enough men to kick back.'[11]

Stories abound about the relative states of mind of the two teams on the day of the Final. One such story centres on the Cup Final autograph book traditionally signed by all the members of both teams before the game. It has been suggested that when it arrived in the Portsmouth dressing room, some thirty minutes before kick-off, the players could hardly recognise the signatures of the Wolves' players, which were as 'shaky as the writing of a centenarian'.[12] Portsmouth were in the 'lucky' No. 1 dressing room, and were being entertained with funny stories and songs by a northern comedian and long-time Portsmouth fan, Albert Burden. The manager, Jack Tinn, also brought his own 'luck' to Wembley by wearing his 'magic' white spats, which he insisted had to be buckled up by the winger, Freddie Worrall, and put on left before right. They were regarded as so lucky that they were stored in the club safe. Worrall had his own supposed sources of good fortune: he played with a lucky sixpence inside one of his boots, a miniature horseshoe in his shirt pocket, a sprig of heather in each sock and a china white elephant tied to one of his garters. Guthrie later recalled a more down-to-Earth aspect of the atmosphere before kick-off: he noticed that the young Wolves players were 'tense and looking pale and drawn'[13] as the teams waited together in the tunnel before the match.

Playing before a crowd of 99,370, the largest gate since the 'white horse' Final of 1923, Portsmouth went ahead in the thirty-first minute through Barlow, who had (as mentioned above) been transferred from Wolverhampton earlier in the season. The centre-forward, Jock Anderson, continued his fine run of scoring in the Cup with a second goal just before half-time, when Cullis misjudged a cross from Worrall. Immediately after the interval a mistake by the Wolves' goalkeeper, Scott, who failed to hold a 30-yard shot by Barlow, let Parker in for his first goal, to make the score 3–0. Parker is said to have told Scott as he retrieved the ball from the net, 'That's my first, Scotty, I'm coming back for another!'[14] While Dickie Dorsett got one back for Wolves in the fifty-fourth minute, to make the score 3–1, Parker lived up to his promise to Scott by making the game safe for Portsmouth with a headed second from Worrall's cross from the right wing. The *Daily Mail*'s match report called Parker 'a brilliant opportunist on this day of days'.[15]

Portsmouth's success on the day has since been attributed to the team's 'piercing, constructive football, using the lines of longitude, whereas Wolverhampton had too often sought the lines of latitude'.[16] However, even while the newspaper reports of the day celebrated Portsmouth's fine achievement, they were at a loss to explain the demise of Wolverhampton. For example, an article in the *Observer* commented:

> the real mystery of the match is how a team which is capable of playing so well could descend to such a mediocre level. The Midlanders contributed to their own downfall by bad tactics, and by individual errors, both of omission and commission. For the greater part of the game it almost seemed as if the Wolverhampton players were so convinced of their own superiority that it was scarcely necessary for them to put forth their most strenuous efforts. Time after time a player of the Midlands side, safely in possession of the ball would lose it to an opponent whose presence in a position to tackle was not even suspected . . . The men of the winning side were on their toes; the men of the losing side were on their heels. That, granting the writer a little licence, is as near a correct summary of the game, and conveying the secret of Portsmouth's success, as it is possible to get.[17]

Reviewing the outcome of the Final, Geoffrey Green has commented that for Wolverhampton 'something snapped at the vital moment. Wolverhampton never came within measurable distance of their true selves that afternoon. Perhaps the label of favourites was a burden too great for their young side to carry!'[18] Cullis's later assertion that his team would normally have beaten Portsmouth 99 times out of 100 is perhaps confirmation of the view that it was complacency that led the Wolves to defeat.

After receiving the Cup from King George VI in the midst of a hailstorm, Guthrie led the Portsmouth players, not on the traditional lap of honour, but straight down the tunnel. Very soon afterwards they were on the train back to the south coast. They were met at Fratton railway station at 11 o'clock that evening by thousands of overjoyed fans. They then boarded coaches for a procession to a civic reception with the lord mayor. An estimated 120,000 people turned out to provide the team with the greatest of receptions and took delight in singing the appropriately entitled popular song, 'Who's Afraid of the Big Bad Wolf?' Throughout the city the famous Pompey chimes rang out in celebration of the team's very first FA Cup victory. Indeed, Portsmouth's performance on that day in late April, just over four months before the war broke out, had brought the FA Cup south of London for the first time. Because of the outbreak of war in September 1939 Portsmouth retained the Cup until 1946, when Derby County beat Charlton Athletic in extra time, also by 4–1.

As might be expected, Portsmouth's success was exploited by local and national businesses. Cliff Parker's 'commanding performance'[19] and his two goals won him not only his winner's medal but also two suits provided by a local tailor. Parker insisted that one of the suits, or the cash equivalent, went to the two Portsmouth reserves, Bill Bagley and Abe Smith. Local press advertisements featuring Jack Tinn and Jimmy Guthrie appeared both before and after the great event. A soft-drink manufacturer linked its Idris fruit squashes with the club under the slogan 'Arduous training calls for cooling refreshment' and used a photograph of the players engaged in jumping, supposedly as part of their training regime. Not all the advertising tie-ups made even that much sense: Tinn was seen praising Pontefract cakes, for example, while Guthrie extolled the virtues of a brand of tobacco and of Van Heusen's semi-stiff shirt collars.

Another commercial dimension of the Cup Final has always been the matter of allocating match tickets. Such allocations represented a once-in-a-lifetime opportunity for players who were on the maximum wage to add some tax-free income to their bank balances, as is still evident in contemporary football, even though wages are now higher than anyone in the 1930s could ever have imagined. In 1939 each club was given 12,500 tickets, far below their normal home attendance figures. Portsmouth's attendances were averaging just under 20,000, despite their poor League performances. The club's directors allowed the players to buy twenty tickets each while deciding upon their own ticket allocations in private. Guthrie later recalled that one of the directors, who ran a pub in the town, seemed to be doing good business in the weeks before the Final. Guthrie also claimed that he gave his own allocation away, while Tinn put half of his allocation back into the pool for supporters to purchase.

Winning the Cup did not bring fantastic rewards for the players. Each received just £20 and a share of the £550 win bonus. Guthrie later discovered that the musicians in the massed bands at Wembley on the day had been paid more than he and his team-mates had. Guthrie passed this information on to Ted (later Lord) Castle, a reporter for the left-wing weekly *Tribune*, which published it under the headline 'They would have been better off playing the cornet'. Income from what press advertising there was did not bring much reward for the players, nor were newspapers asked to pay for the photographs they used.

The war and after

The possibility of war had been in the air as Portsmouth faced Wolverhampton. Even the programme for the Cup Final had carried a notice exhorting all the men in the crowd to register themselves for national service as firemen or air-raid wardens, or to join heavy-rescue squads or decontamination groups. After it actually began Portsmouth adjusted to playing in regional football and in the War Cup. In 1942 the team reached the Final before being beaten 2–1 by Brentford. In 1944 Field Marshal Bernard Montgomery agreed to become the club's president; that year also marked the signing of Jimmy Dickinson, who was to become the club's most famous and longest-serving player.

Jack Tinn, the manager who had steered the club to three Cup Finals in his twenty years' service, resigned during the 1946/7 season. He had not been a great tactician: his skill lay in finding the right players and then motivating them to perform on the big stage. He was succeeded by Bob Jackson, who went on to lead Portsmouth to two League Championships before moving on in 1952 to manage Hull City.

Cliff Parker continued to play for Portsmouth after the war. Between 1946 and 1951 he made 68 appearances, scoring just 7 goals, the last when he was 38. This period proved to be one of the club's most successful. During the 1948/9 season, when the club celebrated its fiftieth anniversary, the team took the Championship with an unbeaten home record and reached the semi-final of the Cup, losing 3–1 to Leicester City. A new club record attendance of 51,385 was set at the sixth-round victory over Derby County. The following season Portsmouth won the Championship again, beating Wolverhampton Wanderers on goal average.

Parker retired from playing in 1951 but remained with the club in a scouting position. During his long career at Portsmouth he had played 241 times and scored 58 goals. His career had been characterised by his ability to cross the ball accurately and to make the most of the half-chance: he had often scored before the opposition even realised that he was there. Over the years he had scored many cheeky goals and had become the joker of the side. Cliff Parker, the Cup Final goal hero, died in 1983, aged 70.

BERT SPROSTON,
Leeds United F.C.

16 Bert Sproston – Leeds United, Tottenham Hotspurs and Manchester City

Bert Sproston, an 'elegant right back'[1] who has also been described as 'cool, a grand tackler and exceptionally quick to recover',[2] and as 'a star of the late 1930s',[3] was unusual among the leading League players of the decade in that he managed to play for three major clubs, as well as achieving recognition by gaining international caps. As a full-back Sproston never received the kind of attention that star centre-forwards or speedy wingers could attract from the media, but he nonetheless provided high-quality defence for successful League teams and for his country. His 'youthful speed and hardness made him one of the very best in his position just before the war, good enough to keep [George] Male [of Arsenal] out of the England team'.[4] The Wolves and England player Stan Cullis described Sproston as 'the fastest full-back with whom I ever played. His speed of recovery was fantastic . . . but his power of tackle was such that he didn't need to recover very often.'[5] Sproston is also an example of a leading player who went on to play a key role in professional football long after he had hung up his boots: he spent almost thirty years with Bolton Wanderers in a variety of training and related capacities.

From Sandbach Ramblers to Leeds

Albert Sproston was born in Elworth, near Sandbach in Cheshire, on 22 June 1915. Like most professional players, he started playing football while he was at school. He then moved on to join the local club, Sandbach Ramblers, which played in the Cheshire League, replacing his own brother as right-back in the first team. He was spotted initially by Huddersfield and offered a trial, but this came to nothing. Leeds United then made contact and its secretary–manager, Dick Ray, signed the 17-year-old Sproston in May 1933. Ray, himself a former player, apparently had control over playing policy and team selection, an unusual situation in an era when the directors closely controlled activities at most clubs.

Leeds had been promoted from the Second Division at the end of the 1931/2 season, when they had been runner-up to Wolverhampton Wanderers. During the 1932/3 season Leeds had consolidated their new status, reaching a creditable eighth place in the First Division, mainly on the basis of their strong defence, which included Wilf Copping, who was soon to join Arsenal and become one of the legendary 'hard men' of the game. The 1933/4 season also turned out to be satisfactory rather than outstanding and Leeds ended it in ninth place, mainly because of their good home record. Sproston made his first-team debut in a 1–1 draw at Chelsea in December 1933. Four more appearances followed during that season, but after Leeds's regular defender George Milburn recovered from an injury Sproston had to return to the reserves.

Sproston and Milburn competed for the position of right-back in the first team for another few seasons. In the 1934/5 season they both made regular appearances; in 1935/6 Sproston appeared in all but one League match; and in 1936/7 they again shared appearances relatively evenly. It was during the 1937/8 season that Sproston secured the position as his own, partly because Milburn left Leeds to join Chesterfield. However, the competition with Milburn did nothing to inhibit the development of Sproston's growing reputation as a high-class full-back.

Leeds suffered their worst season of the decade in 1934/5, ending in eight-eenth place. Plagued by injuries to key players, the team saved themselves from relegation by making a relatively strong finish to the season, losing only one game of their last six. Dick Ray, who was on a salary of £1,000 a year, resigned his post in early March 1935. He went to Bradford City as manager soon afterwards.

The 1935/6 season began with another former Leeds player, Billy Hampson, in the post of secretary–manager and an early season signing, the former international player George Brown from Burnley, as inside-forward. The season once again did not live up to expectations and the team finished in eleventh place. Although Brown led the attack well and scored goals, many observers concluded that the team needed new and younger blood. Sproston, however, tended to be exempted from the criticisms and the Football League's review of the season asserted that his 'youthful promise [had] matured at full-back'.[6]

Leeds's form suffered once again during the 1936/7 season, especially away from home, where the team managed only one win all season. Hampson's role in the club also changed in the close season, when he became 'manager' and C.A. Crowther was appointed 'secretary'. The other significant change early in the season was the loss of George Brown, the leading goal-scorer in the previous season, who left to become player–manager at Darlington in mid-October 1936. Relegation looked a strong possibility for much of the season, but the signing in March 1937 of Gordon Hodgson, a South African who had been centre-forward at Aston Villa, proved to be a crucial move. His six goals in March and April helped Leeds to escape relegation, and the team finished in nineteenth place, just two points ahead of Manchester United. Leeds's half-back, Edwards, stood out, alongside Sproston, as the star of the team, despite the poor performance overall.

In the 1937/8 season Leeds returned to the mid-table performances and final position of earlier years, finishing in ninth place. Led by Hodgson, who scored twenty-five League goals, the team managed to achieve second place by

Christmas 1937, but a slump in form followed between February and April 1938. Sproston continued to shine at right-back.

At the end of the 1937/8 season Leeds found themselves in a poor financial position and were faced with having to sell Sproston. He was transferred to Tottenham Hotspurs, then in the Second Division, for £9,500, which was close to that club's record fee for a signing at that time. He had made 140 League and Cup appearances for Leeds, scoring only once.

At Spurs and Manchester City

This relatively rare venture into the 'big money' transfer market by Spurs, then managed by Peter McWilliam, proved to be remarkably unsuccessful. After playing just nine games for his new club, Sproston told the club that he was having difficulties settling into a London-based life and that he wanted to move back up north. Recognising the futility of trying to hold on to this expensive England star, McWilliam soon struck a deal with Manchester City, during a visit by Spurs to Manchester in November 1938. The Spurs contingent arrived in Manchester on the Friday and the deal was struck overnight. The transfer fee was £10,000, close to the British record at the time. Sproston then turned out on the Saturday afternoon for his third club and helped them to win 2–0.

City, having been relegated from the First Division at the end of the previous season, had started the 1938/9 season poorly and by October 1938 was in twentieth position. Sproston's signing seemed to have an immediate effect in steadying the defence, which had lost Billy Dale (see Chapter 11) to Ipswich Town in the close season. By early December City had risen to the middle of the table. The remaining months saw the team having good and bad runs, which often seemed to hinge on the form of Peter Doherty. By the season's end City had managed to reach a creditable fifth place.

On the international stage

In just 2 years and while playing for 3 different League clubs, Sproston managed to collect 11 international caps for England. He made his England debut on 17 October 1936, in a 2–1 home defeat against Wales, and swiftly came to be regarded as the national team's first choice for right-back. He gained another 7 caps during his time with Leeds, 2 more during his short time with Tottenham and his last while he was with Manchester City.

Sproston's most significant involvement with the England international team came on the continental tour at the end of the 1937/8 season, when the team played matches against Germany, Switzerland and France. England and the other home countries were still maintaining their boycott of FIFA and the new World Cup competition, so such tours were important means of demonstrating the justice of England's claim to be the world's leading football-playing nation. Such international matches also held political significance, just as they do now; as P.J. Beck has put it, they 'came to be interpreted by governments and the media as a reflection of the quality not only of a country's soccer skills but also of its socio-political system and overall power'.[7]

Sproston had been selected to join an England squad that included stars such as Stanley Matthews, Cliff Bastin, Eddie Hapgood, Vic Woodley and Ted Drake. As an opportunity for overseas travel, which was then way outside the experience of most people in Britain, the tour was an exciting if somewhat daunting prospect for most of the players. The FA refused even to consider letting the team travel by air, so the journey to Berlin, the venue of the first match on the tour, was by ferry to the Hook of Holland and then onwards by train. The players were to be paid £8 a game, whether they played or not, and 10s. a day pocket money. They would also be receiving their normal summer wages of £6 a week from their clubs.

The England team was travelling into Nazi Germany at a time when British newspapers were warning daily of the threat of a German invasion of the Sudetenland, the part of Czechoslovakia where most of that country's German minority lived, following on from the Nazi occupation of Austria. In his last of three autobiographies Stanley Matthews claimed: 'I don't think any of the England players knew what Nazi fascism meant, but we quickly came to realise that, whatever it stood for, warm friendship and humour were not on its list of priorities.'[8] In the same autobiography he recalled an incident that occurred on the team's first day in Berlin, involving both himself and Sproston:

> Having booked into the hotel, the players had a bit of free time. I went out for a walk with Bert Sproston, a tough and uncompromising full-back with Leeds United. Bert was a down-to-Earth lad who, according to the joke of the time, lived on a diet of raw meat and wingers like me. Bert and I walked around the streets near our hotel, just to get our bearings, and eventually called into a small café. We had just sat down with a pot of tea between us when the other patrons suddenly leapt to their feet in great excitement. One by one the local customers and the café staff all rushed to the door. Not knowing the reason for such a commotion, Bert and I stayed where we were. I was suddenly aware of a cavalcade of cars going past and, as they did so, everyone who had rushed outside raised their arm in the Nazi salute before breaking into spontaneous applause.
>
> 'Sounds like some *grande fromage* has passed by,' I said to Bert.
>
> A tall man standing by the door heard me and, turning to Bert and me, said in perfect English, 'You underestimate the importance of the occasion, gentlemen. That was our beloved Führer gracing us with his presence.'
>
> Not wanting to cause a scene, Bert and I just smiled and nodded. After all, the guy had been pleasant enough. For a moment neither Bert nor I said anything as the excited café patrons took to their seats once again. Then Bert leaned across the table.
>
> 'Stan', he whispered, 'I'm just a workin' lad from Leeds. I've not 'ad much of an education and I know nowt 'bout politics and t'like. All I knows is football. But t'way I see it, yon 'Itler fella is an evil little twat.'[9]

To what extent this story, recalled more than sixty years later and not mentioned in Matthews's earlier autobiographies, can be relied on as an accurate report of Sproston's words is impossible to say. Nevertheless, it does seem plausible as an anecdote about a more or less typical Englishman from a working-class background suddenly placed at the centre of Anglo-German relations just over a year before the outbreak of war between the two countries.

Neither Matthews nor Sproston could have realised at the time that both governments regarded the forthcoming football match with increasing serious-ness. The British government, surprisingly enough, appears to have heard about the match only ten days earlier. Having decided that, given the policy of appeasement, it was too politically sensitive to cancel or postpone, it still sought to ensure that the FA and its team recognised the significance of what they had stumbled into. A message from the Foreign Office to Stanley Rous, the secretary of the FA, who was in Berlin, emphasised that 'it is really important for our prestige that the British [*sic*] team should put up a really first-class performance'. The FA responded reassuringly that 'every member of the team will do his utmost to uphold the prestige of his country'. While the FA was making sooth-ing noises on the political front, it made no special preparations for this particu-lar match, other than having Tom Whittaker of Arsenal accompanying the team as trainer. The squad had been chosen, as usual, by the FA's International Selection Committee, which had sent one of its number, C. Wreford-Brown, to take charge of the tour, although without the title of manager.

As for the match itself, Germany had yet to beat England, but there was growing optimism among the German officials and the state-controlled media that their team's time had come. The German national side was on an unbeaten run of 14 games, while England had lost 4 of its 6 matches in 1936 and had beaten only weak Scandinavian opposition in 1937. Germany had also been strengthened by one of the side-effects of the occupation of Austria, for former members of Austria's now defunct national team had suddenly become eligible for selection as Germans. It was well understood that a good result against England would 'bring considerable kudos to a regime conscious always of its domestic and international image'.[10] According to Stanley Rous's later account, Sir Neville Henderson, Britain's ambassador to Germany, said: 'The Nazis are looking for victories to boost their regime. It is their way of claiming [to be] a super-race.'[11]

The match between England and Germany, which was played on 12 May 1938, is probably known now, if at all, not because England achieved an out-standing 6–3 victory, but because the England team gave the Nazi salute as the German national anthem was being played in front of a crowd of 110,000 in the Olympic Stadium. Sproston's feelings about this notorious incident have not been put on record, but those of several other players have been, either in their own words or in words provided by ghostwriters. However much their memories must inevitably have been coloured by subsequent events and the passage of time, they probably provide some insight into the responses of international football players caught up in a political maelstrom that they could hardly have been prepared for or equipped to deal with. Sproston's reported remark that 'I've not 'ad much of an education and I know nowt 'bout politics and t'like'[12] could have been made, in a different dialect, by any other member of the team. Certainly, the British government and the FA both regarded it as imperative that 'no disrespect should be offered at such a delicate moment in the affairs of Europe'.[13] Even before the match several British newspapers had run stories about the possibility that the England players would give the salute. On the Wednesday before, G.W. Sinfield of the *Daily Worker*, the paper of the Communist Party of Great Britain, had declared: 'If the FA have not done so already, we strongly advise them [the players] to agree at once not to have anything to do with efforts to embrace them in a political stunt designed especially for the consumption of the German masses, thus kidding them that we in this country are in support of Hitler.'[14] The *Daily Express* suggested that the salute would and should be given, while the *Daily Mail* and the *News Chronicle* both asserted that the players would be breaking with tradition if they did not honour the customs of their hosts by doing what was expected.

However, by the time the press took up the story the players were stuck in a hotel in Berlin with little or no access to British newspapers (and certainly not to the *Daily Worker*). Accounts vary as to when the players became aware that they would be expected to give the salute. Stanley Matthews and Cliff Bastin both stated in later years that the first they heard of the matter was in the dressing room just before the match itself. However, in his autobiography, published only six years after the incident, Eddie Hapgood, the captain of the team, claimed that he was taken aside by the FA officials Wreford-Brown and Rous following a meeting that they had had on the morning of the game with Sir Neville Henderson. According to Hapgood, having been told what was expected of him and his team-mates he expressed his disagreement and went to the hotel to inform the other players. There was then 'much muttering in the ranks',[15] but Wreford-Brown visited the rest of the team and told them that the politicians had taken the decision: they were to give the salute. Stanley Rous provided his own version in 1978,[16] stating that he presented the players with a choice but pointed out that the atmosphere in the stadium might become antagonistic if they refused to salute as expected. He claimed that 'all agreed that they had no objection'. His assertion that they 'no doubt saw it as a bit of fun rather than of any political significance' seems to fit with Cliff Bastin's statement that he 'did not feel very strongly about the incident'.[17]

Matthews, in contrast, claimed that when the players were told that they were to salute the 'dressing room erupted. All the England players were livid and totally opposed to this, myself included.'[18] Matthews also claimed that Hapgood, 'normally a respectful and devoted captain, wagged his finger at the official and told him what he could do with the Nazi salute, which involved putting it where the sun doesn't shine'.[19] Hapgood's suggestion that the players should simply stand to attention during the playing of the German national anthem was rejected by Wreford-Brown and Rous, who, again according to Matthews, effectively issued an order to the players.

Whatever the players really felt as they saluted, their main purpose in being in Berlin was, of course, to play football. With Sproston in defence and 19-year-old Jackie Robinson making a sensational debut, the England team reached half-time 4–2 ahead with goals from Bastin, Robinson, Broome and Matthews. Then, although Bastin had been injured and had to limp through the rest of the match, Robinson got his second goal, followed by another German goal, before the finest goal of the match was scored by the inside-left Len Goulden, with a left-foot volley from outside the penalty area following a Matthews cross. Matthews recalled the match as 'the finest England performance I was ever involved in. Every player was at the top of his game, to a man we played out of our skins and Len Goulden's goal will live forever in the memory.'[20]

The FA was delighted and relieved by this outcome: 'The disciplined performance by both teams, the resulting absence of incident, the impact of the pre-match Nazi salute and the manner of England's victory led [Sir Neville] Henderson to observe that it "undoubtedly revived, in Germany, British sporting prestige".'[21] The International Selection Committee later gave a canteen of cutlery to each player as a mark of its 'special appreciation'.

Bert Sproston was never again involved in such a newsworthy and controversial international match. He remained in the England team for the remaining two matches on this tour, which produced an unexpected 2–1 defeat by Switzerland and a 4–2 victory over France, but it was the match in Berlin that was to figure in the annals of English football as the most famous match involving England until a certain day in 1966.

Sproston made his final appearances for England during the 1938/9 season. With Tommy Lawton making his debut in the side, England lost 4–2 to Wales in Cardiff. This was quickly followed by a match between England and a 'Rest of Europe' side, played at Highbury to celebrate the FA's seventy-fifth anniversary. England's 3–0 win was an ideal outcome to a match that had been arranged to show how far the continental upstarts still had to go before they could challenge England's self-awarded status as the world's greatest footballing nation. Sproston went on to gain his last full international cap the following month, in a 4–0 home win over Norway.

In addition to representing England eleven times, Sproston represented the Football League on a number of occasions. On 22 September 1937, for example, the Football League lost to the Scottish League 1–0 at Ibrox Park. On 5 October the same year it beat the Irish League at Blackpool 3–0. During the 1938/9 season the Irish League was beaten once again, this time 8–2 in Belfast, in a match in which Lawton scored four times in torrential rain. The English team then defeated the Scottish League 3–1 at Wolverhampton.

War-time and after

At the outbreak of war, just weeks into the 1939/40 season, Sproston joined the army and saw service in India, as well as spending time in many areas of Britain. He maintained his links with Manchester City, making more than eighty appearances in the war-time regional league and cup competitions. Like many other players, he also guested for other teams, including Aldershot, Port Vale, Millwall and Wrexham. In addition, he made two further appearances for England, played in an FA Services XI in Belgium and represented the army on twenty-three occasions.

With the resumption of normal League and Cup football in 1945, Sproston returned to Manchester City as a first-team regular. It was during the 1946/7 season that he won his only major club honour, the Second Division Championships, under the club's manager Sam Cowan, who 'rescued City from the doldrums of the Second Division with an impressive string of victories inspired by players such as Eric Westwood, Alan Black and Bert Sproston'.[22]

Sproston left City in August 1950, having played 128 League and 6 FA Cup games as a member of the team, scoring just 5 goals. Before he hung up his boots for the very last time as a player he spent a season with a non-League team, Ashton United. As a full England international with a long track record, he could offer any club a wealth of experience. In the event, it was at Bolton Wanderers that he carved out a second half to his career that spanned almost thirty years. During this time he served as trainer, physiotherapist and scout, and shared in the glory of the Bolton's FA Cup victory over Manchester United in 1958. He eventually retired in the late 1970s, but remained a resident of Bolton.

Bert Sproston died, after a lengthy illness, on 27 January 2000, aged 84. In its obituary the *Bolton Evening News* described him as 'the man who tended some of the most famous players in the history of Bolton Wanderers', and 'one of the most familiar and well-respected figures at the club through three decades'.[23]

17 Conclusion

The purpose of this book has been to examine the lives and times of professional footballers who played in England in the 1930s. The ten 'terrace heroes' profiled here all contributed to the development of the game during this turbulent pre-war decade, playing as they did for leading clubs in the upper reaches of the English Football League.

While these players were regarded within their respective communities as individuals who had gained a degree of middle-class respectability, they still managed to retain connections with the largely working-class supporters on the terraces. The increasingly significant mass media – newspapers, specialist publications, radio, newsreels and (to a limited extent) television – conveyed their images to a wider national audience, but their status as heroes remained primarily grounded in local communities.

Although these players were much more affluent than those who conferred hero status upon them, they remained at the beck and call of their clubs, and, in particular, the directors. The tightly regulated wage structure, coupled with the release or retain system, ensured that they remained assets that the clubs could buy or sell, sometimes with little concern for their social welfare. While membership of the Players Union was on the rise, footballers as an occupational group appear to have had little if any bargaining power in their workplaces. The star players continued to rely on the scarcity of their particular expertise in negotiating contracts. Their room for manoeuvre was constrained, at least officially, by the clubs' rigid adherence to the maximum-wage regulations, but the availability of various non-financial arrangements and under-the-counter deals suggests that it was not difficult to find ways around the restrictions.

The public images of terrace heroes in the 1930s were largely based on longevity of service to one club; 'gentlemanly' behaviour both on and off the field; and a degree of modesty. Jack Crayston, Joe Mercer and Bob Baxter are good examples of the type. However, not all heroes were of this kind: it was their association with, and contribution to, a team's success that enabled other players to acquire hero status. Billy Dale and Cliff Parker, for example, were both relatively modest players, but they gained prestige by association with key events in the history of their clubs: respectively, Manchester City's winning of the Championship and Portsmouth's unexpected victory in the FA Cup.

Individualists, especially goal-scorers and, on occasions, goal-makers, have always attracted hero worship, both on the terraces and in the media, Jock Dodds being a prime example. Dodds's image also benefited, later in his career, from his 'rebellious' attitude to his employers and the football authorities, which also endeared him to many football fans.

While individual players developed this community-based status as terrace heroes, it must be remembered that much of this status was mediated through the actions of the clubs' directors, who saw the benefits to be gained by continuing to employ stars who could draw in the crowds. However, supporters had no direct influence over the business decisions taken by clubs about selling or releasing their assets. The furore that erupted when it seemed that Stanley Matthews might leave Stoke City stands out as an exception in an industry where supporters could make, at most, only a sporadic and indirect impact on decisions, and employees' rights were almost unheard of.

Entry into a footballing career remained haphazard, depending largely on roving managers scouting for schoolboy or youth talent. For many players the next steps along the career path were also haphazard, being determined largely by the annual lottery of the release or retain system that clubs used to balance their books across the summer months. For every Mercer or Crayston there were dozens of journeymen who spent their careers moving between clubs, or from the reserves to the first team and back again, and even having spells when they were forced to return to 'ordinary' jobs. Being a professional footballer carried many benefits and was an occupation dreamed of by many thousands of young men across the country, but it was also characterised by uncertainty and relative brevity. Exit from a playing career could lead on to a smooth transition into other roles within the game, club management being the pinnacle of achievement. However, Crayston's successive moves into Arsenal's back room and then, eventually, into the manager's office were not at all typical. The majority of players had to leave the game and enter 'civilian' life, in factories and offices, returning to football grounds only to cheer on the next generation of heroes.

The 1930s saw the gradual emergence of another key figure within the game, the manager, in line with the increasing division between club administration and team management. The newspaper industry's growing recognition that football coverage was a key ingredient in their search for readers, coupled with club directors' reluctance to permit themselves or their players to 'go public' on club affairs, meant that managers acted more and more as the public faces of their clubs. Success and failure on the field increasingly came to be linked to managers' ability to plot and scheme. For example, Herbert Chapman and his successor George Allison were both seen as 'owning' Arsenal, and their domination of the decade was largely accounted for, in the media and on the terraces, by their actions rather than solely those of the players. That is not to say that 'stars' did not emerge at Highbury, but it was often their contributions on the international stage, when they were outside the clutches of their club managers, that gave them their status.

The growth of the media, and in particular the BBC's radio coverage, helped to institutionalise football as the 'national game', with key events such as the Cup Final and England international matches seizing the attention of many households. Football gambling, especially the pools, also contributed to the forging of a much wider audience for the game, one result being that individual players became better known than ever before, even if just by name. Professional football had always had an ability to generate heroes, but it was during the 1930s that leading players, and managers, started to acquire much higher profiles, as newspaper coverage expanded, and the radio became an everyday source of information and entertainment in the majority of homes. Football became a topic of routine comment and discussion among many who had never stepped onto a terrace on a Saturday afternoon.

Thus it was that players became 'personalities', perhaps especially because many continued to live within their local communities, engaging increasingly in social activities and public events, and, at most clubs, being encouraged to do so. During the playing season they were also expected to live relatively sheltered and uncontroversial lives, and to accept that much of their daily routine would be structured by their clubs. Travelling regularly around the country, living in hotels and, perhaps above all, taking part in end-of-season continental tours were all experiences that set the leading professional players apart, not only from most other players but also from their supporters. The fact that the middle-class game of golf featured as an important pastime for many players, and as part of pre-match 'special' training, indicates that a degree of honorary middle-class status had been bestowed on these sons of the working class, at least while they remained figures of renown within their local communities.

England went through considerable social, economic and political turbulence in the 1930s, both domestically and externally, culminating, of course, in the outbreak of the Second World War. Like members of every other occupational group, professional footballers were inevitably affected by the discontinuity that this engendered. While they remained relatively powerless inside their well-regulated workplaces, they emerged for the first time as significant social figures, both within their immediate milieu and, increasingly, on the national stage. These terrace heroes played increasingly significant roles in the lives of many who could only dream of having the opportunities that they enjoyed. Accordingly, any examination of their lives and times, even if only those of ten of their number, casts some light on the lives and times of millions of their contemporaries.

Notes

Series editor's foreword

1 See Richard Holt and J.A. Mangan: 'Prologue: Heroes from a European Past' in Richard Holt, J.A. Mangan and P. Lanfranchi (eds), *European Heroes: Myth, Identity, Sport* (London: Frank Cass, 1996), p. 2.
2 Ibid.
3 Norbert Elias, 'Introduction' in Norbert Elias and Eric Dunning, *Quest for Excitement: Sport and Leisure in the Civilising Process* (Oxford: Blackwell, 1986), p. 42.
4 Judith Herrin, 'Women and the faith in icons in early Christianity' in Raphael Samuel and Gareth Stedman Jones (eds), in *Culture, Ideology and Politics* (London: Routledge and Kegan Paul, 1982), p. 69.
5 J.A. Mangan and Richard Holt, 'Epilogue: Heroes for a European Future' in Holt, Mangan, Lanfranchi, *European Heroes: Myth, Identity, Sport*, p. 170.
6 Michael Oriard, *Dreaming of Heroes: American Sports Fiction 1868–1980* (Chicago: Nelson-Hall, 1982), p. 5.
7 Ibid., p. 8.
8 Ibid., p. 23.

1 Professional footballers as 'terrace heroes'

1 M.F. Fishwick, *American Heroes: Myth and Reality* (Westport, CT: Greenwood Press, 1954), p. 225.
2 R. Holt, J.A. Mangan and P. Lanfranchi (eds), *European Heroes: Myth, Identity, Sport* (London: Frank Cass, 1996), p. 1.
3 Ibid., p. 161.
4 R. Peskett (ed.), *Tom Whittaker's Arsenal Story* (London: Sportsman's Book Club, 1958), p. 106.
5 Ibid.
6 Holt, Mangan and Lanfranchi, *European Heroes*, p. 5.

2 The career path of professional footballers

1 E.A. Hapgood, *Football Ambassador* (London: Sporting Handbooks, 1944), p. 12.
2 Ibid., pp. 140–1.

3 Footballers as employees

1 D. Russell, *Football and the English: A Social History of Association Football in England, 1863–1995* (Preston: Carnegie Publishing, 1997), p. 76.

2 J. Harding, *For the Good of the Game: The Official History of the Professional Footballers Association* (London: Robson Books, 1991), p. 170.
3 C. Shindler, *Fathers, Sons and Football* (London: Headline, 2001), p. 21.
4 Ibid.
5 G. Hardwick, *Gentleman George* (Liverpool: Juniper Publishing, 1998), p. 29.
6 D.R. Jack (ed.), *Len Shackleton, Clown Prince of Soccer: His Autobiography* (London: Nicholas Kaye, 1955), p. 17.
7 J. Guthrie, *Soccer Rebel: The Evolution of the Professional Footballer* (Pinner: Pentagon, 1976), p. 32.
8 J. Walvin, *The People's Game: The History of Football Revisited* (Edinburgh: Mainstream, 1994), p. 136.
9 Shindler, *Fathers, Sons and Football*, p. 34.
10 Ibid., p. 33.
11 Ibid.
12 Russell, *Football and the English*, p. 93.
13 N. Fishwick, *English Football and Society, 1910–1950* (Manchester: Manchester University Press, 1989), p. 74.
14 Guthrie, *Soccer Rebel*, p. 52.
15 Ibid.
16 Shindler, *Fathers, Sons and Football*, p. 33.
17 T. Lawton, *Football is My Business* (London: Sporting Handbooks, 1946), p. 120.
18 Fishwick, *English Football and Society*, p. 75.
19 S. Matthews, *The Way It Was* (London: Headline, 2000), p. 70.
20 J. Seed, *The Jimmy Seed Story* (London: Sportsman's Book Club, 1958), p. 49.
21 Ibid., p. 50.
22 Fishwick, *English Football and Society*, p. 86.
23 Ibid., p. 79.
24 Guthrie, *Soccer Rebel*, p. 32.
25 S. and M. Matthews, *Back in Touch* (London: Arthur Barker, 1981), p. 40.
26 Harding, *For the Good of the Game*, p. 182.
27 Guthrie, *Soccer Rebel*, p. 13.
28 Ibid., p. 11.

4 Directors, managers, trainers and coaches

1 D. Russell, *Football and the English: A Social History of Association Football in England, 1863–1995* (Preston: Carnegie Publishing, 1997), p. 88.
2 Ibid.
3 S. Wagg, *The Football World: A Contemporary Social History* (Sussex: Harvester Press, 1984), p. 48.
4 Ibid.
5 Ibid.
6 Ibid., p. 57.
7 Ibid.
8 J. Guthrie, *Soccer Rebel: The Evolution of the Professional Footballer* (Pinner: Pentagon, 1976), p. 17.
9 Wagg, *The Football World*, p. 60.
10 E.A. Hapgood, *Football Ambassador* (London: Sporting Handbooks, 1944), pp. 22–4.
11 J. Mercer, *The Great Ones* (London: Oldbourne, 1964), p. 31.
12 G. Tibballs, *Great Sporting Eccentrics* (London: Robson Books, 1997), p. 56.
13 G. Hardwick, *Gentleman George* (Liverpool: Juniper Publishing, 1998), p. 33.
14 R. Taylor and A. Ward, *Three Sides of the Mersey: An Oral History of Everton, Liverpool and Tranmere Rovers* (London: Robson Books, 1993), p. 22.
15 S. Matthews, *The Way It Was* (London: Headline, 2000), p. 43.

16 Taylor and Ward, *Three Sides of the Mersey*, p. 33.
17 *Daily Dispatch*, 1 January 1937.
18 Ibid., 7 January 1937.
19 S. Studd, *Herbert Chapman: Football Emperor* (London: Souvenir Press, 1998), p. 131.
20 Taylor and Ward, *Three Sides of the Mersey*, p. 35.
21 Wagg, *The Football World*, p. 31.
22 Ibid.
23 S. Matthews, *Feet First Again* (London: Corgi Books, 1955), p. 187.
24 B. Glanville, *Soccer Nemesis* (London: Secker & Warburg, 1955), p. 75.
25 Hardwick, *Gentleman George*, p. 37.
26 Matthews, *Feet First Again*, p. 187.
27 Wagg, *The Football World*, p. 63.
28 Ibid., p. 62.
29 Taylor and Ward, *Three Sides of the Mersey*, p. 78.

5 Footballers' lifestyles

1 D. Russell, *Football and the English: A Social History of Association Football in England, 1863–1995* (Preston: Carnegie Publishing, 1997), p. 92.
2 Ibid., p. 95.
3 Ibid.
4 E.A. Hapgood, *Football Ambassador* (London: Sporting Handbooks, 1944), p. 142.
5 F. Swift, *Football from the Goalmouth* (London: Sporting Handbooks, 1948), p. 65.
6 R. Taylor and A. Ward, *Three Sides of the Mersey: An Oral History of Everton, Liverpool and Tranmere Rovers* (London: Robson Books, 1993), p. 20.

6 Footballers and the media

1 R. Holt (ed.), *Sport and the Working Class in Modern Britain* (Manchester: Manchester University Press, 1990), p. 163.
2 J. Hill and J. Williams (eds), *Sport and Identity in the North of England* (Keele: Keele University Press, 1996), p. 86.
3 Ibid.
4 N. Fishwick, *English Football and Society, 1910–1950* (Manchester: Manchester University Press, 1989), p. 113.
5 G. Allison, *Allison Calling* (London: Staples Press, 1948), p. 8.
6 E.A. Hapgood, *Football Ambassador* (London: Sporting Handbooks, 1944), p. 137.
7 Ibid., p. 27.

7 Jack Atkinson – Bolton Wanderers

1 T. Purcell and M. Gething, *War-time Wanderers: A Football Team at War* (Edinburgh: Mainstream, 1996), p. 15.
2 Ibid.
3 Ibid.
4 Ibid., p. 18.
5 Purcell and Gething, *War-time Wanderers*, p. 11.
6 Ibid., p. 12.
7 *Bolton Evening News*, 22 April 1933.
8 Ibid.
9 *Bolton Evening News*, 29 April 1933.
10 Football League (ed.), *The Competitions of Season 1934–1935* (London: Football League, 1935).
11 *Bolton Evening News*, 23 March 1946.

8 Bob Baxter – Middlesbrough

1 www.mfc.co.uk/past/baxt.htm.
2 *Topical Times*, 7 January 1939.
3 www.mfc.co.uk/club/view/past_players.htm.
4 Football League (ed.), *The Competitions of Season 1936–1937* (London: Football League, 1937).
5 Ibid.
6 G. Hardwick, *Gentleman George* (Liverpool: Juniper Publishing, 1998), pp. 28–9.
7 Football League (ed.), *The Competitions of Season 1938–1939* (London: Football League, 1939).
8 Ibid.
9 *Topical Times*, 7 January 1939.
10 Hardwick, *Gentleman George*, p. 37.
11 *Topical Times*, 7 January 1939.
12 Ibid.
13 Hardwick, *Gentleman George*, p. 32.
14 Ibid., p. 31.
15 Ibid.
16 Ibid., p. 29.
17 Ibid.

9 Harry Betmead – Grimsby Town

1 Football League (ed.), *The Competitions of Season 1933–1934* (London: Football League, 1934).
2 Football League (ed.), *The Competitions of Season 1934–1935* (London: Football League, 1935).
3 *Daily Mail*, 2 January 1935.
4 Football League (ed.), *The Competitions of Season 1935–1936* (London: Football League, 1936).
5 Football League (ed.), *The Competitions of Season 1936–1937* (London: Football League, 1937).
6 P. Joannou, *The Hughie Gallacher Story* (Derby: Breedon Books, 1989), p. 98.
7 Football League (ed.), *The Competitions of Season 1937–1938* (London: Football League, 1938).
8 Football League (ed.), *The Competitions of Season 1938–1939* (London: Football League, 1939).
9 Ibid.
10 *FA Cup Semi-Final Match Programme*, March 1939.
11 www.thisisgrimsby.co.uk.

10 Jack Crayston – Arsenal

1 R. Peskett (ed.), *Tom Whittaker's Arsenal Story* (London: Sportsman's Book Club, 1958), p. 106.
2 E.A. Hapgood, *Football Ambassador* (London: Sporting Handbooks, 1944), p. 124.
3 D. Lamming, *An English Football Internationalists' Who's Who 1872–1988* (Beverley: Hutton Press, 1990), p. 78.
4 G. Green, *The Official History of the FA Cup* (London: Sportsman's Book Club, 1960), p. 119.
5 G. Green, *Soccer: The World Game* (London: Sportsman's Book Club, 1954), p. 131.
6 *Topical Times*, 7 January 1939.
7 G. Allison, *Allison Calling* (London: Staples Press, 1948), p. 82.

8 Ibid., p. 83.
9 Peskett (ed.), *Tom Whittaker's Arsenal Story*, p. 106.
10 Ibid., p. 110.
11 N. Barrett, *The Daily Telegraph Football Chronicle* (London: Carlton, 1995), p. 58.
12 *News of the World*, 26 April 1936.
13 Ibid.
14 B. Joy, *Forward, Arsenal!* (London: Sportsman's Book Club, 1954), p. 185.
15 J. Harding, *Alex James: Life of a Football Legend* (London: Robson Books, 1988), p. 140.
16 Peskett (ed.), *Tom Whittaker's Arsenal Story*, p. 108.
17 Joy, *Forward, Arsenal!*, p. 73.
18 Harding, *Alex James*, p. 151.
19 Hapgood, *Football Ambassador*, p. 10.
20 Ibid.
21 Harding, *Alex James*, p. 151.
22 Ibid.
23 Hapgood, *Football Ambassador*, pp. 105–7.
24 Ibid., p. 23.
25 Harding, *Alex James*, p. 164.
26 Ibid.
27 D. Bowler, *Shanks: The Authorised Biography of Bill Shankly* (London: Orion, 1996), p. 74.
28 Ibid., p. 79.
29 Ibid.
30 R. Wall, *Arsenal from the Heart* (London: Sportsman's Book Club, 1971), p. 34.

11 Billy Dale – Manchester City

1 *Bolton Evening News*, 28 April 1933.
2 F. Swift, *Football from the Goalmouth* (London: Sporting Handbooks, 1948), p. 27.
3 *Manchester Evening News*, 14 April 1934.
4 Ibid.
5 Swift, *Football from the Goalmouth*, p. 27.
6 Ibid., pp. 52–3.
7 *Manchester Guardian*, 27 April 1934.
8 Ibid.
9 *Manchester Evening News*, 14 April 1934.
10 Ibid.
11 Ibid.
12 *Manchester Evening News*, 28 April 1934.
13 www.mcfc.co.uk/past/cowans.asp.
14 *Manchester Evening News*, 27 April 1934.
15 *Manchester Evening News*, 28 April 1934.
16 Ibid.
17 *News of the World*, 29 April 1934.
18 Swift, *Football from the Goalmouth*, p. 36.
19 *Manchester Evening News*, 28 April 1934.
20 Ibid.
21 Swift, *Football from the Goalmouth*, p. 39.
22 *News of the World*, 29 April 1934.
23 R. Goble, *Manchester City: A Complete Record 1887–1987* (Derby: Breedon Books, 1987), p. 112.
24 *News of the World*, 29 April 1934.
25 *Manchester Guardian*, 30 April 1934.
26 *Manchester Evening News*, 1 May 1934.

27 *Manchester Evening News*, 18 April 1934.
28 *Manchester Evening News*, 27 April 1934.
29 *Bolton Evening News*, 1 May 1934.
30 Ibid.
31 *Manchester Evening News*, 28 April 1934.
32 P. Doherty, *Spotlight on Football* (London: A & E, 1947), p. 43.
33 Ibid.
34 Ibid., p. 45.
35 Ibid., p. 47.
36 Ibid.
37 *Manchester Evening News*, 15 March 1937.

12 'Jock' Dodds – Sheffield United and Blackpool

1 *Topical Times*, 28 May 1938.
2 Ibid.
3 Blackpool FC match programme, October 1995.
4 Ibid.
5 *Topical Times*, 28 May 1938.
6 Ibid.
7 *Sheffield Green 'Un*, 1 February 1936.
8 *Topical Times*, 25 April 1936.
9 *News of the World*, 26 April 1936.
10 Ibid.
11 *Sunday Chronicle*, 11 December 1938.
12 *Sheffield Telegraph and Independent*, 3 March 1939.
13 Ibid.
14 www.blackpoolfc.co.uk/pastdodds.htm.
15 T. Lawton, *Football is My Business* (London: Sporting Handbooks, 1946), p. 128.
16 Ibid.
17 M. Prestage, *Blackpool: The Glory Years Remembered* (Derby: Breedon Books, 2000), p. 20.
18 Ibid.
19 www.blackpoolfc.co.uk/pastdodds.htm.
20 *Sheffield Star*, 22 July 1982.
21 Ibid.
22 R. Adamson, *Bogota Bandit: The Outlaw Life of Charlie Mitten, Manchester United's Penalty King* (Edinburgh: Mainstream, 1996), p. 107.
23 Anonymous (ed.), *Book of Football*, Vol. 1 (London: Marshall Cavendish, 1971), p. 245.
24 Blackpool FC match programme, October 1995.
25 *Sheffield Star*, 22 July 1982.
26 Blackpool FC match programme, October 1995.

13 Harold Hobbis – Charlton Athletic

1 Football League (ed.), *The Competitions of Season 1932–1933* (London: Football League, 1933).
2 Football League (ed.), *The Competitions of Season 1933–1934* (London: Football League, 1934).
3 Ibid.
4 J. Seed, *The Jimmy Seed Story* (London: Sportsman's Book Club, 1958), p. 51.
5 *Daily Mail*, 3 January 1935.
6 Seed, *The Jimmy Seed Story*, p. 33.

7 Ibid., p. 34.
8 Ibid., p. 51.
9 Ibid., p. 34.
10 Football League (ed.), *The Competitions of Season 1935–1936* (London: Football League, 1936).
11 Ibid.
12 Ibid.
13 Ibid.
14 Seed, *The Jimmy Seed Story*, p. 34.
15 Football League (ed.), *The Competitions of Season 1936–1937* (London: Football League, 1937).
16 Ibid.
17 *News of the World*, 2 May 1937.
18 Football League (ed.), *The Competitions of Season 1936–1937*.
19 Seed, *The Jimmy Seed Story*, p. 35.
20 Ibid.
21 Ibid.
22 Ibid., p. 36.
23 Football League (ed.), *The Competitions of Season 1937–1938* (London: Football League, 1938).
24 Football League (ed.), *The Competitions of Season 1938–1939* (London: Football League, 1939).
25 Seed, *The Jimmy Seed Story*, p. 52.
26 C. Buchan, *A Lifetime in Football* (London: Phoenix House, 1955), p. 125.
27 *Topical Times*, 7 January 1939.
28 Seed, *The Jimmy Seed Story*, p. 44.
29 Ibid., p. 48.
30 Ibid., p. 49.
31 *Topical Times*, 7 January 1939.

14 Joe Mercer – Everton

1 J. Mercer, *The Great Ones* (London: Oldbourne, 1964); G. James, *Football with a Smile: The Authorised Biography of Joe Mercer* (Leicester: ACL and Polar Publishing, 2000).
2 S. Cullis, *All for the Wolves* (London: Sportsman's Book Club, 1961), p. 216.
3 G. Hart (ed.), *The Guinness Football Encyclopedia* (London: Guinness Publishing, 1991), p. 123.
4 I. Ross and G. Smailes, *Everton: A Complete Record* (Derby: Breedon Books, 1985), p. 109.
5 Anonymous (ed.), *Book of Football*, Vol. 1 (London: Marshall Cavendish, 1971), p. 674.
6 R. Goble, *Manchester City: A Complete Record, 1887–1987* (Derby: Breedon Books, 1987), p. 36.
7 N. Walsh, *Dixie Dean* (London: Pan Books, 1978), p. 69.
8 *Liverpool Echo*, 10 August 1990.
9 *Liverpool Post*, 11 August 1990.
10 J. Holden, *Stan Cullis: The Iron Manager* (Derby: Breedon Books, 2000), p. 20.
11 Mercer, *The Great Ones*, p. 19.
12 Anonymous (ed.), *Book of Football*, p. 674.
13 Mercer, *The Great Ones*, p. 18.
14 Everton FC match programme, 3 January 2000.
15 *Topical Times Sporting Annual 1936–37*.
16 Football League (ed.), *The Competitions of Season 1938–1939* (London: Football League, 1939).

17 *Liverpool Echo*, 24 April 1939.
18 Football League (ed.), *The Competitions of Season 1938–1939*.
19 S.F. Kelly, *Backpage Football: A Century of Newspaper Coverage* (London: Queen Anne Press, 1988), p. 73.
20 *Liverpool Echo*, 22 April 1939.
21 Cullis, *All for the Wolves*, p. 217.
22 Ibid.
23 R. Taylor and A. Ward, *Three Sides of the Mersey: An Oral History of Everton, Liverpool and Tranmere Rovers* (London: Robson Books, 1993), p. 37.
24 D. McVay and A. Smith, *The Complete Centre Forward: The Authorised Biography of Tommy Lawton* (Worcester: Sportsbooks, 2000), p. 46.
25 Ibid.
26 Ibid., p. 57.
27 Walsh, *Dixie Dean*, p. 18.
28 Mercer, *The Great Ones*, p. 31.
29 *Liverpool Echo*, 10 August 1990.
30 Ibid.

15 Cliff Parker – Portsmouth

1 *Portsmouth Evening News*, 1 November 1993.
2 Author's correspondence with R.J. Owen, Portsmouth FC's club historian.
3 Football League (ed.), *The Competitions of Season 1933–1934* (London: Football League, 1934).
4 Football League (ed.), *The Competitions of Season 1934–1935* (London: Football League, 1935).
5 *News of the World*, 21 January 1934.
6 Ibid.
7 Ibid.
8 Football League (ed.), *The Competitions of Season 1938–1939* (London: Football League, 1939).
9 Ibid.
10 J. Guthrie, *Soccer Rebel: The Evolution of the Professional Footballer* (Pinner: Pentagon, 1976), p. 17.
11 Ibid.
12 R.J. Owen, *The Official Pictorial History of Portsmouth FC* (Portsmouth: Portsmouth FC, 1998), p. 63.
13 Guthrie, *Soccer Rebel*, p. 16.
14 Ibid., p. 18.
15 A. Thraves, *The History of the Wembley FA Cup Final* (London: Weidenfeld & Nicolson, 1994), p. 50.
16 G. Green, *The Official History of the FA Cup* (London: Sportsman's Book Club, 1960), p. 125.
17 *Observer*, 30 April 1939.
18 Green, *The Official History of the FA Cup*, p. 125.
19 *Portsmouth Evening News*, 1 November 1993.

16 Bert Sproston – Leeds United, Tottenham Hotspurs and Manchester City

1 M. Jarrad and M. Macdonald, *Leeds United: A Complete Record, 1919–1996* (Derby: Breedon Books, 1996), p. 126.
2 D. Lamming, *An English Football Internationalists' Who's Who, 1872–1988* (Beverley: Hutton Press, 1990), p. 233.
3 Ibid.

4 C. Freddi, *The England Football Fact Book* (London: Guinness Publishing, 1991), p. 229.
5 S. Cullis, *All for the Wolves* (London: Sportsman's Book Club, 1961), p. 214.
6 Football League (ed.), *The Competitions of Season 1935–1936* (London: Football League, 1936).
7 P.J. Beck, 'England v. Germany, 1938', in *History Today*, 32:6 (1982), p. 29.
8 S. Matthews, *The Way It Was* (London: Headline, 2000), pp. 81–2.
9 Ibid., p. 82.
10 Beck, 'England v. Germany, 1938', p. 33.
11 Ibid.
12 Matthews, *The Way It Was*, p. 82.
13 D. Downing, *The Best of Enemies: England vs Germany, a Century of Football Rivalry* (London: Bloomsbury, 2000), p. 49.
14 *Daily Worker*, 9 May 1938.
15 E.A. Hapgood, *Football Ambassador* (London: Sporting Handbooks, 1944), p. 27.
16 S. Rous, *Football Worlds* (London: Faber & Faber, 1978), p. 65.
17 Downing, *The Best of Enemies*, p. 50.
18 Matthews, *The Way It Was*, p. 83.
19 Ibid.
20 Ibid., p. 87.
21 Beck, 'England v. Germany, 1938', p. 34.
22 www.mcfc.co.uk/past/managers.htm.
23 *Bolton Evening News*, 28 January 2000.

Select bibliography

Adamson, R., *Bogota Bandit: The Outlaw Life of Charlie Mitten, Manchester United's Penalty King* (Edinburgh: Mainstream, 1996)

Allison, G., *Allison Calling* (London: Staples Press, 1948)

Anonymous (ed.), *Book of Football*, 5 vols (London: Marshall Cavendish, 1971)

Armstrong, G., and R. Giulianotti (eds), *Football Cultures and Identities* (London: Macmillan, 1999)

Barrett, N., *The* Daily Telegraph *Football Chronicle* (London: Carlton, 1995)

Beck, P.J., 'England v. Germany, 1938', in *History Today*, 32:6 (1982)

Beck, P.J., *Scoring for Britain: International Football and International Politics, 1900–1939* (London: Frank Cass, 1999)

Beck, P.J., 'Going to War, Peaceful Co-existence or Virtual Membership?: British Football and FIFA, 1928–46', in *International Journal of the History of Sport*, 17:1 (2000)

Bowler, D., *Shanks: The Authorised Biography of Bill Shankly* (London: Orion, 1996)

Brailsford, D., *British Sport: A Social History* (Cambridge: Lutterworth Press, 1997)

Buchan, C., *A Lifetime in Football* (London: Phoenix House, 1955)

Burley, D., *Playing the Game: Sport and British Society 1910–45* (Manchester: Manchester University Press, 1995)

Butler, B., *The Official Illustrated History of the FA Cup* (London: Headline 1996)

Calley, R., *Blackpool: A Complete Record 1887–1992* (Derby: Breedon Books, 1992)

Crampsey, B., *The Scottish Football League: The First 100 Years* (Glasgow: Scottish Football League, 1990)

Cullis, S., *All for the Wolves* (London: Sportsman's Book Club, 1961)

Doherty, P., *Spotlight on Football* (London: A & E, 1947)

Downing, D., *The Best of Enemies: England vs Germany, a Century of Football Rivalry* (London: Bloomsbury, 2000)

Fabian, A.H., and G. Green (eds), *Association Football*, Vol. 2 (London: Caxton Publishing, 1960)

Fishwick, M.F., *American Heroes: Myth and Reality* (Westport, CT: Greenwood Press, 1954)

Fishwick, N., *English Football and Society, 1910–1950* (Manchester: Manchester University Press, 1989)

Football League (ed.), *The Competitions of Season* . . . series, *1931–1932* to *1938–1939* (London: Football League, 1932–9)

Freddi, C., *The England Football Fact Book* (London: Guinness Publishing, 1991)

Glanville, B., *Soccer Nemesis* (London: Secker & Warburg, 1955)

Glanville, B., *Soccer: A Panorama* (London: Eyre & Spottiswoode, 1969)

Glanville, B., *Football Memories* (London: Virgin, 1999)

Goble, R., *Manchester City: A Complete Record, 1887–1987* (Derby: Breedon Books, 1987)

Green, G., *Soccer: The World Game* (London: Sportsman's Book Club, 1954)

Green, G., *The Official History of the FA Cup* (London: Sportsman's Book Club, 1960)

Guthrie, J., *Soccer Rebel: The Evolution of the Professional Footballer* (Pinner: Pentagon, 1976)

Hapgood, E.A., *Football Ambassador* (London: Sporting Handbooks, 1944)

Harding, J., *Alex James: Life of a Football Legend* (London: Robson Books, 1988)

Harding, J., *For the Good of the Game: The Official History of the Professional Footballers Association* (London: Robson Books, 1991)

Hardwick, G., *Gentleman George* (Liverpool: Juniper Publishing, 1998)

Hart, G. (ed.), *The Guinness Football Encyclopedia* (London: Guinness Publishing, 1991)

Hayes, D., *Bolton Wanderers* (Stroud: Sutton Publishing, 1999)

Hill, J., and J. Williams (eds), *Sport and Identity in the North of England* (Keele: Keele University Press, 1996)

Hodgson, D., *The Everton Story* (London: Arthur Barker, 1979)

Holden, J., *Stan Cullis: The Iron Manager* (Derby: Breedon Books, 2000)

Holt, R., *Sport and the British: A Modern History* (Oxford: Clarendon Press, 1989)

Holt, R. (ed.), *Sport and the Working Class in Modern Britain* (Manchester: Manchester University Press, 1990)

Holt, R., 'Heroes of the North: Sport and the Shaping of Regional Identity', in J. Hill and J. Williams (eds), *Sport and Identity in the North of England* (Keele: Keele University Press, 1996)

Holt, R., J.A. Mangan and P. Lanfranchi (eds), *European Heroes: Myth, Identity, Sport* (London: Frank Cass, 1996)

Hugman, B., *Canon League Players Records, 1946–1984* (Feltham: Newnes Books, 1984)

Inglis, S., *League Football and the Men who Made It* (London: Willow Books, 1988)

Jack, D.R. (ed.), *Len Shackleton, Clown Prince of Soccer: His Autobiography* (London: Nicholas Kaye, 1955)

James, B., *England v Scotland* (London: Sportsman's Book Club, 1970)

James, G., *Manchester City: The Greatest* (Leicester: Polar Print Group, 1997)

James, G., *Football with a Smile: The Authorised Biography of Joe Mercer* (Leicester: ACL and Polar Publishing, 2000)

Jarrad, M., and M. Macdonald, *Leeds United: A Complete Record, 1919–1996* (Derby: Breedon Books, 1996)

Joannou, P., *The Hughie Gallacher Story* (Derby: Breedon Books, 1989)

Jones, S.G., *Sport, Politics and the Working Class* (Manchester: Manchester University Press, 1988)

Joy, B., *Forward, Arsenal!* (London: Sportsman's Book Club, 1954)

Keith, J., *Dixie Dean: The Inside Story of a Football Icon* (London: Robson Books, 2001)

Kelly, S.F., *Backpage Football: A Century of Newspaper Coverage* (London: Queen Anne Press, 1988)

Lamming, D., *A Who's Who of Grimsby Town AFC, 1890–1985* (Beverley: Hutton Press, 1985)

Lamming, D., *A Scottish Soccer Internationalists' Who's Who, 1872–1986* (Beverley: Hutton Press, 1987)

Lamming, D., *An English Football Internationalists' Who's Who, 1872–1988* (Beverley: Hutton Press, 1990)

Lawton, T., *Football is My Business* (London: Sporting Handbooks, 1946)

Lawton, T., *My Twenty Years of Soccer* (Norwich: Heirloom Library, 1955)

Ledbrooke, A., and E. Turner, *Soccer from the Press Box* (London: Nicholas Kaye, 1955)

McCarthy, T., *War Games: The Story of Sport in World War Two* (London: Queen Anne Press, 1989)

McVay, D., and A. Smith, *The Complete Centre Forward: The Authorised Biography of Tommy Lawton* (Worcester: Sportsbooks, 2000)

Marland, S., *Bolton Wanderers: A Complete Record, 1877–1989* (Derby: Breedon Books, 1989)

Marland, S., *Bolton Wanderers: One Hundred Years at Burnden Park* (Derby: Breedon Books, 1995)

Matthews, S., *Feet First Again* (London: Corgi Books, 1955)

Matthews, S., *The Way It Was* (London: Headline, 2000)

Matthews, S., and M. Matthews, *Back in Touch* (London: Arthur Barker, 1981)

Mercer, J., *The Great Ones* (London: Oldbourne, 1964)

Miller, D., *Stanley Matthews: The Authorised Biography* (London: Pavilion Books, 1989)

Neasom, M., *Pompey: The History of Portsmouth FC* (Leeds: Milestone Publishing, 1984)

Ollier, F., *Arsenal: A Complete Record, 1886–1990* (Derby: Breedon Books, 1990)

Owen, R.J., *The Official Pictorial History of Portsmouth FC* (Portsmouth: Portsmouth FC, 1998)

Pawson, T. (ed.), *The Observer on Soccer* (London: Unwin Hyman, 1989)

Penney, I., *The Maine Road Encyclopedia* (Edinburgh: Mainstream, 1995)

Peskett, R. (ed.), *Tom Whittaker's Arsenal Story* (London: Sportsman's Book Club, 1958)

Phelps, N.A., 'The Southern Football Hero and the Shaping of Local and Regional Identity in the South of England', in *Soccer and Society*, 2:3 (2001), pp. 44–57

Prestage, M., *Blackpool: The Glory Years Remembered* (Derby: Breedon Books, 2000)

Price, N., *Gritty, Gallant, Glorious: A History and Complete Record of the Hearts, 1946–1997* (Edinburgh: N. Price, 1997)

Purcell, T., and M. Gething, *Wartime Wanderers: A Football Team at War* (Edinburgh: Mainstream, 1996)

Rollin, J., *Soccer at War* (London: Willow Books, 1985)

Ross, I., and G. Smailes, *Everton: A Complete Record* (Derby: Breedon Books, 1985)

Rous, S., *Football Worlds* (London: Faber & Faber, 1978)

Russell, D., *Football and the English: A Social History of Association Football in England, 1863–1995* (Preston: Carnegie Publishing, 1997)

Seed, J., *Soccer from the Inside* (London: Thorsons, 1947)

Seed, J., *The Jimmy Seed Story* (London: Sportsman's Book Club, 1958)

Sharpe, G., *Gambling on Goals: A Century of Football Betting* (Edinburgh: Mainstream, 1997)

Sharpe, I., *Forty Years in Football* (London: Sportsman's Book Club, 1954)

Shindler, C., *Fathers, Sons and Football* (London: Headline, 2001)

Soar, P., and M. Tyler, *Arsenal: The Official Illustrated History, 1886–1996* (London: Hamlyn, 1996)

Soar, P., and M. Tyler, *The Official Illustrated History of Arsenal, 1886–2000* (London: Hamlyn, 2000)

Studd, S., *Herbert Chapman: Football Emperor* (London: Souvenir Press, 1998)

Swift, F., *Football from the Goalmouth* (London: Sporting Handbooks, 1948)

Tabner, B., *Through the Turnstiles* (Harefield: Yore Publications, 1992)

Taylor, M., 'Beyond the Maximum Wage: The Earnings of Football Professionals in England, 1900–39', in *Soccer and Society*, 2:3 (2001)

Taylor, R., and A. Ward, *Three Sides of the Mersey: An Oral History of Everton, Liverpool and Tranmere Rovers* (London: Robson Books, 1993)

Thraves, A., *The History of the Wembley FA Cup Final* (London: Weidenfeld & Nicolson, 1994)

Tibballs, G., *Great Sporting Eccentrics* (London: Robson Books, 1997)

Triggs, L., *Grimsby Town: A Complete Record, 1878–1989* (Derby: Breedon Books, 1989)

Wagg, S., *The Football World: A Contemporary Social History* (Sussex: Harvester Press, 1984)

Wall, R., *Arsenal from the Heart* (London: Sportsman's Book Club, 1971)

Walsh, N., *Dixie Dean* (London: Pan Books, 1978)

Walvin, J., *The People's Game: The History of Football Revisited* (Edinburgh: Mainstream, 1994)

Watt, T., and K. Palmer, *Wembley: The Greatest Stage* (London: Simon & Schuster, 1998)

Wright, B., *Captain of England* (London: Stanley Paul, 1950)

Index